SEX
SHAMANS

"A fascinating and informative look at the lives of the sex shamans of the International School of Temple Arts tribe. As you pore over these pages, you will be entertained, educated, and have your mind blown open to new possibilities."

CHARLES MUIR, PRESIDENT AND DIRECTOR OF STUDIES AT THE SOURCE SCHOOL OF TANTRA YOGA

"The sexual and the spiritual are connected, and the importance of ritual in sexuality is a potent truth. *Sex Shamans* helps us move toward that great truth, through personal stories and accounts of transcendence through sex, the divine in the erotic, and the rituals that have helped many seekers and teachers to meet their own divinity through sexual energy, power, and expression"

AMY JO GODDARD, AUTHOR OF *WOMAN ON FIRE*

"Incredible and profound stories with something to offer anyone exploring their sexuality. These stories are bound to titillate your imagination, while providing you new insights into what is possible to experience in your body."

DESTIN GEREK, AUTHOR OF *THE EVOLVED MASCULINE*

"There are tons of stories about shamans who cultivate plant medicines or use psychedelic drugs for shamanic journey, but there are too few accounts about those who truly know the power of using sex as medicine. This book is an invaluable resource on many such taboo topics, helping one to come into right relationship with their own primal power and magic."

KATIE WEATHERUP, AUTHOR OF *PRACTICAL SHAMANISM*

"This intriguing book of diverse personal stories is a vital awakening call for the return of the sacred fire, the transformative element so needed in our sacred culture. As we enter into a new era that values one's energy and vibrations more than gender orientation, we must celebrate the feminine and the masculine energies within each of us. Only then can we bring a real balance and a lasting peace to our societies. I highly recommend it."

ITZHAK BEERY, AUTHOR OF *THE GIFT OF SHAMANISM*, *SHAMANIC TRANSFORMATIONS*, AND *SHAMANIC HEALING*

"This book busts through myths, stereotypes, and stigmas around sexuality as a career path. I'm profoundly grateful that KamalaDevi and all the contributors are coming out of the shadows, with their heads and hands up high, to show us how sex as a healing profession is just as important as school teaching, doctoring, cooking, or any other valuable profession."

MICHAEL ELLSBERG, AUTHOR OF *THE EDUCATION OF MILLIONAIRES* AND COAUTHOR OF *THE LAST SAFE INVESTMENT*

"If you're still imprisoned by your sexual wounding, *Sex Shamans* delivers hard-won wisdom from a remarkable array of the liberated, a deep dive into the river of healing, and an utterly daring road map into the reclamation of the magic we're all born with—our original innocence."

STEVEN STARR, PRODUCER OF *FLOW: FOR LOVE OF WATER*

"We are entering a real revolution based on a new culture of consent, particularly in the realms of power and sexuality. With her new anthology of parables, myths, and stories, KamalaDevi seeds the growing field of spiritual sexual consciousness on Earth. Let her take us spiritually into the caverns of consciousness together!"

KELLY BRYSON, AUTHOR OF *DON'T BE NICE, BE REAL*

"Be very careful when you choose to sit down and read this book, as you will not be able to put it down. And, it could just change your whole life. Set aside the time to dive into a new world of possibility for your future."

ALEXIS KATZ, FOUNDER OF EYES WIDE OPEN LIFE AND AUTHOR OF *WEAR CLEAN UNDERWEAR!*

SEX
SHAMANS

True Stories of Sacred Sexuality and Awakening

EDITED BY

KamalaDevi McClure

Destiny Books
Rochester, Vermont

Destiny Books
One Park Street
Rochester, Vermont 05767
www.DestinyBooks.com

Text stock is SFI certified

Destiny Books is a division of Inner Traditions International

Welcome to My World! online newsletter and *Love Without Limits* blog by
   Deborah Taj Anapol.
Excerpt from theoerotic.olterman.se reprinted with permission from Patrik
   Olterman.
Letter on page 57 © Robert Osborn, CelticTantra.com, used with permission.
   All rights reserved.
Osho's Dynamic Meditation and other teachings by Bhagwan Shree Rajneesh
   can be found on www.osho.com.
Embodiment exercises 4, 5, 6, 8, 13, and 17 are reproduced with permission by
   the authors of *Sacred Sexual Healing: The SHAMAN Method of Sex Magic,*
   Baba Dez Nichols and KamalaDevi McClure.

Cataloging-in-Publication Data for this title is available from the Library of Congress

ISBN 978-1-62055-921-5 (print)
ISBN 978-1-62055-922-2 (ebook)

Printed and bound in the United States by Lake Book Manufacturing, Inc.
The text stock is SFI certified. The Sustainable Forestry Initiative® program
promotes sustainable forest management.

10 9 8 7 6 5 4 3 2 1

Text design and layout by Priscilla Baker
This book was typeset in Garamond Premier Pro with Tide Sans, Avant Garde,
Gill Sans, and Legacy Sans used as display typefaces
Cover art titled *Ida & Pingala* by Mukee Okan, ThePussyTalks.com

To send correspondence to the author of this book, mail a first-class letter to the
editor c/o Inner Traditions • Bear & Company, One Park Street, Rochester, VT
05767, and we will forward the communication, or contact the editor directly at
www.KamalaDevi.com, and learn more at **www.ISTA.life**.

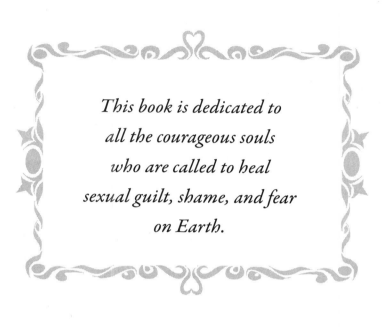

*This book is dedicated to
all the courageous souls
who are called to heal
sexual guilt, shame, and fear
on Earth.*

CONTENTS

Embodiment Exercises

All Our Subtle Bodies

By Bruce Lyon

Each of us is like a radio that can be tuned to different frequencies. Many people in modern society have tuned out all higher and lower frequencies and live within a narrow band of their dulled outer senses. Doing so seems to be required of them to earn a living, and this tuning out is reinforced by the surrounding culture, protecting them from their fear of death.

A shaman is someone who has learned to listen to many stations at once, integrating the different music and news broadcasts into a coherent whole. Being a shaman does not, however, protect us from our humanness and the often intensely vulnerable experience of showing up within the so-called normal bands of experience. If anything, it increases the shaman's sensitivity because the extraordinary is curled up inside the ordinary.

Working. Eating dinner with family. Sitting in traffic. Making love. Shopping for groceries. Riding the subway. When the channels are open, all experiences ride the edge of the miraculous; all encounters are soaked with possibilities, endlessly dynamic. The joy of true meeting is enhanced, and so is the tragedy of all the missed meetings. Also intense is the waste of lives unlived and uncelebrated. Time alone in meditation, in nature, in the presence of others who love solitude—or all three together—is a balm for the spirit that helps recalibrate the sensitive instruments of body and soul.

In these pages are the different stories of intimate beloveds. One of the beautiful things about this tribe-of-no-tribe is that there is little in our personalities that unites us. We do not share the same ideologies, and we have each forged paths in our own unique and wild ways, breaking free into authentic lives that we know to be sourced from our own cores. These words also represent only the surface of our profound journeys.

Core recognizes and resonates with core, and we share that essential aliveness, but we also celebrate the real diversity in expression. We all have different keys to the sacred locks of the soul and body. We all serve as reference points for one another's journeys, not to emulate but to stimulate and awaken the many qualities inherent in the human experience. What we begin to appreciate in others eventually emerges through the center of our own being.

Biological sex allows for the sharing of DNA in such a way that the endless diversity of life can continue to be creative. The same principle applies to shamanic sex. When we meet as energy beings with a mutual willingness to share with one another what has been harvested in our own deep experience—our soul DNA—then humanity can quickly create better software for integrating its sexuality and its spirituality.

I invite you into a shamanic experience with me right now, if you have the desire to meet in this way. First, we need to slow down and take time. You have probably been eating these words with speed, so I invite you to slow down, slow right down, dropping out of the mind and into the heart and body.

Take a few deep, conscious breaths and feel the air breathing you. Feel the same air I am breathing as I write this, sitting up in bed on a luminous morning, with the sun lifting above the horizon and shining through a light mist still clinging to the rose garden. We are both on this incredible blue-green jewel of a planet, whirling through an immense cosmos. The material of our bodies was partly fashioned in supernovas, grown and developed through millions of years of biological evolution, flowing down the bloodlines of our cultures and families.

Our souls are ultimately one with the universal consciousness; the same awareness reading these words permeates all space and time. We are love—impossible, irrepressible, eternal. We are the great dance of matter and spirit, masculine and feminine, light and dark. We delight in all polarities and are the spark between them. We are sex. Eros was the child of Mars and Venus, and to the Greeks, sexual attraction meant being in the presence of a god.

Sex is not just one person doing something to another, the transactions of sexuality. It is what happens to both in the presence of their shared divinity. When we surrender together to the wisdom of the erotic current of the universe, transformation occurs. In that state, this is my prayer: "Whatever is *in me* or *of me* that is of benefit to this *other me* and serves the evolution of love, may it be given."

Sex as love generates life—the moment of ejaculation, the final push of a woman in labor, the sacrifice of parents to serve and save a child. These are unconditional, all-in expressions of the life that is beyond life and death.

In this moment, you are the *other me* that I have the great pleasure of offering myself to in this unconditional way. I don't just want to write to you, but to well up inside you. I want to be that tingle that starts in your body and turns into the warm honey of arousal. I want to be there in that exhale that is a little fuller and in the sigh of the heart as it opens in the presence of love. I want to celebrate the mutual penetration of souls as we reach through the veils of time and space and begin to touch each other intimately.

I want to know you, in the biblical sense, from the inside, arising as you and tasting the delight of being this unique one and, at the same time, all ones. I yearn to be known by you—not for you to hear my story through the exchange of clumsy words and symbols, with their conflicting meanings, but to be known from the inside, to let you into and through the most intimate places of my being that have walked this sacred path. I invite you to come inside me and be me.

In this way we pierce for each other that sacred hymen of separate identity, which is the source of the deep loneliness present at the core of every human soul. As our souls consent to let each other in, our hearts can't help but blow open to each other. The intimacy of the heart is not in loving each other as separate selves but in falling through each other's hearts into the common mystery that resides in each of us.

And then comes the delight of the bodies opening. Yes, the warm honey, the ripening rush of blood, and the warm arousal. Yes, the deeper currents of Earth and kundalini awakening. Yes, the rush from base to crown and the defibrillation of the heart, so that it explodes even more.

The core of each atom then starts to reveal that it too is guarding a secret portal into the void. The dark rushlight of matter itself begins to shine through everything. Our bodies seem to pass through each other effortlessly so that we are truly inside each other and somehow inside matter itself. The emptiness of spirit at the heart of the soul meets the bliss of matter and the heart of the body, and nothing remains but love, dancing in us, as us, as everything.

Aroused

We who stand up for love
are the pink bits
the erogenous zones
the erectile tissue
of humanity
the rush we feel
is the passionate blood
of a second coming
lifting us swollen
with the sap of freedom into
an ecstatic cosmic embrace
we stand naked
vulnerable and unafraid

for we rise on an invincible tide
we are the first rosy blush
of an awakened earth
aroused and ready
for the ride

Bruce Lyon explores places where the personal, planetary, and cosmic meet, guiding others on initiatory journeys around the world. An international teacher and author of numerous esoteric books, he is a member of the wisdom council that advises ISTA's governance and a lead faculty member. As cofounder of Shamballa School, he is seeding a modern temple and mystery school called Highden in New Zealand. He is also a contributor to this book (see chapter 19).

INTRODUCTION

How to Begin
a Story That
Never Ends

This book is the culmination of my deepest desire to belong to something bigger than myself. Perhaps it's also an attempt to prove, once and for all, that I am not crazy and, more importantly, that I am not alone.

I spent most of my early years seeking acceptance, connection, significance, and some way to contribute. Like many people, I longed to fit into a family, school, church, community, and society. I participated in the culturally constructed notion that there is such a thing as normal. Yet I carried the haunting feeling that just underneath the surface of what could be sensed, I somehow belonged to another unseen world.

While dreaming at night and sometimes while making love, I'd journey into invisible realms with revelatory significance, but upon returning, in order to participate in consensual reality, I'd make the psychic agreement to leave that world behind.

How could I feel so connected yet suffer so much separation? This enigma only grew more puzzling when mixed with the subject of sex, which holds so much social shame. Nearly everyone I've met has had some kind of mystical experience during lovemaking, usually more than one, but they rarely talk about it. The taboo is too thick. Sacred sex becomes even more unspeakable when it involves deviant desires. Why is this enigmatic realm shrouded in so much shadow?

When I first encountered it, shamanism seemed like a faraway concept, a throwback to some backward village. I couldn't imagine that it had anything to do with me. I was a modern woman, an educated entrepreneur, a Mexican American writer intent on becoming a wife and a mother. I didn't know how to handle myself when guides, gifts, visions, and voices started arriving at my doorstep. It seemed easier to dismiss these visitations and "return to sender" rather than to unpack and learn to live with them.

I suspected something was wrong with me. Maybe it was my mental health. I sought professionals for help with my dyslexia, gender dysphoria, and massive depressive disorder. There were many helpful healers on my journey, but there was still something invisible that they couldn't seem to touch. An unnamed fear followed me around like an untamed dog nipping at my heels.

I worried that I'd end up like those people who live in the streets yelling at their invisible adversaries or, worse, locked up in a room with padded walls. After all, what was the difference between the mystic seers revered by the world's religions and the crazy people I saw preaching gospel on the corner? Where is the line between insanity and truth telling?

Driven by strange voices, my soul carried me through decades of deep work, acquainted me with tantric masters, and inspired me to create performance art and even to write a number of books. Truthfully, however, it wasn't until I found myself in a like-minded community of sacred sexual visionaries that I no longer felt crazy. Today, I work with a modern mystery school called the International School of Temple Arts (ISTA). (See section titled "What Is ISTA?" on page 15.)

This anthology provides an intimate portrayal of the life of the modern sex shaman. Since academic attempts to define sexual shamanism can kill the living transmission, I felt it important to ask my peers about their firsthand experiences. In the spirit of oral tradition, I had to shut up and listen. I listened to my students as well as my mentors. I opened my heart to their shamanic storytelling. Then, instead of trying to be a lone star shining a single light on this vast subject, I invited a whole constellation of luminaries to share their stories as well.

This book is a compilation of twenty mini memoirs by pioneers from around the world, all of whom are practicing sexual shamanism in the ISTA field. Each chapter reveals the author's unique journey to realize their calling as a modern sex shaman.

The intention of this collection is to demystify sexual shamanism and to release the shame surrounding the journey of sacred sexual awakening. By revealing the intimate details of our lives in these pages, we hope to empower you to inquire more deeply into your own sexual wounding as well as into your mystical awakenings, thereby inspiring more sexual liberation.

We also aim to address the provocative questions that friends, students, fellow educators, and even people sitting next to us on airplanes frequently ask, such as:

- What is sexual shamanism?
- How did you get into this work?
- What typically takes place in a session?
- What are some common sexual wounds that need healing?
- Did you have a personal crisis that led you to this calling?

There are also the deeper questions. The ones that people are afraid to ask.

And then there are the questions that have no answers. Beyond that, there are questions that only serve to generate more questions.

Studying sexual shamanism is like observing steam. It quickly evaporates into invisible realms: dreamtime, vision, myth, and incomprehensible paradox, which is ultimately impossible to capture in words.

On Sexual Shamanism

What arises when you hear the term *sex shaman*? Are you intrigued? Uncomfortable? Excited? As you might imagine, this question has elicited a wide range of reactions, such as: "It sounds like a New Age hippie starting a cult." Or "A quack who's trying to have sex with you to hustle you out of money." And of course, we've heard this: "It's clearly cultural misappropriation; a real shaman would object to being called a sex shaman."

Despite all the stigma and confusion surrounding sexual shamanism, this book intends to provide clarity and insight into an emerging new culture that is part of a growing international movement. Throughout these pages, we use the term *shamanism* to refer to a way of being, not to any specific religion, culture, or wisdom tradition. A shaman is someone who goes into an ecstatic trance to act as an intermediary between the natural world and nonordinary reality. The term *sex shaman* is used to describe someone who uses sex as medicine. Eros, kundalini, and orgasmic energy can all induce an altered state and be used for journeying, divination, healing, and/or alchemy.

My favorite interpretation of the word *shaman* is "self-healed madman." Traditionally the term comes from Siberia and has been defined as "one who knows." Anthropologists have applied it to various cultural practices from ancient times, which have been observed throughout completely unrelated parts of Asia, Africa, Australia, and the Americas. Yet, Aboriginal, Native American, indigenous, and First Nations peoples use the equivalent of the term *shaman* in their own languages to describe tribal healers, seers, medicine people, elders, and the like.

The term *sexual shamanism* has been popularized by Kenneth Ray Stubbs, PhD, who is a mentor to many practitioners in the ISTA tribe and the author of ten books, including the groundbreaking *Women of the Light: The New Sacred Prostitute*. The cover copy of this book describes it as follows: "Eight women who exchange sex for money share their lives and insights. Without a continuing lineage, without a temple, the contemporary sexual healer has many faces. Today she is a sex surrogate, sexual meditation teacher, call girl, porn star, or even a shaman."

I also want to acknowledge the work of Stephanie Rainbow Lightning Elk Wadell, MA, who is the pioneering sex shaman referred to in Stubbs's anthology and who presented on the topic of spiritual sexual shamanism at various academic conferences from 1987 to 1997. She was initiated as a Fire Woman in the tradition of Chuluaqui Quodoushka and has made it her life's work to help clients heal from the sexual wounding of our culture.

Serendipitously, the first time I ever heard the term *sex shaman* was in 2001, when I met my life partner, Michael, who was writing a book about sexual intuition—and he already owned the domain www.SexShamans.com. Even though the remarkable story of his sexual awakening didn't make it into this first volume, he was an enormous source of inspiration for the visioning and editing of this book. And he has generously offered his website www.SexShamans.com as the official home for all offerings related to this book and its collaborating authors.

It is also worth noting that most of the authors of this book are not writers. Except for a handful, they are mostly teachers, orators, and even performance artists, but not necessarily wordsmiths. I wanted to preserve their unique voices in hopes that you, dear reader, can get a sense of their energetic transmission. I selected the storytellers that touched and challenged me the most. Somewhere along the way I lost my critical objectivity and surrendered to the irrational magic of this co-creation.

The collaborating authors come from a range of spiritual lineages and religious backgrounds, including Jewish, Pagan, Christian, Hindu, and New Age. We embrace a wide spectrum of styles and practices. We also recognize that other paths to sexual shamanism exist, which are not represented in this book.

We do not claim to represent any indigenous culture or any traditional practices. Each author has a unique and direct connection to the Divine. As such, we are not bound by the tribal beliefs, dogma, or superstitions of ancient shamanism.

Every shamanic path comes with its own light and shadow. Ancient practices developed for the survival of the tribe. Although practitioners were intimate with the local landscape, they lacked education, and many of their teachings and practices operated from prerational consciousness. As shamanism became more conventional, practitioners gained more education, but they were also socialized within their specific cultures and limited by their individual creeds.

The move toward a postconventional practice of shamanism means that we seek to include the best teachings from all over the world and to transcend the disadvantages of each. Our intention is to use the tools and practices that serve to awaken humanity, which may include modern sciences like neurobiology, pharmacology, psychotherapy, and quantum physics, along with the ancient healing arts. We are honoring the unknowable mystery of the universe while riding the frothy edge of human evolution.

A Note on Ethics

A strong grasp of ethics is imperative when it comes to sexual shamanism. Cross-cultural controversies rage over topics such as gender identity, sexual orientation, dual-role relationships, transference, and the imbalance of power. As a global community, ISTA remains sensitive and flexible to subtle differences between populations, where cultural norms, morality, and laws may vary. We seek to offer ethical considerations to inform sovereign decision-making as opposed to imposing a rigid set of rules.

As a guiding principle, ISTA endeavors to be impeccable about teaching boundaries, agreements, consent, nonviolence, and personal responsibility. We attempt to offer services with informed consent only and for the highest good of all.

Inherent in the practice of shamanism are dynamics of power and vulnerability. Great responsibility, trust, and discernment are required of anyone in the position of a spiritual adviser, guide, or seer. In every session, ceremony, or ritual, it is up to the shamanic practitioner to uphold the highest good.

We do not condone the misuse of power for any kind of gain whether it be personal, financial, sexual, professional, social status, or otherwise. People who misrepresent themselves or falsify the truth to exploit the mystique of indigenous cultures and/or traditional practices are dangerous to themselves and to others.

In a context where people access guidance that they believe to be of a higher power, such as ancestors, animal guides, angels, or any other spirit entities, it is crucial to uphold clear ethical principles. Beings of other dimensions are not necessarily bound to the same ethics as humans. One of the essential roles of the shaman is to be a bridge between ordinary reality and other worlds, maintaining awareness and choice about what to say and do with the information they gather from other realms. We maintain that all shamanic healing, divination, and spiritual guidance require clear permission from everyone involved.

Many self-identified shamans may not recognize their own shadows, especially in the area of sexuality. For this reason, a rigorous feedback method is necessary. ISTA has a built-in wisdom council with appointed elders who provide checks and balances to help guide the lead facilitators and governance circle. It's an evolving community of empowered individuals that offers guidelines for ethical behavior, but we are not a governing board that regulates the behavior of others.

As a culture, we share values of love, freedom, truth, integrity, sovereignty, synergy, and reverence for what is considered sacred.

If you choose to practice any of the rituals or practices offered in this book, we implore you to use the highest ethical standards and take full responsibility for your own actions. This book contains narratives that are intended to inspire, entertain, and educate the reader. It is not intended as a substitute for training in sexual shamanism. If you feel a sincere calling to this work, you are welcome to contact the authors to seek mentorship on your shamanic path.

How This Book Was Conceived

The trajectory of my life was forever altered the day I read *Women of the Light: The New Sacred Prostitute*. I still remember being mysteriously drawn to it from the window display of a used-book store. At the time, I was working as a yoga teacher, and I used to feel so confused when my eros would arise in a private session with a client. This spontaneous burst of shakti energy always seemed to bring a higher state of consciousness into my instruction. I'd feel inspired to try a new posture or practice, but cultivating my arousal was beyond the scope of anything taught by my classical yoga mentors and spiritual texts, both of which preached celibacy.

Finally! A book that validated my sexual energy as a healing gift. This book gave me the courage to offer myself more freely. My private yoga classes evolved into partner yoga workshops, and together with my husband, Michael, I started teaching tantra. Tantra is an esoteric path to enlightenment that involves the integration of opposites (such as the sacred and profane, light and dark, partial and whole, male and female.)

In 2003, seeking support as an aspiring professional in the realm of sacred sexuality, I did some online research and discovered that author Kenneth Ray Stubbs would be speaking at a conference in Arizona. I dialed the number for what used to be called the Sedona School of Temple Arts (ISTA before it became international), and the founder, Baba Dez Nichols, picked up his private cell phone. After getting over the shock that I was speaking with the handsome man from the website photos, I told him that I was an aspiring sexual healer. He told me that I was in the right place.

I went to my first Daka/Dakini Conference in 2004 (a gathering for sacred sexual healers, teachers, and practitioners) and felt a significant resonance in my soul, reminding me of the first time I went to a LGBTQ pride festival. I felt like I was coming home. These were the souls with whom I shared a purpose, and I immediately felt the urge to co-create with them. When Baba Dez invited me to coauthor a book with him the following year, it felt preordained.

We combined our life's work with various esoteric oral traditions and added hands-on tools for a practical guidebook titled *Sacred Sexual Healing: The SHAMAN Method of Sex Magic*. It contains details for dozens of embodiment exercises. Unlike most how-to books, which only point at the moon, this book is an invaluable resource for anyone thirsty for a real transmission. Nevertheless, we maintain that books can never capture the fullness of these embodied arts. Therefore, *Sacred Sexual Healing* became the foundational text for ISTA's Level 1 Spiritual Sexual Shamanic Experience. This practitioner's training guide has since been translated into Spanish and Portuguese.

Ten years after the book was born, after a full decade of guiding people into the mysterious terrain of sexual awakening, I woke up from a deep, dreamless sleep with the clear instructions to co-create a new book. And that is how *Sex Shamans* was conceived!

I carried this sparkly new idea with me to Brazil, where ISTA was holding its annual core gathering with faculty and organizers from around the world. Unlike the proceedings of traditional board meetings, ISTA members use eros, pleasure, and play to envision, dream, and synergize about how resources are to be directed for the coming year. Our planning meetings were held between swimming naked on the private beach and dancing around the community fire.

I enthusiastically pitched my new book project to a few colleagues whom I had preselected as prospective coauthors and quickly learned how the ISTA culture deals with new ideas.

There is a key distinction between "birds" and "dragons." An idea is like a bird. Bird medicine is about flying between higher and lower worlds. Birds represent freedom. There are lots of ideas flying around.

While birds are common, dragons are rare and harder to train. A dragon is like a dharmic calling; riding a dragon takes dedication. You must be passionate, fearless, and willing to face dangerous obstacles.

This book is my dragon. Over the past two years, I have dedicated myself to long hours of spearheading, managing, coordinating, editing, and cheerleading this project. My original call for submissions sounded like a rallying cry for shamans to reveal their most intimate secrets.

To appeal to the mythological spirit of the tribe, I spoke of the hero's journey. I sniffed around in each contributing author's personal affairs, looking for the first moment he or she heard the call to adventure. I pried about when the author had crossed the threshold or took a magic flight or mastered two worlds, as if I were Joseph Campbell himself.

Fortunately, this community is rich with risk-takers. Stories poured in, surprising me with their depth, insight, and truth. Most of the contributors are teachers, not writers, who wanted to transmit philosophical truths about collective consciousness. But I insisted on hearing their personal stories, not their transpersonal teachings. The more vulnerable the stories, the more universal the book. Further, I believe that recounting one's personal history is a rite of passage. By shining a light on where we come from, we can release attachments to our old identities.

Together we've been through multiple meaningful revisions, revealing and polishing each gem. For the sake of unveiling these untold stories and discovering new ones, I am holding a future vision for a multivolume series.

How to Read This Book

You are invited to join our tribe around the metaphoric campfire as we share our stories. We'll be entering unknown, exotic territory that may feel uncomfortable at first, so we'll start off with a fun icebreaker to introduce ourselves.

At the beginning of each chapter, alongside each author's photograph, I've made a quick list of fun facts that I like to call "shaman stats." I asked contributing authors for their knee-jerk response to the questions on the following list.

Perhaps you can play along by answering these questions yourself, without overthinking. Have fun!

Shaman Stats

YOUR NAME:

TRANSPERSONAL NAME: (Have you ever taken a spiritual name or an alternate name that extends your identity beyond the personal level of the psyche into a larger realm?)

YEAR OF BIRTH:

SUN SIGN: (What is your zodiac sign, based on the sun's position at the time of your birth?)

HOMETOWN: (What town holds the most memories of growing up?)

RESIDENCE:

ARCHETYPE: (Is there a universal, mythic character or prototype that best describes you?)

SUPERPOWER: (Do you have any extraordinary gifts, skills, or strengths that define you?)

LINEAGE/TEACHERS:

EPITAPH/MOTTO: (Is there a phrase or mantra you'd want to have inscribed on your tombstone?)

SHAMANIC TOOLS: (What sacred objects do you use in ceremonies or healing sessions?)

HOBBIES: (What do you enjoy doing for sheer pleasure?)

If you are resistant to answering the above questions, you are not alone. Some of the contributing authors protested that it sounded like a dating profile; several weren't comfortable revealing their age; others didn't want to trivialize their lineage or their superpower. I asked everyone to answer only those questions that felt authentic, so not all contributing authors answered every question.

The purpose of this little literary device is to help you create a first impression. I recommend reading the shaman stats with attention toward your own preferences and aversions, then notice how your prejudices dissolve while reading deeper into the stories.

At the end of each essay, you'll find a brief biography for the contributor, which will allow you to reach out and continue a connection with any of the contributing authors.

At the end of each chapter, you'll also find an "Embodiment Exercise," which will include detailed directions on how to deepen your participation on the path of sexual shamanism. As the editor, I chose each of these specific techniques because of their relevance to the preceding chapter, and many of the contributing authors recommend these practices as well.

These are not traditional techniques.

All the Way Up, All the Way Down

Spiritual practices tend to fall into two basic approaches. The majority of spiritual schools that teach contemplative practices, such as meditation and yoga, are ascending in their ideology. An ascending path emphasizes transcendence of the physical world, wherein spirituality is independent of the material universe. In contrast, the descending path emphasizes immanence or the embodiment of the Divine into physical form. Examples of descending paths include animistic, druid, pagan and some occult schools. Both of these spiritual approaches offer potent gifts; however, in our view, both of them offer only partial truths.

When either path is practiced to the exclusion of the other, there can be dangerous consequences. The ascending path leads to ecstatic communion with expansive nonphysical energies, but if you disconnect with the body and Earth, the disconnection can result in health issues, repression of bodily pleasure, and desecration of the planet.

On the other hand, the descending path may ground us in our earthly experience, allow us to savor the richness of the material world, and enjoy bodily pleasure in the present moment, but when practiced without sufficient spiritual awareness or consciousness, it can also lead to hedonism and lethargy and can stunt the practitioner's spiritual evolution.

The path of the sex shaman is nondual. This means that it's both ascending and descending, light and dark, masculine and feminine. By practicing the embodiment exercises offered in this book, you will learn to dance between these two worlds. Underlying all these exercises is the belief that the body is a temple that we open with pleasurable worship so that spirit may dwell more fully within. As you practice, you'll begin to realize that you are not only the body, but you are also transcendental consciousness entering into your felt experience. A sex shaman brings the infinite to the finite, boundlessness into boundaries, formlessness into form, and heaven to earth.

Around the world, wisdom traditions create elaborate temples to help seekers turn their senses to God. Catholics, Hindus, Muslims, and pagans alike fill their temples with stimulation for all five senses. Incense for the nose. Devotional music for the ears. Stained-glass windows and ornate sculptures for the eyes. Fine fabrics and textured woodwork for the fingers. Even the practice of fasting before Communion enhances our sense of taste.

Now imagine your body as a holy temple. How can you cleanse, decorate, and activate your form in ways that invite more devotion, passion, and ecstasy? You'll find that the exercises offered in the book are designed to progressively deepen your experience of embodiment, connecting you to both spirit and matter.

To get the most out of these teachings, we recommend that you schedule a specific time and place to practice and take time to try each ritual several times before deciding whether it works for you. Many of the practices ask for you to self-reflect and record your thoughts. We recommend getting a journal and dedicating it exclusively to whatever arises in your life as a result of this book. You may actively seek guidance from a teacher, or you may find that additional guides spontaneously show up to help you on your path.

To support your ongoing study of shamanism, we've included an extensive glossary of occult concepts at the back of the book. Whether or not you encounter unfamiliar terms in the text, we encourage you to use this alphabetical list of esoteric terms and definitions as a resource that points toward more advanced initiations into the temple arts. It reaches beyond the scope of this book to offer explanations of hidden, mystical, metaphysical, supernatural, and paranormal concepts.

I highly recommend reading this book in sequence. Although each chapter was written independently from the whole, each is like a unique gem specifically placed into a particular pattern to create the overall effect of a larger mosaic. Each story touches on multiple overlapping themes, such as orgasm, birth, death, initiation, rebirth, ego death, soul loss, reclamation, love, community, the collective awakening, and beyond.

Several chapters refer to sexual abuse and childhood trauma, which may trigger feelings or memories of your own experience. You may want to read the book with a partner, friend, or community member who can support a conversation about your healing and awakening. Because many of our experiences go beyond reason and run counter to mainstream thinking, you may be called to question some of your own spiritual cosmology. We are not trying to convert or recruit. We simply invite you to release any limiting beliefs that no longer serve you and to open your heart to new possibilities.

As you read, you may resonate deeply with one shaman's story and loathe the next. Take note of how you *feel*. You may find yourself in disbelief or in judgment. Try turning the judgment around: *What is it about myself that I admire in this one? What is it about myself that I judge in that one?* Our reactions provide valuable information about how we can become more whole.

Even if you have no intention of practicing sexual shamanism, the messages in these stories can inspire your life in unimaginable ways. You may need to take a pause from reading for a while or skip a few stories, but we encourage you to come back when you are ready. This book is an ally for your soul and should not sit on your shelf unread.

Sexual shamanism is a vast terrain, and our various voices are here to inspire your journey, with both timeless truths and timely answers. We sit at a crossroads in the evolution of humanity, and if this book has found its way into your hands, your participation is needed for that transformation.

What Is ISTA?

The International School of Temple Arts is a collective of awakened beings around Earth who operate as a mystery school, offering a variety of immersive experiences. ISTA uses group practice, ritual, and initiation to embody the feminine and masculine energies in communion with spirit and form.

ISTA recognizes that the deep self is already free, inherently loving, and dynamically creative. As a movement, we are constantly growing, and at the time of this printing, we have thirty facilitators, thirteen lead faculty members, and a rotating governance, along with twenty apprentice faculty members and dozens of organizers who are active in more than thirty-five countries.

We do not have a physical headquarters, central office, or manager. Instead of seeing ourselves as a business enterprise, we operate as multiple arms of a living organism that shares one group heart. We allow ourselves to be informed by the empty center or void. Our creative community, including thousands of allies and contributors, is experimenting with innovative ways to make sacred temple arts more sustainable.

We offer three distinct immersions: Level 1 is the Spiritual Sexual Shamanic Experience (SSSEx). Level 2 is the Spiritual Sexual Shamanic Initiation (SSSIn). Level 3 is the Spiritual Sexual Shamanic Seeding (SSSeed). We also offer an ISTA Practitioner Training Program. And we are in the experimental stage of developing an ISTA Family Fusion Coming of Age Camp.

We share a vision of a world in which humans have a peaceful, guilt-free, shameless, fearless, and loving relationship with their own bodies, sexuality, emotions, hearts, minds, and spirit as well as the ability to harmonize with other sentient people, animals, and dimensions. For details, visit www.ISTA.life.

INITIATION INTO THE ART OF LOVE

By Lin Holmquist

Jenni Taube

TRANSPERSONAL NAME: Ananda

YEAR OF BIRTH: 1979

SUN SIGN: Cancer

HOMETOWN: Örebro, Sweden

RESIDENCE: The heart

ARCHETYPE: The queen

SUPERPOWER: Shape-shifting

LINEAGE/TEACHERS: From the foundation of Advaita Vedanta philosopher Adi Shankaracharya, through the crazy wisdom schools of neotantra, to trusting the life force within.

EPITAPH/MOTTO: The world needs love right now: let's start the love revolution together!

HOBBIES: Practicing tantra and yoga and exercising.

It was spring, and the hovering buds on the apple trees in the garden slowly unfurled under the sun. Ängsbacka was one of my favorite places on Earth, a center for spiritual growth in the middle of Sweden, and this week we had an Easter gathering with dance, yoga, and *bhajan* (devotional singing). I was there to teach yoga in the mornings.

I arrived in the afternoon and ran into Raven, one of my friends for many years, in the west corridor, just outside my room. Raven came from Germany, and we only met at Ängsbacka's gatherings a few times every year. We had a little flirt going on—nothing serious; we enjoyed dancing together and playing with our mutual attraction on the dance floor. To be honest, I would never engage more deeply than that. He was the kind of man who knew he looked good and didn't hesitate to use his looks to get what he wanted. Raven was a womanizer!

This time, though, I immediately felt that something had shifted in him. He was so relaxed, his eyes were so soft, and his energy worked as a magnet to my core. I dropped my bags on the floor to receive his welcoming embrace, and I couldn't leave. His warmth was so comforting, and I could feel his heartbeat in his chest. I was mesmerized by his fragrance, and as he held me close, I could feel him all the way down in my pussy.

For a while, my mind tried to come up with all sorts of excuses to leave his arms. Who was I to take up his time? What if he had other places to go or other people to embrace? What if he thought that I was in love with him or wanted something from him or . . . I am too much, too close . . . but I couldn't leave. For thirty minutes or so, I fell, breath by breath, deeper and deeper into a space of melting silence. Time and space ceased to exist, and my whole being surrendered to him.

After a while, we looked at each other with stars in our eyes, and I asked him frankly, "What the hell happened to you since we last met?"

Raven told me that half a year back he had started to practice tantra. I was puzzled. At that time I had been into yoga for many years, and I also practiced a tantric meditation technique that took me nowhere but into strain and compulsion. Raven's tantra, however, was a sexual practice, and according to him, it was a fast track to enlightenment. I didn't believe him. I had been living in celibacy for a year, and I was very proud of myself.

I had always loved sex, but I had repeatedly found myself in bed with the "wrong guys." I was attracted to men who used me, and I abused myself in that way for many years. I didn't believe in sex as a spiritual practice; it sounded absurd. In the tradition of yoga that I practiced, *brahmacharya* (celibacy) was very important for the purpose of sublimating sexual energy and converting it to creativity or stillness. Nevertheless, Raven had changed a lot since we last met, and I was curious.

The next morning, some friends and I gathered around Raven in the garden for breakfast. He told us about polarities, the attraction between the masculine and the feminine energy, and how the dance of polarities merges in the heart as love. I was all ears; it reminded me a lot of yogic philosophy, and I wanted to know more. Raven asked me if I wanted a private session with him after dinner that night, and I said yes. We agreed to meet up in my room at eight.

I didn't see Raven during dinner, so I went straight to my room to prepare myself for the session. I took a shower and shaved my legs and my pussy. I dressed in clean clothes and lay on the bed with a book to wait for him to arrive. It was with great exhilaration that I called him in when he finally knocked on my door.

There he was, more gorgeous than ever. His masculine face was framed by long hair like a lion's mane, and his arms hung relaxed by his sides. He closed and locked the door behind him and called me to stand up from the bed and step out on the floor. And so I did.

"Undress for me," he said and gave me a commanding nod.

I took off my dress and let my leggings fall to the floor. I shivered when I realized that he expected me to take off my bra and my panties as well. So there I stood, naked in front of him.

He didn't move, just stood there by the door and looked at me. What did he expect from me now? Were we going to have tantric sex right away? And how would that be? Did he want me to approach him or not? My mind was totally confused, and the room started spinning, but he didn't move; he just stood there and looked me in the eyes. I had never felt so naked in my entire life.

Suddenly, I felt him. I could feel that he didn't want anything from me; he didn't expect anything from me. He didn't want to kiss me; he didn't want to touch me; he didn't want me to do anything to him. He just wanted to see me and look at me with reverence and awe. I could see in his eyes what he saw when he looked at me.

He saw God.

When I realized that he saw God in me, I suddenly felt God looking out of my eyes as well, and I saw God in him and God everywhere.

Rays of light sprang out of the halo of gold that surrounded us, and I could feel myself in every breath. There we stood like divine embodiments of man and woman; then he bowed in gratitude to me and left the room. I stumbled back to my bed and lay down on my back with one hand on my beating heart. I couldn't grasp what had just happened, nor the rushes of energy coursing through my body. I couldn't sleep that night, tossing and turning in my bed, wondering . . .

The next day, I met up with Raven at breakfast and sat down close to him. We didn't mention the session from the night before, but he kept on talking about tantra and sexuality as a spiritual practice. He talked about the importance of presence and surrender, and everyone around the table seemed very interested. When we went to leave our dishes, he asked me if I wanted to try another session that night, and, of course, I said yes. In fact, the whole day I couldn't think of anything else besides the promised session. I was so curious and excited.

He came shortly after eight o'clock. This time, he actually sat down on my bed. We didn't talk, but he caressed my face and my neck and started to take command of me in a way that I really enjoyed. He bent my head back and kissed me on my neck and my shoulders. Then he looked me in the eyes, deep and long, and he didn't let go of my gaze. He lifted me up on his lap and started to arouse me, looking me straight in my eyes. He started to touch my spine in a way that I had never felt before. He knocked his knuckles on my breastbone and made my spine move in waves. I gasped in delight, and then he started to move my hips on top of his hips in spirals and circles. I could feel his erection under my pussy, and I closed my eyes and leaned my head back as I moaned with pleasure.

Immediately, he snapped his fingers in front of me and pulled my neck back so he could gaze into my eyes again. We were breathing rhythmically together, and I felt totally confused. I had so much resistance in my muscles, so much control. When I was about to let go of control and be fully under his command, a wave of bliss came over me and made me close my eyes and drift away. But he wouldn't let me go. As soon as he felt that I lost presence, he snapped his fingers in front of my face and commanded me to look him in his eyes. Waves of pleasure and joy broke my patterns of control and confusion, and he took command of me and kept me present. After a while, we rested together in silence, gazing at the stars in each other's eyes. He didn't want to make love to me this night either, which was a big surprise to me. I had never met a man who wanted a date from me and then left unfucked or unsucked, but Raven did. He said good night and left for his room.

I couldn't sleep. My body was so hot and burning. The whole night I tossed and turned, and at 4:00 a.m. I had to give up on the idea of sleeping. I had too much energy in my body, so I went up to one of the balconies to meditate. In my meditation, my mind bombarded me with thoughts of what had happened the night before and what secrets Raven could teach me. I wondered if he would meet me again, and if I could gaze into his eyes forever. I realized that I was starting to fall in love with him. Or was I? I started to evaluate our future together. How would it be to spend the rest of my life with him? We could have great tantric sex in his house in Germany every night and have long romantic weekends in bed. Our kids were almost the same age and would probably get along just fine, and I could look for a job as a yoga teacher in his town. They had really good yoga studios there; it would be so perfect.

Suddenly I became aware of my own thoughts. How could I project a whole future onto someone just because he had given me two of the most beautiful experiences of my life? What was this invisible contract that I constructed in order to love? I realized that whenever I experienced love, this was the detour I took in my mind. I immediately calculated whether this person could be the love of my life and how our lives could be woven together. I realized that I was used to putting love in a small box with walls that represent certain projections and demands, a secret contract of love.

Suddenly I felt as if I had been struck by lightning. My whole body opened, and through my nose I could smell the most exquisite fragrance from the opening flowers in the garden. I heard bees humming in the morning sun, and the birds sang as loud as an orchestra with hundreds of voices.

I could hear what the birds were singing: "Come, sit with me on my branch, sing with me. Make love to me. I love you, come, come."

I opened my eyes and saw the apple blossoms opening their petals, and all their delicate beauty was revealed to be seen and loved. "Come," they said. "Come and love me, make love to me. Drink of my sweet nectar and enjoy me. This is how beautiful I am. I am alive."

The whole of nature vibrated with love, and I was overwhelmed by it. After a while, other people woke up and entered the garden with their breakfast. They sat beside one another in the sun and talked about the weather and the news, the workshops and their memories, but I could hear, behind the words, what they really said.

"Come, sit beside me. I want to know you. I want to feel you. Come love me. Let me love you."

I started to cry as my heart cracked open to the truth that had been unseen for so long, and from deep inside of me, a voice came. I trembled from the power of it.

> *If you don't believe in love, you don't believe in me.*
> *If you don't believe in love, you don't believe in me!*
> *I am love.*
> *I am love.*
> *I am love.*

The voice inside me was so strong that I couldn't hear anything else. My heart was pounding, and waves of heat rolled from my lower back up to my face, again and again.

I saw Raven from the balcony. He was surrounded by people who were eager to feel him, love him, and be close to him, and I could see his love pouring like an infinite stream out of his whole being. As I went out into the garden, I saw him sitting with a young man in front of him, deeply gazing into the young man's eyes. Tears were rolling down the young man's cheeks. I realized that Raven's love was not mine to take for myself alone. It belonged to the world.

Nevertheless, I enjoyed bathing in the love we shared whenever we met in the garden or on the dance floor. We flirted as usual, but there was a new kind of spark between us, like a secret that no one shared except for us.

One day, we both decided to go to a *bhajan* class. He held my hand as we walked up the stairs to the room where the music played. I felt his presence as Shiva, and I was his Shakti; we were the divine couple, and I felt chosen. I felt special. Even if his love poured out into the world so freely, I was special to him. He had chosen me.

We sat down in the front row and started to sing, and our voices merged with each other and danced in harmony with the rest of the room. After a while, another woman sat down beside Raven. They greeted each other lovingly, and she started to touch his spine. I saw the delight in her eyes, and their bodies moved softly together to the music.

Suddenly, I was struck by jealousy. Who the fuck was she? Didn't she see that we were at the concert together, me and my Shiva? She disturbed our harmony, and maybe she wanted to take him away from me. A cold hand of loneliness, rejection, and jealousy took a firm grip on my belly. My breath became shallow, and I felt so ashamed. Then, everything shifted. Raven had his hand resting on my knee, and I could feel his pleasure. Through his hand, I could literally feel him being touched on his spine. Not only could I feel his pleasure, but I could also feel the other woman's love flowing through him too. My body opened again with bliss and streams of heat. My voice opened to God, and together we sang the sounds of love, all three of us.

That same night, Raven invited me to come to his room for our last session. The retreat was over the day after, and we were about to go home. When I came to his room, I was full of expectations as well as a touch of fear. His roommate was in the other bed, ready to go to sleep, but he gave us his blessing to do what we wanted by putting in earplugs and turning his face to the wall. Raven and I drowned in each other's eyes for the last time. Softly he touched my whole body under deep presence, not leaving my eyes for a second. He kissed my hands and my arms and touched my spine in a way that rippled delight all the way down to my pussy. We were breathing together, deep and soft, and after what seemed to be eons of time melting under his hands, he rolled over onto his back and lifted me to sit on top of him. Slowly, he entered me with his cock. He didn't move; he gazed into my eyes, breathed with me, and stayed still. At first, I didn't feel much. I attempted to move like I used to, but he stopped me, holding my ponytail firmly at my neck and looking deeply into my eyes. "Do not move," he said, and then I could feel him. Even though his cock softened inside me, I could feel its energy rising. Like a silver ray of clear light, he illuminated my insides, and I trembled. My skin felt electric, and all the little hairs on my arms rose.

"If you move, I will come inside of you, so please be still," he said, and another shot of electricity vibrated inside me. I drifted away in the bliss of the sensations of the beginning of an orgasm inside me, but he would not let me go. He held my hair firm and forced me to look into his eyes as I came in a way that I had never experienced, like soft waves all inside my pussy, waves that made my whole body relax deeply.

"I am sorry, I can't fuck you like other people do," he said. "I have a problem with premature ejaculation, but I really love being inside of you."

My heart opened with such love and gratitude. My pussy vibrated with orgasmic waves, and tears filled up my eyes for the honesty and vulnerability this strong and loving man showed me.

After making love, we rested beside each other before he asked me to return to my room. My dreams were vivid and weird that night.

After leaving Ängsbacka, I went home to my daughter and my ordinary life. Little did I know that nothing would ever be the same again.

In the morning the day after the retreat, I rode my daughter to school on my bike, and riding downhill on the way home, something really strange happened. Suddenly, my whole spine started to vibrate with electricity. It jerked and shook with such power, and the shaking spread out to my chest and down my arms and into my hands. I had never felt such a feeling before; my whole spine was spastic and my hands vibrated. At the same time, this feeling was so familiar to me as if it had been a part of me forever. When I got home, my whole body was vibrating with ecstasy. My sister was visiting me, and I spent the whole day in deep and soulful conversations with her, with music, drawing, and creativity just pouring out of me. The day after, when I got back to my work as a yoga teacher and gym instructor, I was high, as if on drugs. I felt like I had made love to the whole world, and the participants in my classes came up to me afterward and asked what had happened to me. I couldn't answer, but I felt something deep and powerful moving through me.

I started to wake up around 4:00 a.m. every morning. My body would be spontaneously orgasming; it moved like a snake, undulating and dancing in bed. My need for sleep reduced to a maximum of five hours a night, and for a few weeks I was high and vibrating with light. I felt on top of the world in a way that I had never experienced before. It came out in such a natural and centered way, and it enhanced my life experience tremendously.

I tried to call my friend Raven through Skype to ask him what this wonderful energy was, but as soon as I saw him online, time and space ceased to exist, and we ended up eye gazing in silence for hours. There was no way that I could put words to my experience.

One day when I arrived at work, I felt really raw. It was as if I could feel all the people around me right inside me, and there was so much pain and confusion. The people who go to the gym are mostly doing it to correct something they don't like about themselves or to escape something painful, and I could feel every single bit of their pain. Once in a while a contented person walked by, and I could exhale. But when the phone rang, I could feel it cut my flesh like a knife, and when I touched the computer to do some administrative work, the computer shut down. I had to go and hide in the staff kitchen to get away from it all.

The next day, when I took the bus to work, the light started to illuminate the shadows inside me.

I walked through the square to take the bus, when suddenly I felt as if everyone was staring at me. As I continued walking, I felt as if even the houses came closer to me. My heart started to beat fast, and my breath got shallow. The houses rushed in toward me, and I couldn't breathe. I felt as if I were dying. But I also realized that I knew what was going on. This seemed like a panic attack, something that I had only heard about before. So I stayed cool, got on the bus, and went off to the gym. Instead of going to the reception desk, I went straight to my boss and explained the situation. I was shaking from the inside out, and she sent me home immediately.

When I woke up the next morning and opened my eyes, my room did not look the same. The roof was not a roof; I could see the open sky above me. When I looked at the walls, I saw them fall down, brick by brick. I couldn't leave my bed for several hours, the walls puzzling me, but I stayed centered and realized why I had had those experiences. The panic attack was a message from my subconscious mind, and it told me that I had been lying to myself for too long. I had been going to a job that was nice: I had my yoga groups, my training, and a good income. But I had no freedom: I couldn't speak completely freely at work; I couldn't be myself. If I kept on selling my soul for safety and money, if I continued this lifestyle, I would end my life in depression or even worse. I had to wake up and be true to myself, 100 percent. The walls that fell down and the open sky above symbolized my belief system, which was dismantling, and my ego, which was falling apart.

When I woke up the next day, I was a man, a young man around the age of twenty. I felt my body, and yes, under my hands I felt my soft and feminine shape, but somehow I knew that I had a slim and muscular male body and a cock between my legs. I spent the day as a man, exploring my masculine energy as it pervaded every part of my being.

The next day, the room was shining as if it were polished. The door handles, the walls, the furniture—it all sparkled and vibrated with light. I stayed in bed that day and observed the beauty of a mindless being.

The days went on with those extraordinary experiences of being in a heightened consciousness. One day I spent on the floor in my living room, and everything around me was empty. No walls, no floor, no roof; it was all gone. I felt so alone, as if floating in space, timeless, endless. I realized that this is the core of my being. I am alone; I am the creator. I am everything and nothing. Since I am the creator, the one who creates everything out of nothing, I can create whatever I want. I suddenly felt such a tremendous power.

The next day I told my boss that I wouldn't come back to work for another nine months. I realized that I needed to go deeper and follow the flow of energy that made my body dance in bed at night and my mind open to the journey beyond.

I consulted a psychiatrist with the concern that my hallucinations might be a psychosis or schizophrenia, but she reassured me of my sanity and told me that as long as I was not suffering from this condition and was able to manage my life, I would not be considered clinically ill. I decided to follow the flow and spend the coming months discovering the mysteries that had opened up to me.

I felt alone in this experience. I tried to talk to Raven about it, but I couldn't put it into words, and I was longing to fully understand what I was going through.

I asked the universe for guidance, and the next day I woke up unusually late. I felt heavy and tired. I heard my eight-year-old daughter calling me from the bathroom.

"Mom, why am I black around my nose?" she called. "And Mom, why is the toilet seat black?"

I went into the bathroom and saw that not only was she black around the nose, but I too had small black rings around my nostrils, and I had a big black ring around my mouth. I smelled smoke in the air, and when I touched the mirror, I realized that there was a layer of black dust covering its surface.

I went through the whole apartment, running my finger along the walls, the curtains, the sofa, and it was all covered with a thin layer of black dust. When I came into the kitchen, I realized an advent candle, in a candlestick filled with traditional Christmas moss, had burned all the way down and created a big hole in the table, but the curtains were untouched, the letter to the tax office that lay on the table was burned only in one corner, and somehow the fire had magically gone out.

I was stunned and called the insurance company. After a few hours, the sanitation firm came to sanitize the whole apartment, and my daughter and I went to Ängsbacka for the Christmas holiday.

When I came home from Ängsbacka, I automatically found myself packing the apartment into moving boxes, and the first thought that struck my mind was, Who is moving? It took me a moment to realize that I was the one who was moving. I was moving on!

I couldn't live a life that forced me to sell my soul any more. I was no longer able to maintain a lifestyle that was only for show—a facade with a big fancy apartment that I spent all my free time cleaning, just in case someone might visit. I was a slave to my need to be seen as perfect and successful, to prove my worth by accumulating material things. All my true values had been forgotten for too long, so I made a phone call to terminate the contract with my landlord, and I rented a storage room for my boxes. I bought a ticket to India for myself and my daughter and wrote an email to her school telling them that we would not be returning for three months.

From that day on, I promised myself to heal my relationships to life, to myself, and to my child and to follow my heart's truth no matter what. Starting that day, my life turned around, and I have lived a life of joy and freedom ever since.

I devoted myself to giving back to life all the gifts that life had given me. I started to walk the path of a dakini and began to support the kundalini awakening process in other people. I recognized my gifts as a healer but also saw myself as someone who brings people together in love. Now I travel worldwide, giving workshops and arranging festivals in the name of love, and the more I give away from this well of joy, bliss, and love, the more I receive. Many times I have called Raven back, wanting to thank him for the precious gift he gave me, but whenever I do, he just turns it back to me.

"You were ready, you know that. It's not because of me, it's because of you."

Lin Holmquist is a yoga teacher, yoga therapist, tantric therapist, and dakini devoted to unconditional love. Lin's passion is connecting to the Divine source and meeting from that place. She makes her contribution through workshops and sessions and by organizing tantra events, including the Ängsbacka Tantra Festival—the biggest tantra festival in Europe.

Soul-Gazing

PURPOSE: This simple and powerful technique can cut through illusion and open the heart, allowing you to see the Divine in yourself and others. When done regularly, it can transform your understanding of who you are. Prolonged gazing can induce trance and accelerate your awakening. It can also increase bonding between people.

PREPARATION: Eye gazing can be done with a partner or as a solo practice in front of a mirror. If you are working with a partner, adjust your bodies to be as close as you comfortably can, while looking into each other's eyes. Drop into deep belly breaths and feel what is going on in your body, heart, and sexual center. Ask your ego to step aside for the duration of the ritual.

PROCESS: Start by softening your gaze. This is not a staring contest. Look into each other's left eye. The left side of the body is considered to be the receptive side. It is okay to change eyes, if and when you feel called to. Just relax, breathe, and allow the experience to unfold. Notice what arises without judging it. Be open and curious, like a child.

If you feel resistance, see if you can allow it to melt. How does it feel to be seen? How does it feel to look deeply into another person? Afterward, discuss your experience with your partner.

VARIATIONS: Once skilled at gazing from the soul, you may advance to gazing upon a partner's genitals. Or you may use a mirror to gaze upon your own sex organs. Yoni/lingam gazing can melt years of body shame and allow us to experience reverence and awe for the human form. Not only are we the embodiment of the Divine, but our sex organs are also portals where spirit comes into form.

Start by preparing a sacred space where you will have no interruptions. Find a comfortable position in which your body can relax for at least 15 minutes. Begin slowly with a namaste to recognize the Divine in yourself and your partner. Observe all of the details; see if you can sense or feel the energetic essence of the sex center. What arises in you as you witness or feel yourself being witnessed? Notice your internal experience without attaching any meaning to it. Afterward, you may want to share with your partner. Or if you're alone, you can journal, draw, paint, or write poetry.

NOTES: You can do this practice for as long as you want. I suggest that the first time you begin with 5 minutes of eye gazing. Then close your eyes, go inside yourself, and reconnect internally for a few minutes. When you are ready, open your eyes and begin again. Extend the gazing time as you get more comfortable with the process. Soul gazing for an extended period can take you to new levels of connection. By extending to 30 to 60 minutes, you may find yourself in an altered state. Soul gazing is naturally trance inducing. As your inner eye opens, it may have hallucinogenic effects. You may see aspects of your own face or your ancestors' faces projected onto the face in front of you. Your sense of time and space may melt. Or you may have other sensory experiences such as smelling phantom scents or hearing voices.

RESOURCES: Crystal Dawn Morris writes in detail about this practice on www.ISTA.life.

2
TALES OF A JUICY CRONE

By Laurie Handlers

A. J. Vitaro

TRANSPERSONAL NAME: Latihan

YEAR OF BIRTH: 1947

SUN SIGN: Sagittarius

HOMETOWN: New York City

RESIDENCE: Phoenix, Arizona

ARCHETYPE: Magician

SUPERPOWER: I'm able to read people. My hands can feel trauma. I listen and speak clearly.

LINEAGE/TEACHERS: Carl Rogers, Isabel Hickey, Robert Gass, Malidoma Some, Werner Erhard, Bodhi Avinasha, Deva, and Lakshmi

MOTTO: "We don't stop playing because we grow old; we grow old because we stop playing" (attributed to George Bernard Shaw).

HOBBIES: Meeting people, dancing, practicing radical life extension, writing, working out, drinking red wine, swimming, collecting art, and hosting my radio show

I posed as a naked centerfold for a women's magazine. I love my body and deserve to show it off. When the editor invited me, I responded yes, without hesitation. She nearly fainted when I told her my age. I recently turned seventy and regularly attract men (and women) half my age, wherever I go. I'm happy to share my sexy escapades, but the real proof of my sexual shamanic secret is the fact that I am vital, full of life, attractive as ever, and loved beyond my wildest imagination.

I grew up in the 1950s and '60s in New York. My family moved from Brooklyn to Long Island to experience a "more idyllic life." I remember being an extremely precocious little girl in every way.

My mother worried about me, especially when it came to sex. I discovered self-pleasure at an early age and used to lock myself in the bathroom for hours.

My mother would call, "Laurie, what are you doing in there?" When I think back, I realize, even then, I had discovered how to take my sweet time for my own pleasure.

I would respond, "Nothing, Mother."

Here are a few memories that stand out from my early sexual development:

My grandmother watched me like a hawk and told my mother that I was going to be "trouble" when it came time for dating.

My mother washed my mouth out with soap when I was five years old for saying a bad word.

I had my very first partnered orgasm in seventh grade on the dance floor, dancing slow with a boy, when he rubbed his knee against my pubic mound.

The first boy I met who had a car became my lover, and the backseat became a safe haven in which to explore.

Although I had been sexually active, I was still technically a virgin when I began my first year of college. Back home on a semester break, as I walked along the beach with my father, I had an urge to tell him that I was planning to have intercourse. "Pop, I'm going to experience sex when I go back to college," I blurted out.

He responded, "Laurie, sex is not the best thing in the world, and it is not the worst thing in the world. It is part of life, so do enjoy it, and remember you are responsible for your actions. If you should get pregnant, you'll have to deal with it."

I thought, *Great, my father approves.*

When we got back to the house, I told my mother of our conversation. She took out every pot and pan from the cupboard and threw them at both of us! So much for my parents' guidance and blessings on sex.

After I had my first experience with intercourse while a freshman—and by the way, it was a terrible experience—I sought my pleasure with a number of other young men. Because I had been masturbating at least since I was five, I knew something about my budding sexuality. I remember having sex with a football player, a law student, a frat boy, and a grad student, to name a few. I can't say that they turned me on that much; they seemed to rush into intercourse. Although I was new to intercourse per se, I had certainly experienced more variety than that with my high school boyfriend. It seemed to me that everybody was in a hurry to reach the goal of ejaculation.

What about kissing? What about heavy petting? What about using fingers? What about oral? These all seemed to go by the wayside once people had experienced intercourse. I didn't like it.

Back then, I intuited that sex was far more than the in-and-out friction of intercourse, but no matter who I invited to go deeper with me, I got blank stares. None of the young men I dated had any interest in going deep at all. When I look back on it, my notion of going deep was something akin to prolonging orgasm for as long as possible for both partners, after hours of foreplay. It was a deep, spiritual experience for me even then, though I didn't know how to put it into words.

Not much later, when psychedelics became the rage, I was able to touch the kind of experience I had been longing for with a partner or two. Since it was the time of "free love," I didn't have to get into a relationship with these partners. But when I fell for someone, I was pretty much monogamous. Back then, I never even considered anything else.

Anyway, I recall one such experience in grad school where my partner at the time and I dropped acid and began having sex. By the time the drug came on, we were melting into each other and the cosmos all at once. After one of these acid experiences, we emerged from my bedroom to discover that humans had actually accomplished putting a man on the moon—at the same time that we were melting! We looked at each other and said what hippies said back then: "Far out!"

Things got better for me in terms of my sex life in those days, but I'm sad to say that that period didn't last.

I lived through both the women's liberation and the sexual liberation. But the loosening of attitudes toward sexuality wasn't exactly liberating for women. When I entered my twenties and thirties, sex for the most part wasn't that great for women. With the introduction of the birth control pill, we could now control our own destinies, but I felt I didn't have permission to ask for what I specifically desired. Being direct about what I wanted was sometimes met with disdain from my partners. I think my sexual appetite scared them. Several times, well-meaning guys told me that I was too forward, and that was enough to shut me down for a while. My friends were not much help in this department either. Suppression from every direction!

I figured that this state of affairs was just the way it was. The other thing I knew was that I was not at all "normal."

In the '70s my lover gave me a copy of *Liberating Masturbation* by Betty Dodson, later renamed *Sex for One*. Now I was on to something. I wrote letters to Betty telling her how cool she was—and she responded. I got so many ideas from her and felt that at last somebody was saying something about women's sexuality that was in line with what I felt. I treasured my letters from Betty, and today I still have the front and back covers of her book, but the inside is missing because I lent it out so much. I guess the book finally wore out.

One day in the '80s, I read an article about Margot Anand in *Yoga Journal*. I read it over and over. It described what I knew in my heart existed, something that went beyond what Betty Dodson was saying.

There was something called tantra, sacred sexuality that connected body, mind, and spirit with the act of sex. I wept with joy! I had no idea how to access her or her classes about this subject, but I was determined to keep my eyes open, and I knew that eventually I would find a way to experience tantra.

At last, in 1996, a friend of mine mentioned to me that a tantra class was coming to Silver Spring, Maryland. It was going to be taught by Bodhi Avinasha of the Ipsalu Tantra School. I lived in Washington, DC, at the time, doing government contracting work for Bill Clinton's welfare-to-work initiative, so I was close enough to attend for the weekend. After that first experience, I knew I had found what I'd been longing for. Once again, I wept with joy. I remembered who I was. I turned on my feminine. I felt whole and complete and connected to every drop of water in the ocean.

I immersed myself in the study of tantra. There is, of course, much more to it than exotic sexual practices. I was so hungry for this knowledge that I blasted through all three levels that my teacher offered. Then I completed her teacher training program, and in a couple of years I had to leave her. I needed to find other teachers or strike out on my own, and that's exactly what I did.

I incorporated knowledge from my many years of seeking personal growth and awareness into my own workable—and pleasurable—map for life.

The first tantra course I ever taught was in January 1999. I was a bit nervous, but nothing could stop me. I taught tantra part-time and continued to do government contracting work until the next presidential election. When George W. Bush was elected, all of the welfare-to-work contracts went to churches, and I didn't belong to a church, nor was I going to. So I said to myself, *Sex always sells. No government will determine whether I can make a living. I will become a full-time tantra teacher.* I have never once looked back.

I even wrote a book called *Sex and Happiness: The Tantric Laws of Intimacy*. It's a book about happiness, communication, self-expression, and sex. My book isn't your typical tantra book. I believe that what sets me apart from other teachers is not just that I am writing from my own personal experience and in-depth study but also that I am offering a road map to creating possibilities while working with people's intentions. This comes from years of working for Landmark, a worldwide personal growth company, as well as my own corporate consulting business. The way that I teach transformation is to use whatever has actually worked for me in shifting my own life.

When I was first teaching tantra, I was having less, not more, sex than I anticipated I would. I wasn't interested in sleeping with my students, and I rarely met anyone else I was interested in. What to do?

I got into a five-and-a-half-year-long relationship with a man who helped me create everything I am now. He taught me how to run a business, how to do marketing, and how to branch out to different locations and even foreign countries. From him, I learned to multitask and to tackle difficult projects that, before I met him, I wouldn't have believed myself capable of completing. This was a pivotal relationship, because I got my first taste of what it meant to be limitless.

Unfortunately, our sex life sucked. He was not a very attentive lover, and he cheated a lot to boot. I think his idea was quantity, while I was still seeking quality. When we broke up, I thought once again, *There has to be something more to this whole sex thing.* I felt so unfulfilled.

So, I decided, one way or another, to explore the deep cosmic places that my soul craved. I had a talk with myself and decided to take things into my own hands, literally.

A couple of these experiences stand out.

Once, with my crystal wand and my vibrator in hand, I squatted over the floor and began to self-stimulate. As I turned myself on with my vibrator, I used my wand on my G-spot, and before long went into a multiorgasmic state. Soon, I noticed a puddle on the floor. I could hardly believe my own eyes. I had taught myself to ejaculate!

Then, one night after smoking a joint, I asked myself, *How can I fool myself into thinking someone else is making love to me the way I want them to?* I answered, *I know: I'll wear surgical gloves! Then I won't recognize my own hands.* And so I did. I took myself to peak and over, to peak and over, to peak and over . . . again and again. I experimented with different textures and temperatures on my body. I used my hands and different vibrators. I came standing, sitting, and lying down. What a night!

All of my exploration helped me know the exact speed, intensity, and pressure that brought me the most pleasure, and I knew that I could never be silent again. I was determined to tell my lovers exactly what I liked and how I liked it. I benefited tremendously from this particular night and so have my lovers. It was absolutely game changing.

I say "lovers" because I would never want just one, never again.

Another chapter of my life opened when I met Baba Dez Nichols, and he invited me to present at a conference. I didn't know it then, but our meeting would later change my life. (It's not what you think—I am one of the few women I know who hasn't had sex with him.) But I am jumping ahead of myself.

This conference was significant because it gave me the opportunity to meet a sex shaman. He lived in LA, and I was living in Phoenix. He visited me often for about a year and a half. He taught me all the secrets he had under his kimono, and I finally had someone with whom to share mine. Together, we created a form of sex magic that I both practice and teach to this day.

I started manifesting things I had hardly dared to dream about. I have created a book, a DVD, a successful radio show, and a Shangri-la house, and I have starred in three movies. I use sex magic to manifest everything. I use it so much that I can be heard yelling, on occasion— just at the point of orgasm—"How much money do you want?" Then my lovers and I break out in laughter.

When I was living in New York City, I participated in the OneTaste community as a part-time resident. OneTaste, founded by Nicole

Daedone, has been dedicated to teaching and spreading the practice OM, or orgasmic meditation, which focuses on female pleasure. One night, Alan Steinfeld, creator of New Realities TV and a member of the OneTaste community, invited me out to a potluck and presentation. Alan is something of a spiritual vortex for New York City, and he's like my brother. He said he wanted to introduce me to the physical immortality community, and my first reaction was, "I don't want to meet any vampires."

But he was persuasive. "I'm telling you, you need to meet these people."

So, I went to a dinner party with forty-five savvy people from the sacred sexuality community, and I became intrigued with the people dedicated to super longevity.

That evening, they talked about the importance of having a community that holds you to living an unlimited life.

I was very impressed because I've been through every "spiritual" conversation—Landmark Education, opening the heart, bodywork, astrology, tantra, orgasmic meditation—but I'd never heard about physical immortality.

So, I enrolled in their workshop that Sunday with about thirty-five people, and after listening to them speak, I took the mic and said, "Let me get this straight, if I continue to teach tantra the way I know it, but take out the part about Hindu reincarnation or heaven or hell, which I don't believe in anyway, I'll be able to be an immortalist?" They said, "Yes."

And they looked me in the eye and posed the basic question: "Why do you have to die?"

I replied, "Because everyone else does. It's written at the end of the unspoken plot about humanity. We're told that we all get old and die."

And they asked, "What if you don't have to?"

I laughed, "I'm certainly interested in that. My life is great!" And that's how they started encouraging me to think beyond the programmed script. I came to realize that physical immortality is not some faraway, distant goal in a future beyond this world; it's a bodily feeling, right now in this moment, that we are timeless and free of any obligation to die.

I became obsessed to learn everything I could about super longevity by traveling back and forth from New York to Scottsdale, Arizona. I had to consider that I had "made it" in New York City and that there was something more for me to learn.

So, I decided to move closer to Scottsdale, and I talked to a real estate agent and found that the prices of houses in Phoenix were like the price of candy compared to a house in New York. I took one quick look around and found my tantric home. I now live in a sprawling ranch house with two wings, four bedrooms, and a backyard that is perfect for hosting tantric parties. The pool, the Mexican-tile bar, the sunken fire pit, and the thatched roof *palapa* each serve as intimate areas to have sensual encounters, or "puja stations," as I like to call them. I can have parties and events under the stars in the desert. And I do. I've learned so much living here in the past ten years.

- I now exercise five to seven days a week.
- I restrict my caloric intake to a mostly Mediterranean diet.
- My nutritional supplementation optimizes my vitality.
- I've consciously eliminated negative talk about aging.
- I like what I see when I look in the mirror.
- I take immune-boosting IVs, especially when I come home from being on the road.
- I break old routines because people grow old with unbroken habits.
- I have broken my habit of workaholism. I used to work until 11:00 p.m., but now I stop at 5:00 p.m. (No matter what I'm working on—it'll be there tomorrow.)
- I sleep seven to nine hours each night.
- I've learned to treat my body better than ever before.
- And I earn more money too!

About five years ago, I was presented with a challenge. Someone said: "It's going to take a lot of money to live forever, so what are you going to do to increase your abundance?" That's when I realized that I had to stop working alone, doing everything myself.

That was the year I started my apprenticeship program, and with the help of my apprentices, I actually get more done while working less.

Just about that time I received the life changing phone call from Baba Dez, where I finally said yes to joining the ISTA faculty. He had invited me multiple times before, but I wasn't ready to surrender to learning the core curriculum. As I immersed myself in spirituality, sexuality, and shamanism, I found myself working as part of a team, and now I have a much bigger reach than "Little Laurie" used to have all by herself. This changed everything in my world.

My main community is ISTA. There are a lot of people in the world of sacred sexuality who don't even know about my pursuit of immortality. Some of my colleagues think I am crazy to pursue it. I'm not going to stop being me. I'm not going to hold back. I'm a crone. You can't shut me up. I enjoy living into the unknown.

There is a Sufi meditation called *Latihan*. I've made it my primary practice of fearless movement into the unknown in preparation for radical life extension. It's usually done blindfolded or with eyes closed. You simply allow yourself to be moved by the mystery. Rather than thinking about the movement, you allow it to arise organically from within itself. There are no dance steps, no yoga postures. One authentic movement leads to another. It's totally spontaneous, without planning—and that's how the immortals live. Like shamans, they question everything.

My other main practice is sex magic. When I'm self-pleasuring, I often visualize living forever. I can't do this with all my partners, but my current partner, Michael Gibson, is into it. When we make love, we start off by stating our desires and intentions, and I'll say, "I want to enjoy optimal health and live forever." And then we'll surrender and enjoy it. Afterward, I might say, "I'm seeing myself in this wonderful body that's very limber and keeps living forever."

I am an ambassador of immortality around the world. I speak my truth. I'm sexually free.

Another place that I travel to regularly is Hedonism in Jamaica, a clothing-optional swingers' resort where I feel great. Although I wouldn't call myself a swinger, I wouldn't want to go without this yearly visit. Each time I return home from Hedo, as it is affectionately called, I feel like the sexiest and most beautiful woman in the world. Everybody comes home feeling like this. At Hedo, there is total acceptance for every age and every body type. It is truly a sex-positive environment, and it feels good to be there in spite of any personal boundaries I may have. Nothing is wrong there. Nobody is judged. There is no shame or guilt. I can't say that I experience this unlimited acceptance so completely in any other place.

In the past year I have even been a poster child for the Sybian, the Lamborghini of vibrators. It's a saddle-style riding machine designed for women's maximum pleasure. When I first received mine from the company, I entered myself into a thirty-day challenge and blogged about it so the entire world could have a peek into my sex life. Sometimes I ride the Sybian solo, and sometimes I invite a partner to join me, which may involve completely surrendering the controls to someone else. My life is an open book.

One of the hottest things I've ever done was to play out a fantasy with a man I hardly knew. This man and I scripted out the scene in advance and then played it out. I invited him to my home. I left the front door open, turned on sound machines, and closed all the other doors, so when he arrived, he couldn't hear me and didn't know which room I was in. He had to search the house to find me.

Meanwhile, I was scantily clad and riding my Sybian, while blind-folded, ear-plugged, and listening to music. I had no idea when he arrived or entered my room. When he did enter the room, I'm sure his heart stopped for a second at the sight of me. The first moment I felt his presence was when he started breathing next to my ear and neck. It was so exciting that I almost jumped out of my skin. Then he began to gently touch me and stroke my body all over. I was already gently climaxing as he stroked me and kissed me with the wettest kisses. He literally picked me up off the Sybian and carried me out to the backyard—where the lawn resembled a green carpet—and made love to me on the grass, while I was still blindfolded. Then he removed my blindfold, and we continued having sex for hours. When we finished, he said, "Wow! I'm thinking . . . bucket list!"

Later, I went outside to look at the spot in the grass. It resembled a snow angel. There was our imprint in my beautiful lawn. I snapped a picture and sent it to him. I'm sure when he was at the airport and saw the shot of the imprint on the grass it excited him once again. I like this sort of thing, and what's more important is that I give myself permission to be the kind of person who would do it.

So that's the story of how I personally went from a life of sexual frustration to the life of a sex and happiness coach. I've found the perfect occupation for me. Not only does it transform those who seek my services, but I am the direct beneficiary of everything I do.

I tried being a schoolteacher. I piloted antidrug programs and taught self-esteem to at-risk youth. I took people off the welfare rolls. I did all of this in an effort to make a difference, but I can say for certain that what I do now does make a clear difference in the world. First, I set myself free, and then I helped set thousands of other people free over the course of the past twenty-two years. People become focused, empowered, happy, and healthy as a result of my being in their lives, whether I am their lover or their teacher. Sex is the most powerful force on the planet. Harnessing sexual energy and giving it the credit it deserves is my life's purpose.

Laurie Handlers is the author of the Amazon number one international bestseller *Sex & Happiness*. She hosts a weekly podcast, Sex and Happiness, and stars in three independent films: *The Big T: Testosterone* (2017), *Beyond Dinner* (2012), and *Tantric Tourists* (2009). She offers Butterfly workshops throughout the world and is focused on sexual ecstasy at any age and developing The Academy for Men.

Latihan: Moving into the Unknown

PURPOSE: Beyond preconceived notions about sex and lovemaking, this practice allows you to open to all of existence and feel the life-force energy flowing through your body. The more you practice this, the more you will be able to make love to the mystery.

PREPARATION: You can practice alone, with a partner, or with more people. Set aside at least half an hour. Put on ethereal music. Wear comfortable clothing or go naked. Stand blindfolded in a room that's large enough to move around in without bumping into things. Understand ahead of time that the energy can become intense, and it's not always pleasant. (As with sex, of course, you want it to be effortless and pleasurable, yet sometimes it just isn't.)

PROCESS: This practice begins with guided imagery: imagine yourself standing at the edge of a precipice. As you look over the edge, you see only darkness, the void. Notice that you are strapped into a harness attached to a cable on a zip line that stretches across the void.

Let go of your footing and allow yourself to swing out, dangling over the unknown. Feel the void. Then look up and notice a red button. This button unfastens you from the zip line. Now, bravely reach up and push the red button. Feel yourself falling fast, into the unknown. Feel the wind on your face and hair as you fall.

Allow the hands of spirit or your inner guidance to guide you into the unknown by moving your body, slowly at first.

There are no prescribed steps or postures. Only move when the impulse to move moves you.

In *latihan,* energy can take any form, such as laughing, dancing, singing, and/or crying. Anything can happen. You may feel the urge to moan or scream. Your body may go into spontaneous yoga postures or spasms. Nothing is taboo or inhibited. You can be as wild or as gentle as you give yourself permission to be.

If your body bumps into another body, follow your inner impulse. Don't try to direct your energy; simply let the energies meet and part, and meet and part, naturally.

If you want it to stop, just stop.

Allow your body to do what your body does, without evaluating or judging. Just be present in the now, again and again. When the mind steps in, tell your thoughts to come back later, and sink back into the present moment.

RESOURCES: Some people refer to this practice as authentic movement. Latihan is an international spiritual movement that began in Indonesia and is associated with an amalgam of Javanese animistic, Buddhist, and Hindu traditions.

3
WELCOME TO
MY WORLD

By Deborah Taj Anapol, PhD

Bodhi Kerlin

TRANSPERSONAL NAME: Taj Mahalo

YEAR OF BIRTH/DEATH: 1951–2015

HOMETOWN: Honaunau Bay, Hawai'i

RESIDENCE: San Rafael, California

ARCHETYPE: Earth mother

SUPERPOWER: Visionary oracle

LINEAGE/TEACHERS: Pelvic-Heart Integration with Dr. Jack Painter, goddess Kali worship, and early pioneers of the polyamory movement

EPITAPH: Imagine a culture where the body is sacred, love is abundant, and spirit is honored.

SHAMANIC TOOLS: Organic coffee and homegrown cacao from the farm

HOBBIES: Traveling to explore goddess temple sites and hot springs, swimming with dolphins, farming, reading, kirtan, and practicing ecosexuality

This chapter is a posthumous tribute taken from Deborah Taj Anapol's journals. She shared her travels and her teachings online, and sometimes she'd give the world a glimpse into her private musings. This is a mosaic of her last ten years of shamanic self-reflection on the subjects of love, sex, life, and death. Each paragraph was plucked like a gem from her blog, *Love Without Limits;* her Facebook notes; and her online newsletter, Welcome to My World!

∽

Hi Everyone!

If there is a single thread running through my entire life it would be the rediscovery of the essential union of sex and spirit. Yes, there are other polarities or seeming opposites, but the core of the quest is to merge the often-separated worlds of spirituality and full embodiment. We call this embodied spirituality, erotic spirituality, or sacred sexuality. All of these concepts point to the same reality, and all of them are often empty words, hopelessly mired in the duality of thought from which they arise.

My personal story is much more complex than what I'm about to share here, but I give you this outline as a context from which to understand. My history spans this amazing diversity of experiences— some sublime, some disastrous—and had left me quite sober as far as romantic illusions go.

When I was seventeen years old and had just graduated from high school, I knew I had a college dorm room in the heart of New York City waiting for me in the fall, but I didn't know if I wanted to go there. I knew I could always land at my parents' home, and I didn't want to go there. With the whole summer, and in fact my whole life, stretching out ahead of me, I felt the excitement of unimagined adventures. I set out with my army surplus backpack, sleeping bag, and fifty dollars stashed in a pocket in case of emergency. I intended to live by my wits and allow myself to be guided toward the greatest opportunities for self-awareness. Life was much simpler in those days: no home computers, no internet, no cell phones, no credit cards, no responsibilities.

It was the summer of 1969, and I took full advantage of the chance to explore psychedelics, sex, synchronicity, and rock and roll. A lover gave me a copy of *Pilgrim's Progress.* I witnessed (on someone else's TV) a man walking on the moon. I discovered chakras, opened my heart for the first time, became a seasoned hitchhiker, and found myself in the midst of what would soon become the world-famous Woodstock music festival. Everything I needed was provided, and even potential dangers were transformed into empowering initiations.

My first child was born when I was twenty-one. When she reached high school, I realized her whole childhood had gone by and I'd spent at least half of it absorbed in career and erotic adventures. I didn't know each precious moment would be gone before I knew it. My second child was born when I was thirty-six. I was grateful to have a gainfully employed husband so I could immerse myself in domesticity—and more erotic adventures—for the next five years, and again, before I knew it, she was all grown up.

Now a new realization is coming to me. It's not just childhood that goes by in a flash; in fact, I remember my own childhood as moving very, very slowly, especially the long days of springtime, trapped in a classroom and waiting for summer vacation. My own adulthood has gone by in a flash, and I don't remember the parts I wasn't truly present for—which is most of it.

Up to the age of about thirty, I had close and harmonious relationships with many girls and women. Childhood best friends who explored forests, beaches, and Barbie dolls, rode bikes, and giggled about boys; teenage partners in crime sharing outrageous adventures; mentors and colleagues in my early professional circles; and a mother who would do anything for me—my world was abundant with feminine grace. Men were the spice, the icing, the boyfriends and husbands, brothers and father. Sometimes exciting, sometimes disappointing or infuriating, sometimes enlightening, but not fully integrated into my world.

In my thirties and forties this reversed. Suddenly my life was full of amazing men—husbands, lovers, healers, fans, and teaching partners. Women all but disappeared and seemed suddenly envious, competitive, even dangerous. With a few notable exceptions, my growing success and expansion in life was not celebrated by my sisters but magnetized so many men.

In my fifties, I again experienced a reversal. As my hair turned gray and my body slowly lost its youthful allure, I became invisible to men who'd automatically pursued me as a potential sex object and threatening to many men who'd found strength and intensity enticing in a young, inexperienced woman but feared it in one who was older and wiser. Once again, the women who showed up bearing gifts of love, appreciation, and companionship began to outnumber the men. And then events unfolded that shook me to the core. Interestingly enough, it was women who nearly brought me down and mostly men who lent their strength, clarity, and professional skills to help me carry on.

At sixty, I can let go of any illusion or pretense of being a young woman. No hair dye or facelifts for me! What you see is what you get, and I do believe I'm aging gracefully. I still practice bikram yoga nearly every morning when I'm not on the road, but I've made peace with the fact that most of my life, in this body at least, is behind me, not ahead of me.

If I'm tuned in and present in my body, I sense small dysfunctions that can easily be healed before they turn into disease. People call this "sensitive," and it's the same capacity that shows up as empathy for others, which makes me a talented healer and group facilitator and has led to many erotic adventures. This ability is also one of many reasons I value my yoga practice, and why breaking my leg five years ago was such a challenge. After all, healing—sexual or otherwise—can best be defined as making whole, reintegrating parts that have been cut off from conscious awareness.

I feel blessed to have led an extraordinary life in so many ways. I know I've been more alive and aware than most, and even so, I look back and realize I sleepwalked through so much of it. I hope I can be present in gratitude for each precious moment still to come.

I find myself wondering how it is that so many people have forgotten, or perhaps never knew in the first place, that the sexual revolution of the '60s and '70s held an intention for liberation—not just sexual freedom as an end in itself but as a means to spiritual liberation. It's always tricky to speak of spiritual liberation because of the tendency to hijack these lofty words and make them into another bogus mental concept or commodity to be sold to the highest bidder. Perhaps it's better to say that the slogan "Make Love, Not War" has yet to be realized. It seems the "making love" part has been much more successful than the "not war" part. Maybe the majority of people are still having sex instead of making love, but even love, and especially free love, has been radically misunderstood by many. Please join me in holding space for deep transformation and world peace instead of more of the same old, same old in the ways that we live, love, and heal together!

Some early spiritual friends of mine who went by the name UV Family when I encountered them in the early 1980s focused my attention on the need for a new sexual ethic. Their self-imposed standard was no sex before marriage. Before you tune out this teaching, let me clarify that they did not mean legal marriage, which they had absolutely no use for, nor was their concept of marriage limited to one person at a time or implying any kind of financial dependency. Rather, they were pointing to the reality that engaging sexually creates a lasting energetic bond and were suggesting that we not share sexually with anyone we were not willing to be permanently connected with. The purpose of this standard was not to limit the number of partners—they had many—but to put forward some selection criteria and to formalize the sexual sacrament with a simple, private ritual acknowledging a conscious choice to create a bond.

In this way, relating becomes a foundation for giving your gifts to the world. Committed sexual relationship serves to nurture, empower, and enlighten lovers as well as all those coming into contact with lovers who stay present and embodied while strongly activated erotically. When high-voltage sex is approached with presence and the merging of both physical and energy bodies, direct contact with the Divine becomes possible. Now the erotic energy—whose function is connecting heaven and earth—is truly serving our spiritual evolution!

The most important selection criteria for the UVs was shared purpose. Rather than depending upon and identifying with visual stimulation, fantasy, conditioning, emotional desires, acquired information, or hormones to shape our erotic experience, they were suggesting that we choose others who are aligned with our values and intentions for being here. Of course, this implies that you know your own purpose and that it is more specific than simply to love and be loved—that would include everyone and put you right back where you started: confused!

This *hieros gamos,* or sacred marriage, is a transcending of our dualistic thought patterns, an end to the battle between our animal and our spiritual natures, a simultaneous embrace of both the wave and the particle. It is a melding of the right and left brains, a fusion of ego and essence into one harmonious whole. It's about changing your mind and your heart. It's about mating with your own soul. It's about experience, not words—but hopefully these words can point you there. In any case, this fusion is what's next on my horizon. I'll let you know what I find there.

Ever since the early '80s, I'd believed that my purpose in life was to create more peace in the world by expanding the boundaries of the family; raising awareness that there are many possibilities for honest, intimate relating; and supporting people to heal sexual trauma, limitations, and conditioning by reuniting sex and spirit. Last year, when I heard spiritual teacher Isaac Shapiro sharing about how the idea of having a mission is really ego-driven, it made an impression on me because I'd already started noticing how this is so. While many people might benefit by giving more attention to discovering their life purpose, my ego had definitely gotten hold of this concept of purpose and was using it in ways that were not entirely joyful.

Just as people can create a spiritual ego that very effectively keeps them apart from the oneness they seek, my mission-driven ego had become a barrier to my own self-love and union with the Divine, not to mention a human beloved. I was too busy taking care of people and running every aspect of my publishing and seminar business and the farm to stop and smell the roses. Worse yet, I'd sacrificed several relationships on the altar of leading seminars on tantric sex and polyamory.

If you don't understand what I'm talking about, think of it this way. Let's say you're an ordinary person who loves to ice skate and your partner does too. You have a wonderful time playing around at your local rink or lake; you totally enjoy yourselves. You sometimes skate with others, and no one pays any attention to you. There is no stress involved, and if you're having a bad day, you just take a break and wait for a better moment. This is a completely different experience from skating with a partner professionally or in the Olympics. Suddenly, the pressure is on. It's your duty to get that gold medal. Your time is no longer your own. You have to practice, travel, and perform whether or not you feel like it at that moment. You are so busy preparing for the next event that you no longer have time to enjoy each other. Your flight is canceled due to bad weather, and you don't know if you will arrive in time for the competition. Judges are scrutinizing your every move, and the crowds are for or against you. Fans tell you to get a new partner if you want to win. Other fans tell your partner the same thing. Your partner misses a beat, and your chances of winning are threatened. You have a misunderstanding at an inconvenient time, and your whole career is threatened. This isn't an exact analogy, but you get the idea: not the easiest conditions for undertaking explorations that are already challenging to begin with and for which there is no road map.

One thing I've realized on this journey: I myself have no roots and come from many generations of rolling stones. Hawai'i felt like home to me for a while, but it became clear that my destiny is to travel the world, weaving the threads of the new culture even as I discover the unique flavors of each part of the planet.

When my older daughter was small, I used to read aloud to her from a book called *Emir's Education in the Proper Use of Magical Powers* by Jane Roberts. It's the story of a young boy who decides to use his magic to eliminate rain so that he can travel the world in his open boat in greater comfort, not realizing the far-reaching consequences of his self-centered desire. It's a wonderful fable about ecosystems and sustainability and applies just as well to the unintended results of our attempts to dictate the nature of love.

Life is short and precious and wants your full attention and engagement right now. Our whole culture seems caught between the paradox of the living-for-tomorrow, goal-oriented rat race and the steadily increasing sense that there may be no tomorrow if we don't clean up our act today. Rumors fly about the economy, the climate, the escalation of conflicts. I have been living on the flank of the world's most active volcano, and over the past month it's been kicking up more gas and lava than it has for a long, long time. This is not a rumor, and while I'm not supersensitive to the fumes—the very same kind of fumes the Oracle at Delphi went into a cave to breathe before making prophecies—I've found myself realizing that I need to put at least a little distance between my body and Kilauea. Hence my trip to Maui!

Meanwhile, more and more people are being squeezed to the tipping point with challenges of all kinds. In these turbulent times, it's crucial that we take the space to center ourselves, breathe (clean air) deeply, and allow our intuitive knowing to speak.

I'm dreaming of a world where opposing polarities have evolved into loving inclusion, where the war between the sexes has become history so incomprehensible that people doubt it ever existed, where our human nature and spiritual nature blend in perfect harmony, where the union of sex and spirit is experienced routinely, where every child is consciously and lovingly conceived and raised by a whole village. I'm dreaming a dream where reciprocity, sustainability, and integrity inform every heart, mind, and action. I'm dreaming a dream where everyone knows that love is the answer, where *lokahi* (Hawai'ian for "unity in diversity") describes everyday life and no one goes without clean water, healthy food, and a home to call their own. I'm dreaming a dream of abundance and enoughness. I'm dreaming a dream without wars and without violence and with plenty of leisure time for art, beauty, and hanging out. I'm dreaming a dream about people prioritizing purpose and meaning and connection over consuming and competing. I'm dreaming a dream where people share their dreams with each other and create nurturing communities and tribes, and together dream a bigger dream. I'm dreaming of living in paradise with my soul family as we co-create heaven on earth. I have no clue when these dreams will appear in 3-D, but I hope it's soon.

Life has been pretty nonstop ever since I left Hawai'i at the end of 2011. Within this, I do take time for my daily hatha yoga practice—at least when I'm at home—but downtime where I have absolutely nothing to do and nowhere to go is becoming more scarce than I would like. It's a luxury I value and savor more than ever. Rushing around is such a way of life for most people, especially in urban areas, and even for those who have retired from busy careers but are still very active in their pursuit of life's pleasures. In my experience, it's only in the quiet nondoing times that I discover the unknown treasures within and get a sense of my true purpose.

I'm finding myself cutting the cords of attachment to Hawai'i with the awareness that infatuation with a place, a culture, and a people is no different from infatuation with a person. The place is as beautiful as ever, maybe even more so, now that the veils of illusion have dropped. At the same time, I notice that the attachment to my own identity, my comfort, and my habitual patterns is far deeper than the attachment to anything outside myself.

As I'm extricating myself from the past, I'm exploring working with a group called ISTA, International School of Temple Arts, founded by Baba Dez Nichols in Sedona and now expanding into a larger vision of collaboration with a variety of dynamic teachers from every continent who share a passion and talent for integrating ancient wisdom with today's cultural peculiarities. I'm excited to find others who share the dream of co-creating a synergistic group and maybe have the understanding, wisdom, and personal power to do it. I am certainly an elder in this group. Though many are only a few years younger than me, some are at least a generation younger. In this context, everyone's gifts and wounds are quickly coming to the surface as we explore the dance of weaving visions and sharing leadership as well as team teaching, strategies, and, to varying extents, everyday life.

It's scary, to say the least, to let go of the past and jump into this evolving and still fragile container, not knowing the extent of everyone's commitment to the group versus their own personal agendas. Resolving issues of trust, competition, responsibility, and, most of all, integrity will either bring the whole group into a higher alignment or spin some or all of us off on our own trajectories.

I'm hopeful that we're on the cusp of yet another wave of development in human life. If enough of us recognize that now is the time to come home to who we really are, just maybe the overall consciousness of humanity could evolve in amazing ways. That is what the world needs now! I totally support everyone's efforts to love and heal themselves and by extension to love and heal others, and I know that this happens most naturally and effectively when we humbly surround ourselves with others who are willing and able to point out our blind spots while loving us unconditionally.

The four genders (wounded and healthy, masculine and feminine) and the four main archetypes (king/queen, lover, warrior, and magician/sage) have been in my awareness a lot lately, along with the concept of initiation. Nearly a year ago, Bruce Lyon, my colleague at ISTA, proposed that the new ISTA training be based around three initiations. Since that time, I've been deeply contemplating what it really takes to offer an initiation, not to mention receive one. Most of the conversation going on about initiations revolves around the importance of receiving them and the gaping holes in a culture that no longer understands their importance. For me, stepping into elderhood is partly about preparing to experience the big initiation still ahead of me—commonly known as physical death—but also the humbling realization that I don't know how to properly *give* initiations, and it's high time I mastered this art.

Now that I've hit the road, or, more accurately, the skies, I have a wonderful sense of freedom. I'm beginning a new cycle with no clue where it will lead. All my efforts to create or maintain some sense of control or security about the future have been reduced to knowing that the only real protection is in following my inner voice and surrendering the deep-rooted desire to know how it will unfold. In other words, existence is demanding that I volunteer to trust in life.

Having always lived close to the edge, I'm relatively comfortable with not knowing. My experience has been that when I surrender and tune in to the signals of ease and attraction, everything works out better than I could have imagined.

I will not be surprised if death continues to stalk us. I confess I'm at least as uncomfortable with the whole experience as most people, though I don't have any difficulty talking and writing about it. My mind is fine with it, but I'm not sure about my heart. More and more people I know seem to be leaving this world, and not just as a function of old age, so those of us who are still here are going to have to get used to it. While some of my friends are convinced that immortality is their destiny, in my humble opinion it's only a matter of time for all of us before our time is up, and we can only live well once we've made peace with death. What's on your bucket list? What do you really want to contribute to life before you're gone?

The closer I get to death and the older I get, I come back to purpose and what I consider my purpose to be—which is to die consciously. My purpose is not to go around being obsessed with death all the time but to actually be ready to die—and therefore ready to live—at any moment.

The following letter was written by Robert Osborn of Celtic Tantra. Taj had become a very dear friend of Robert and his partner Marta, and they were all due to run a workshop together. Taj was staying at their home on the edge of Dartmoor the night she died. This private letter was written by Robert on the morning of Taj's death, August 19, 2015, and was intended only for the eyes of the members of Taj's Pelvic Heart

Integration Teacher Training Course, who needed to know what had taken place.

> Dear friends,
>
> I have some very sad news to share with you.
>
> After two wonderful days staying with us in our old Devon house, Taj died suddenly in her bed last night. It was totally unexpected— she went to bed well and happy and looking forward to her work and travels.
>
> Taj spent her last day with us walking and meditating in what she felt was one of the very oldest of the Dartmoor stone circles, and having lunch in a lovely café in Totnes and a candlelit dinner in our farmhouse kitchen. She was very happy feasting on local lamb and homegrown vegetables while we all chatted about the workshop to come and how Marta and I would be running it.
>
> It was an extraordinary evening. Before she went to bed, Taj wanted to show us a short film about ecstatic death. We watched this together in front of the wood fire, and afterward she spoke a little more about death and the possibility of letting go into it. "If you live your life orgasmically, your death will also be orgasmic" is what she said. She went off to bed later with a warm hug. In the morning, we found that she must have died shortly after she went to bed.
>
> In the light of the extraordinary quality of this last day, the joy she took in it, and the things she spoke of as the day ended, I cannot but feel that Taj at some level knew and embraced the point she had arrived at, even so wonderfully in love with life as she was.
>
> This death was truly a conscious one.
>
> Much love,
> Robert & Marta
> www.CelticTantra.com

A Benediction from Taj

My cats, Tillie and Frances, are named for my grandmothers, invoking their presence daily and not just on this annual Day of the Dead. The Hawai'ians, along with many Pacific Islanders and indigenous peoples, consider their ancestors, or *aumakua,* to be their personal link to the Divine. You don't need to believe this to give it a try. Just ask your ancestors or those who have passed over to the other side and "changed address" for messages to guide you and protect you and see what happens!

ALOHA IA *O'KOA PA'ULO**

Deborah Taj Anapol, PhD, (1951–2015) was a psychologist, pioneer of the polyamory movement, and a recipient of the Vicki Sexual Freedom Award from the Woodhull Freedom Foundation. In her own words: "I've worn many hats in this earth walk—relationship coach, seminar leader, spiritual seeker, author, farmer, management consultant, deep ecologist, mother, traveler—the common thread is sustainable living." (Love Without Limits website)

---

*Editor's note: Taj always signed her letters with this Hawai'ian greeting. It translates to: "When we meet in love, we shall be whole."

Contacting Your Spirit Guides

PURPOSE: To gain a broader perspective, guidance, protection, and/or inspiration. This practice can radically accelerate your spiritual growth.

PREPARATION: The first step is to release any doubt and judgment you may have toward channeling. For this practice to work, you must believe that spirit guides exist. And you must have a strong desire to make contact. It helps to feel gratitude, in advance, for the messages you are going to receive.

Cultivating a reliable link with higher realms takes practice and should be done for at least 20 minutes on a daily basis. Have a journal and pen nearby. Crystals can also be used to enhance receptivity. Amethyst, apophyllite, quartz, and selenite can help you communicate with higher realms. And dark stones like tourmaline or hematite can help with grounding afterward.

PROCESS: Connecting with spirit guides may take different forms but always starts with clearing the mind. Meditation or prayer is necessary to open a channel because spirit guides exist beyond. Start by slowing down and opening all your senses. You may start with an invocation in your own words. Ask for energies that are equal to or greater than your own vibration. You can always choose whether you want to invite spirits into your body.

Sexual shamanism is an embodied practice. You may want to be open to spirit guides who want to link with your energy or step into your energy field so that you may hear, see, and sense what they sense. You do not need to give your body away; instead, be aware of what you pick up when this happens: this is their gift and message. When this happens, you may feel ecstasy, crowded, or pressure on your chest. If you have a difficult time breathing or start to feel anxious, you can express your boundaries and break the link and ask them to communicate with you, not through you.

Once you have made contact, you can ask for your guides to reveal themselves with a name or a gesture. Ask them to show you how they look or sound or feel. Ask what you wish to know and wait to be told what they wish you to know and when.

Listen not only to the sounds around you but also the sounds of your inner ear. What do you smell or taste in your mind? Use your journal to capture your gut feelings. Jot down details that you wouldn't normally notice. It doesn't have to make sense. It may or may not sound like your voice or look like your handwriting. Don't try to interpret it until you are done.

Afterward, be sure to thank your spirit guides, whether or not you got anything valuable.

NOTES: The more you practice this, the more aware you become of the symbolic language of your spirit guides. Continue listening for daydreams, pictures, numbers, or signs throughout the day and into dreamtime. It may take several seasons before you can accurately decipher and understand these messages.

RESOURCES: This practice has been popularized by the Seth Speaks series by Jane Roberts, the book *Many Lives, Many Masters* by Brian L. Weis, and by Jerry and Esther Hicks.

4

THE SECRET PORTAL

By Ohad Pele Ezrahi

Dawn Cherie Ezrahi

YEAR OF BIRTH: 1965

SUN SIGN: Libra

LINEAGE/TEACHERS: Kabbalah. Ordained as a rabbi in 2000 by the late R. Zalman Shakter Shalomi. I've had more teachers than can be named in shamanism, Zen, and sexuality.

SHAMANIC TOOLS: Ears and heart, drum, guitar, plant medicine, and sacred fire in ceremony. I sometimes read palms.

HOBBIES: Nude photography, drawing, writing, composing, and playing guitar

It happened under a warm waterfall in Guatemala. I was part of a group of spiritual teachers who were invited to journey to Mayan sacred sites. The year was 2007, and Barack Obama had just been elected president of the United States. I met up with others who were walking the path of shamanism, touring the sacred temples together. Of all the great ruins we had visited, none were as meaningful as this sacred place in the forest, where a cold and a hot stream merged into a warm waterfall. We had been brought here to refresh ourselves, a place where local families come to bathe, swim, and have fun.

I had spent the night before with my friend's daughter. My friend was the one who had organized the tour and invited me to join. At the time, his daughter was in her early twenties, and she came along with her father and his spiritual friends. As she and I were driving through the forests of Guatemala and chatting, I could feel her interest in me and my work in sacred sexuality growing. We talked about my open marriage, about sexual healing and the ways to invite spirituality into our sex lives. When we arrived at the venue where we were to spend the night, she came over and asked me if I was open to making love to her. Her experiences with men and sexuality so far had closed her heart and had scared her soul. I accepted the invitation, and we spent the night making love on her balcony, under the full moon. She opened to my penetration, and I invited her to expand this opening to the Divine beyond me, to make love with the moon and the stars—not only with me, but with God. She was filled with bliss, and she glowed like the Moon herself.

The following day, I swam under that warm waterfall with some folks from our group. The minerals from millions of years of a running river had created smooth rock in the shape of a cave. Standing under it with the water gushing in front of me, I was amazed to find that this rock was not only very smooth but also pink inside. I was standing under a pink smooth rock, surrounded by warm water, my fingers touching and feeling its curves and my mind in total amazement—I was standing inside Mother Nature's yoni. As my fingers caressed the pink, smooth veins of the rock, I closed my eyes and started to pray. Water was gushing from above into a pool where children were swimming and yelling to one another. This was for me the most sacred of all the sacred Mayan sites. I didn't care that the Mayan people built all those amazing cities and temples—this was a temple of Earth herself. My heart was in awe. My lips started kissing the rock and whispering prayers. Tears rolled from under my closed eyelids as I prayed to learn the deep mysteries of the yoni and how to bring healing to women through sexuality.

I was aware that all I know is nothing. And the mystery of the yoni is so vast. I don't know how long I was standing in prayer, but at a certain moment, I felt someone by my side. I opened my eyes and saw our host, the Mayan shaman. He looked at me and said, "If you dive under the rock, you will find places where the ceiling of the rock goes up and creates a room filled with air." I needed nothing more.

Thanking him, I dove down and swam under the rock in the opposite direction from the pool. Indeed, it wasn't difficult to find a place where I could stand up and breathe again. My body was in the warm water, but my head was in a big bubble of air under the rock. I felt so privileged. As I was praying at the entrance of the Earth yoni, I was invited into its inner chambers!

Light came into the chamber from underneath the water; above was a sealed rock. The light was turquoise blue, full of mystery, and my heart was exploding from feelings of gratitude.

I took off my swimsuit and left it there; I did not need it. I was alone in a water cave, alone in the inner chamber of Earth's vagina, alone in her sacred yoni. The sound of the children disappeared, replaced by the sound of warm water kissing the mineral rock.

My eyes started to get used to the dark. I felt called to continue diving in under the rock, looking for more chambers like this one. I dove under and indeed found another place, deeper inside, where the rock curved up above the surface of the water and created another pocket of air. It was smaller than the first one and darker, and the sounds of the families out in the pool disappeared completely into the deep silence of the rock chamber itself. It was me and nature, and nature was a huge, wet, dark, and pink yoni holding me inside and seducing me to enter even deeper.

I continued diving again and again to find deeper and darker chambers of the yoni. I released all awareness of time. It was total ecstasy, as defined by the Latin root of that word, *ex-stasis,* meaning "to stand outside oneself." All I wanted was to be totally absorbed by the magic.

I ended up in the far end of a cave, in total darkness, squeezing myself into the last wet hole, curled in the fetal position. For a moment, fear flashed into my heart, irrational fear: What if some kind of poisonous South American creepy-crawly creatures were here? I was happy to meet my fear. This is the fear of dying. *Good,* I said to myself. I knew something needed to die so that something new could be born. I curled up and pushed myself into the darkest womb of Earth, surrounded by mud and warm water, silence and magic. I have no idea how long I stayed there, but at a certain moment, I felt the impulse to be born.

The journey back was different. The sun had gone down, and by the time I reached the waterfall, the other visitors had left. My heart was so expansive I felt it would explode. My eyes had grown accustomed to the dark, and the evening seemed to be illuminated by the stars. I found a note from my group, saying they had left for dinner and would come later to check on me. I was filled with bliss and total humility.

When they returned, my friends were very happy to see me, but I couldn't say a word. I was literally speechless. I had just died and been reborn. How could I speak as I was just born? I had given myself to the Goddess, and I was different from the one who had entered the cave. This was an initiation into a new dimension.

Days before, I had walked with the group through the temple ruins of Tikal, the ancient Mayan city. In the jungle, I found one pyramid not visited by tourists. I left the group and wandered off the main track to climb up the steep stairs. At the top of the pyramid was an empty chamber. I entered the abandoned chamber with a bow and a prayer and felt called to perform a sacred ritual. Feeling into myself, it became obvious what I needed to do: I disrobed and stood naked, looking out from the top of the pyramid into the wild jungle. Inspired by my love for nature, I started self-pleasuring. Nature was seducing me with her purity, wild power, and dark mysteries. As arousal spread throughout my body, I did what I usually do: I expanded it through all my systems, letting energy run from the engine of the genitals to all of my extensions and beyond, beyond the physical body and into the subtle realms, the beautiful weaving of my own energy with the radiant field of the forest. My lips were whispering prayers and praises of the Goddess, and my energy was rising. The time came for my life-force offering. In the ancient Mayan temples, humans were often sacrificed; now, it was my turn. I allowed myself to ejaculate, giving my sacred juices as an offering of life force onto the altar. Humble tears of joy were rolling down my cheeks as I sent my energy from the tip of the pyramid temple into the forest.

Suddenly, I saw something that I could not figure out. Some creature was coming out of the jungle and flying directly toward me. It was the size of a bird but didn't fly like one. What is it? Is it dangerous? It was flying in a straight line toward me. I stood mesmerized. Only when it came very close could I tell—it was a huge butterfly! It flew toward me and hit my right shoulder. It fluttered around me and flew back into the trees. *What the fuck?* I thought, but then it did it again, the same pattern. Really? What is that? When it flew toward me for the third time, I asked the butterfly out loud, "Is there something you are trying to tell me?" It hit me on the same shoulder and whispered in my ear, "*You* are a butterfly too!"

It made sense. When I took LSD for the first time, years earlier, the trip started with a moth—in Hebrew, both are called "butterfly"— fluttering in a corner of the room, attracting my attention. When I came near, the moth unfolded its dull gray wings to reveal a glittering bright blue that opened the portal to another dimension where all that seems dull is actually so colorful.. The veil to the other worlds has been, for me, the wings of a butterfly or moth, and here it came again, in response to my sexual shamanic offering, telling me to open my wings. The butterfly was calling me home.

I needed it. I needed these blessings from nature in addition to the blessings I got from the elders, because my self-doubt is a pyramid of its own. When my beloved Dawn and I got together and started to share the work of kabbalah in the realm of sexuality and relationship, we received the blessing of our late Rebbe Zalman Schakter-Shalomi, who told us, "Do not forget to let people know what the holy Ba'al Shem Tov, a Jewish mystic who lived in the eighteenth century, said, that the reason for the late coming of the messiah is that people do not spend enough time in the art of hugging and kissing before they go to penetration."

Transitioning from a kabbalist rabbi in Jerusalem to a sexual shaman was not easy. I was excommunicated from the village where I used to live. Rabbis warned their students never to study with me or read my books because I was a dangerous person. Even my one and only blood sister and her religious family shunned me as a traitor, and I became persona non grata. I was fired from religious institutions because of my openness in the realm of sexuality. This impacted my self-esteem and made me question if I'd ever be accepted and understood. For years, my long journey was a lonely one, full of what I call social suicides—until I found my beloved Dawn. We became two crazy people who cleared a path in the jungle of life for radical, sacred shamanic sexuality. Still, we were pretty much alone within the Israeli spiritual communities and the Jewish world. The doubts weighed on me, despite my determination to walk this path. Loneliness was a constant pain in my heart. Even when surrounded by friends, I questioned the extent to which my friends really understood what I stood for. That's why I felt I needed those blessings from spirit and from Nature herself. In my early years in the Hasidic world of Jerusalem, in the most ultraorthodox sect of Beltz Hasidim, the rebbe of Beltz once told my friend, "Ohad? No, he can never be captured . . . his soul is a butterfly." When the big butterfly tapped on my shoulder and I heard her whisper, it was both a reminder and an affirmation for me to be who I am in the world and fly.

I sometimes require nature's approval to trust myself, ever since I was burned by the bright light of the sun. When I was about nine years old, a full eclipse occurred in the sky above Israel. The teachers at my elementary school warned us not to look directly at the sun as it might damage our eyes. I never really trusted authorities and wanted to test it for myself. I remember standing with my classmates, who were holding up dark film to gaze through, but I ignored the teacher's words.

Squinting my eyelids, I noticed that I could actually see the eclipse with no protection. I believe it was my soul's yearning to connect to the source itself, with no mediation, no filters between us.

To this day, I carry the consequence of this experiment burned within me. The retina on my right eye carries a scar in the shape of the eclipse when the moon was covering part of the sun. That was a high price to pay for my hubris and rebellious nature; I think it made me doubt myself from that day on. I resented the fact that I had proved the adults right. I remember lying on my bed and weeping with agony because of that burn and the self-doubt that was tattooed into my psyche along with it.

Still, I long for direct communication with the source. I hate that we cannot look directly at the sun, that humans need filters to protect us from the intensity of nature.

Spirituality was not part of my upbringing, and as a child I thirsted for it like hell. I couldn't bear the boring life of all the humans I knew around me. Like many other spiritual seekers, at the beginning of my journey I was seeking the light. I longed to transcend the material world and connect with spirit, the source of all life, and to divine wisdom. As a teenager, I left my parents in a mediocre suburbia in the north of Israel and moved far away, to a boarding school in the southern desert. It was in nature that I found my haven. When I finally made it to the desert, I started to really breathe. I do not remember my first experience of ecstatic joy in childhood, but I will never forget when I was fourteen, when my soul met the desert. When I left home, I found home.

Where springwater spouts out of big rocks, where little birds chirp and big birds soar, where silence dwells in the vast openness of naked grounds—this was wild innocence. School was merely an excuse for me to be out in the desert. As a thirsty teenager, I found the Eastern philosophy bookshelves in the local library and started to drink them up. Terms like *meditation*, *shunyata*, *satori*, *moksha*, and *nirvana* filled up my inner realms. I read these books and had solitude in the desert to practice what I read about. Other than spirituality, only one thing interested me: girls!

At age fifteen, I had a lover who had another lover who was her first choice, but he had another girl who was his first choice. So, when he was with his first, my lover would spend the night in my bed, but when he was unoccupied, my lover would go to him, and I would invite one of the other two lovers I had to sleep with me. We didn't call it polyamory; we didn't call it anything. It was just how life presented itself to us, and it was fun—until it wasn't.

There was a big clash between my desire for spirit and my desire for girls. Vaginas and boobs distracted me from the Divine. My rebellious character wanted to find a way out of the labyrinth. I felt like a slave to my own hormones, addicted to the body's urges. A war was being waged between spirit and matter.

At age seventeen, I found Hasidic mysticism—similar in many ways to Zen Buddhism—and decided to dive into the religion of my ancestors. Learning more of the kabbalah, I discovered that masturbation is considered a sin because it is an addiction to carnal pleasures that take the place of spiritual pleasures. I felt addicted and decided to overcome it. I turned myself over completely to the Jewish religion. My desire for God won in the first round against my desire for girls and genitals.

It took me years of studying in the most conservative Jewish institutions in Jerusalem, dedicating myself to the mystery school of my ancestors, to realize that, at its core, it is all about sex. Not about the sex of humans on Earth, but about divine sex, cosmic sex, the sacred union of masculine and feminine and divine emanations in worlds so abstract that no form, no matter, and no energy can be related to them. "It is totally abstract," the traditional kabbalists will strongly claim, "and if you think it has anything to do with carnal life, you are so mistaken. Some great mystics of the past thought it actually has something to do with human love, but they were shunned, excommunicated, and persecuted. You don't wanna be like them."

I thought to myself, *Well, maybe I do. I'm searching for truth, whatever the price.* After years of dedicated learning and yearning to know the light of God, I started suspecting that the secrets of kabbalah are so hidden that even all the righteous sages may never have truly touched them. Could it be that those fallen mystics, those bad guys of the past, might have discovered some unpleasant truth that didn't agree with organized religion? Is that why they were shunned and ridiculed? I started to put the puzzle pieces together in a different way from what my teachers suggested. The new picture was intriguing. I looked for hidden notes and texts from the forbidden rabbis and found them fascinating. I considered the idea that, despite what all the traditional kabbalists were saying, it *is* about sex—but not just sex itself, because sex is more than that. In other words, what if sex is a secret portal that can bring us into divine realms?

In my obsessive research, I found a radical note from R. Baruch of Kosov, Poland, a known nineteenth-century Hasidic master, who said that in his early days he thought like everybody else: to become more holy, he needed to bypass sexual pleasures. Then, with the pure grace of God, he realized that the true meaning of sacredness is allowing oneself to deeply *feel* sexual pleasures—"and this is a very deep secret."

I also found forbidden texts of kabbalists from the seventeenth and eighteenth centuries that claimed that masturbation holds deep secrets; one need only know how to hold presence and intention through it.

I found academic scholars who claimed that in the very ancient days, orgiastic rituals actually took place and that the Judaism of the past two millennia is very far from the rituals of our tribal Hebrew ancestors. The deeper I delved into this scholarly research, the wider my spiritual world cracked open. I disassembled into pieces the history my research was revealing, and then the pieces started to reorganize and come together again in a much different way from before. Everything I once knew seemed to be untrue, and there was so much to learn about and no one to teach me. I realized I would need to pave my own way and find teachers in spirit realms.

In the meantime, I was shunned. My religious village excommunicated me and my family. We were considered dangerous thinkers. I was fired from my job as a rabbi in one of the more open-minded Orthodox study places. My rabbi, who liked me personally but was forced to fire me from my teaching position, warned me that I'd be very lonely out there. My inner world was built on subtle kabbalistic concepts I had turned upside down, but rare are the people who can grasp those concepts in the first place. Who would I be able to associate with if I left the world of Talmudic and kabbalistic scholars?

"Welcome to Beltane!" cried the heavy woman who stood on a bridge in a forest camp in Oregon, opening her big arms and flashing her naked body before everyone. The year was 2000, and I had miraculously been invited to be a scholar in residence at the University of Oregon for the spring term. As I followed my inner truth and left my secure rabbi position, falling toward the void, the invitation to Eugene, Oregon, caught me like a safety net.

Prior to that, I had published two books based on my deep research. One was about the central role of eros in the ancient mysteries of Judaism, as reflected in the texts about King Solomon's temple, the Song of Songs, and the Merkaba. The other book was about Lilith. Yes, Lilith, the dark demoness whose name faithful Jews do not dare to mumble, fearing her evil sexual temptations. My studies led me to find important kabbalistic texts that claimed that she—the dark one, the devil's whore, the bad girl archetype—has a higher divine source than the feminine archetype of Eve, the good girl accepted by society as a devoted wife and mother.

At the time, I was married with three little children, and my sex life was not so exciting. Even though my wife was a dedicated partner in all of my explorations, her constitution was very different from mine. I needed to explore sexuality out of the box and longed to meet Lilith in real life, off the pages.

Beltane is great for this! Men and women dance naked around the maypole in a forest rich with spirit beings and flowing streams of water. I drank it all in. My heart had a hard time coming back home to Israel. My wife suggested I take some time for myself at the beaches of Sinai, and so I did.

Walking on the beach, at dusk, I prayed to find my new path. Suddenly, I had a hunch to call Lilith to meet me in my dreams and teach me. I curled into my sleeping bag, and while listening to the sea waves crashing on the shore like a goddess breathing beside me, I fell asleep. A strong and painful bite on my neck woke me up. My hand flew up to cast away the creature biting me and found nothing but blood. Was it a scorpion or a snake? I got up quickly and pointed my flashlight at the ground, searching for the creepy-crawly, but found nothing. I walked to the Bedouin guardian of the land, showing him my neck and asking if he was familiar with this kind of bite, but he said he had never seen such a thing.

I turned to Lilith and prayed, "Okay, my dear, so it is *you,* huh? You think I'm going to be afraid of you now? You think I'm going to buy into the story of you being an evil, dangerous creature who comes at night to kill babies in their sleep? I am not afraid of you because I know who you really are. You are not evil! I am going back to sleep, and I invite you to come again. Come show me new realms that I do not yet know." And so she did.

Soon after, my wife and I decided to move away from the Orthodox world. We sold our house to the first buyer at a very low price and moved out. I decided to open an ashram, a Jewish ashram, that would be a living lab for a new vision for human existence. People joined us, and a community was established in the desert by the Dead Sea. It was that area where, for thousands of years, seekers, prophets, and mystic groups, such as the Essenes, would retreat to and live in solitude with God. One of the realms I needed to explore was that of sacred and not-so-sacred sexuality. I started to have lovers out of my marriage, some with the consent of my wife and some beyond it. Yes, we experienced everything, from the beautiful to the ugly: tears, jealousy, betrayal, lies, deep truths, and heartfelt mutual understanding, ending up in the realization that with love we would soon need to let go of each other and our family would no longer be one unit. Lilith was a tough teacher, but I was a devoted student.

I was invited to teach a seminar at Elat Chayyim, a Jewish Renewal retreat center in Upstate New York. Sitting on the stairs, I took my guitar and played a tune. She walked across the lawn as if she didn't see me, but she did. The line from the Beatles' song drifted through my mind: "Something in the way she moves, attracts me like no other lover." Her name was Dawn, I learned the next evening when we sat at the same table for dinner and chatted. She was there to take a course on prayer leadership. She wasn't supposed to come, but her grandfather came in her dream and sang some Jewish prayer tunes, so she woke up and registered at the very last moment. I told her about a Hasidic text that claims that prayer is lovemaking with Shekinah, the feminine aspect of the Divine. One night later, we practiced some of that prayer together in her tent.

It's been seventeen years, and we are still practicing. We are both lead facilitators for ISTA, sharing sexual shamanism with thousands of people around the world. She came to me as an embodiment of Lilith, in a shining feminine form: wild and gentle, wise and silly, devoted and slutty, heavenly and beastly, caring and not giving a fuck. From the first day, we said to each other, "No monogamy here!" and started our journey together. When she came to Israel to visit my ashram, my noble wife welcomed her with open arms. My other lovers examined her with cautious eyes. My wife and I ended our eighteen-year relationship with a private ceremony of divorce held by friends of our ashram. "This divorce was more loving than most weddings I've seen," said one of the women witnessing.

Most of what I know and share today clicked into my consciousness while making love with Dawn. Things I learned before from texts all of a sudden made new sense. I channeled images of ancient temples and even poems came to me during lovemaking with her. I met Dawn with very little sexual experience and a lot of mystical ideas about sex and relationships. She loved it, smiled, and showed me in her own way what it all really means.

During our years together in this nonmonogamous marriage, I met with many other lovers. As an artist in the field of love, I needed to explore everything I could, including jealousy. For instance, when she went on a trip to Jamaica with a rich American who was an experienced lover, that's when I met my rage—especially when he fell in love with her and tried to take her away. I discovered this dark part of myself who wanted to be a kung fu sword master and slice his red-haired head in two with one swift, clean stroke!

This lover of hers came into our life just when I decided to put an end to my ashram and move away with Dawn to start a new life together. My marriage was over, my community was falling apart, and my friends were upset with me for forsaking the project. There was no one and nothing to hold on to except my love to Dawn, but she was in America, for fuck sake, falling in love with this other guy who thanked me for my openness, and then admitted he wanted to take her away from me. At least he was an honest jerk! I had nothing to hold on to. I was falling into the void again. I called my friend, a well-known teacher of love and relationships, and he wisely told me, "I love you, brother, but you're on your own now." Falling into the dark, I called my other friend, a local Israeli tantra teacher, and he told me, "You have nothing to do so just surrender!" This is what I did. I surrendered into the dark nights of my soul. I knew that I had ordered it—the whole way down. I was the one who had called Lilith to be my teacher, and I trusted that this *was* the right path for me, even when it hurt like hell. That was one of many shamanic deaths I experienced on this path.

Ten years later Dawn, my son Yehoo (age seventeen), and I went on a community retreat to the Mediterranean Sea. During a lunch break, we went for a short swim. It was stormy, and the waves were high, but nevertheless, we dived in. At first, I didn't realize how much danger we were in, and then as I saw just how strong the waves were, I swam to Dawn and Yehoo, shouting above the waves that we should all get back to shore.

I, however, was already exhausted. Waves were coming from all sides, collapsing onto each other and creating whirlpools, and I couldn't make it to dry land. The current was taking me farther and farther away from the beach, and I couldn't swim against it. Everywhere I looked I saw a wall of water coming at me. I realized this was probably it for me. In my last moments before drowning, I looked back at my life and felt happy. I caught a glimpse of Dawn and Yehoo safe on the beach, and I relaxed. I felt complete. I surrendered myself to the loving hands of the Divine. I thanked the gods and goddesses of the sea. I thanked the spirit of the waves. I thanked the wind. I had no hard feelings about ending my life there. In many ways, I realized I had given my gifts, and if this was it, I was ready to go.

Just then, a memory came to me: a woman from my community had just asked me to make love with her! She was someone I had always wanted to make love with, but the timing hadn't been right. That woman had asked me right before we left for the beach. And there I was, swallowing and spitting saltwater, preparing myself to die! *What a pity,* I thought to myself, *to die without having sex with this woman.* This thought gave me a boost for life, and so I said to all the powers of nature and all the gods and goddesses of the sea, and all that is one, "I *am* indeed ready to die, but if you want to know what I want—I choose life!"

In a matter of moments, a big wave came and delivered me to the shore. I was nearly thrown onto the rocks! People came and dragged me to the beach. My body was exhausted and half dead, but I was a happy man who had gotten his life back! Everything was shining again; I was a newborn. I told God, "That's it! The rest of my life, I'm gonna live fully! I have no time to waste on pleasing others." I was smiling from ear to ear when my wife and son came to welcome me back to the world.

"So who died?" asked the forum leader in my community gathering as we joined them later. I couldn't stand or sit, but I was absolutely present.

"Rabbi Ohad Ezrahi died," I answered.

"So who is here? Who are *you*?" asked the forum leader, and I answered in the words of a well-known Hasidic master, "Ani Pele."

It means, "Who am I? I am Pele. I'm a wonder. My soul is a great miracle."

Ohad Pele Ezrahi is a lead faculty member at ISTA. He is the author of the historical novel *Kedesha,* a musician, and an artist. His background is as a kabbalist rabbi in Jerusalem. His understanding of the mysteries led him to leave religion and dedicate his life to love.

Self-Pleasuring Meditation

PURPOSE: This practice promotes self-love and induces an extraordinary state of being so that you can enjoy longer-lasting lovemaking. This is not a genital-focused exercise but instead a whole-being experience.

PREPARATION: Create a sensual ambience; you must feel totally safe and relaxed. Select a room that feels comfortable, turn off your phone, lock the doors, play soft music, light candles or incense, deepen your breath, and, if appropriate, say a prayer. Above all, take your time. No particular moment is more important than the next. If you find yourself rushing, stop, take a breath, and remind yourself to rejoice in the journey.

PROCESS: Caress and explore your entire body for as long as you can before arriving at your genitals. This includes your own face, neck, arms, belly, and lower back. Perhaps even give your entire body a pass from head to foot. Experiment and see what feels good to you. Nobody is watching or judging you, so allow your body to do whatever it wants, but do not hold your breath.

Breathe into your pelvic region and keep the belly soft. Keep the pelvic floor, or pubococcygeal (PC) muscles, active. As you breathe, engage the PC muscles at the top and bottom of the breath for additional potency. You can even exaggerate your contractions of this muscle and coordinate the movement with your breath, while making a sound to arouse your creativity. Stimulate your sex. Notice if you make different sounds and movements during masturbation from those you make during sex. Give yourself over to God.

When you are very near orgasm, direct all your sexual energy into the heart and/or spread it around the body. Come to the edge of orgasm and slow down, but don't cool off—allow yourself to build energy at least two more times before releasing, if you are moved to orgasm.

Imagine your heart bursting forward with light or warmth. Send loving intention to whatever place in your body needs the most healing. After you climax, lie still and breathe healing energy throughout your body. Drink lots of water and be gentle with yourself.

VARIATIONS: Self-pleasuring is different for everyone; there are as many variations on this practice as there are people.

RESOURCES: Chapter 6, "Masturbation Meditation" in *Sacred Sexual Healing: The SHAMAN Method of Sex Magic* by Baba Dez Nichols and Kamala Devi.

5

QUEEN OF THE UNDERWORLD

By Dawn Cherie Ezrahi

Ohad Pele Ezrahi

YEAR OF BIRTH: Twentieth century

SUN SIGN: Scorpio

HOMETOWN: Buffalo, New York

RESIDENCE: East Coast of the United States, Israel, and the world

ARCHETYPE: Innocent, timeless one, angelic being who isn't afraid to go to the dark, Persephone, Demeter, Lilith, sexy clown

SUPERPOWER: Feeling the space and shifting the energy, bringing depth or light

LINEAGE/TEACHERS: Gloria Maddox, ALisa Starkweather, David Deida, R. Zalman Schechter Shalomi, Arkan, Jerzy Grotowski, Bruce Lyon, and nature and water in all its forms

EPITAPH/MOTTO: If you can dream it, you can be it.

SHAMANIC TOOLS: My voice, a rattle, and a boa constrictor who accompanies my healing work

HOBBIES: Listening to music, traveling, making tea, swimming, and dreaming

I'm fascinated by myth and ritual. In some ways, you could say that it guides my life. If you really want to know my journey into sexual shamanism, you must recall the myth of Persephone. Remember the Greek goddess Demeter, sister and consort of Zeus, who lost her daughter, Persephone, to Hades, the god of the underworld?

Persephone's descent has many interpretations, most commonly that she was abducted against her will, raped, and tricked into eating pomegranate seeds. However, the interpretation that I personally resonate with is not the one of victimhood but rather of empowerment. It's about a woman who needed to go to the underworld to claim her dark wisdom and divinity. Compelled by compassion, Persephone dove into darkness and explored every shade of imperfection and thus became queen of the underworld.

As the legend goes, mother and daughter were so inseparably close that Persephone was almost never out of her mother's sight, just like my mom and me. One day, while harvesting, Persephone was snatched up and taken to the underworld. Demeter, being the powerful goddess of earth and grain, was so distraught about her daughter's disappearance that she searched after her high and low, far and wide. Once she understood that her daughter had been taken to the underworld, she appealed to the great Zeus, father of Persephone, to intervene and help bring her back. Not getting the results she wanted, she created a perpetual winter until her daughter's return.

After much time in the underworld with Hades, Persephone reemerged with pomegranate juice dripping from her mouth. She had ingested six pomegranate seeds, thereby creating her destiny of living six months of the year in the underworld with her now-beloved Hades. The other half of the year she could return to her mother's side to usher in the spring and bring life to the world above, the land of the living.

Whichever version you choose, Persephone always represents fertility and the joy of life. Hades is often associated with Dionysus, hedonism, ecstatic abandon, and bacchanalian revelry. I'm irresistibly drawn to this myth because of my own eternal search for the ecstatic pulse and its hidden treasures.

My initial descent occurred in my late teens, while attending a fashion school in New York City. I'd often go to Danceteria and Limelight, downtown nightclubs. I was the center of my social hub and loved to party. As a runway model, I could have any sexual encounter I desired. Back in those days, I went for the expansive drugs and luckily avoided the so-called stupid drugs, such as cocaine. Only later did I realize the real power and potential for ecstasy and personal growth that medicines could offer. Through my twenties and early thirties, I was escaping into ecstasy, craving it, and even taking it in pill form. I was modeling and clubbing, loving that I had to choose between Madonna or Johnny Sex on the first floor of Danceteria or head on up to the second floor to dissolve into dance, my favorite pastime. Everything would become clearer after dancing. Late-night revelry often ended up at after-hour clubs such as 8BC or Save the Robots, with our final destination of breakfast being Kiev or Yaffa in the East Village. If you pressed me for all my lovers, I wouldn't be able to remember. I'm sure they were meaningful at the time, or I made them feel special, but I probably used many of them unconsciously for my own validation.

Going to a fashion school where 90 percent of the available men were gay, in the age of AIDS, I was hyper aware of the need for safer sex practices. This inspired me to get even more creative with my sexuality. I loved flirting and kissing even more than the act of sex. I used my sensuality for power and freedom. I had more than my share of lovers but always wanted something deeper and more connected and more inclusive of spirit.

After modeling for years, it's no surprise that I started seeking peace and solitude from New York, leaving it to go to college in Maine and live on an organic farm. My biggest break came when I stopped looking in a mirror to know myself from the outside and discovered that my self-worth was deeper than that which was reflected back to me. I began unraveling the me inside.

After college, I found myself back in New York and spent many years working as a commercial actress and running several theater companies. I found a home in ritual theater, but I was torn: I felt that I either needed to be in pure theater or immerse myself fully in ritual. That's when my soul led me to my ultimate descent, to Israel.

The Dead Sea. The lowest place on Earth. From there you can only ascend. This is where I journeyed with Ohad Pele, a polyamorous, unconventional rabbi, the bad boy of the Jewish Renewal world, a trans-denominational approach to revitalizing Judaism. He had an iconic resemblance to Dionysus, and he identified with him as well. He was the perfect combination of holy and naughty. His creativity spoke to my soul.

When we first met, it was in Upstate New York, right after 9/11. The world seemed upside down, and I needed a drastic change. As an actress in New York, going on countless castings for commercials, I felt called to dive deeper into the traditions of my ancestors. On the way, I met a cute guy on the set of *Sex and the City*. I dragged him upstate with me to a freestyle dance. We spent that night together in my tent, and my very Jewish grandpa Max Mandelbaum came to me in a dream. I got clear guidance to show up that very morning at Elat Chayyim, the Jewish Renewal retreat center, and at the last minute I decided that I *must* enroll in a course during the week of Davvenen (Yiddish: "prayer") on the art of leading prayer.

I met Ohad Pele on the Hebrew Valentine's Day of love, Tu B'Av. He had been invited to the retreat center as a rabbi to teach the kab-balistic tale "The Lost Princess." Looking at him, I could feel my spirit craving and crying out for this inevitable coming together. I had a pic-ture of where we were when we were both nineteen. We couldn't have been more different, me in the fashion world and him in the ultra-orthodox world. Meeting Ohad Pele was like walking into my destiny. It shook me to the core.

Later, at the dinner table with our mutual friends (who warned me about this polyamorous man), hearing that I was enrolled in the prayer leadership course, he teased me, "You know, in Hasidic mysti-cism, it is written that prayer is lovemaking with the Shekinah, the divine feminine." It made sense to me: prayer is lovemaking as lovemaking is prayer.

It resonated as truth within my heart and body. I had known it all my life. By the end of the week, I also knew that this was one love I was not going to be able to turn away from. We both knew it, and yet through this apparent depth, we both knew it was not going to be a monogamous one.

An amazing thing happened when his lingam entered me for the first time: I felt purified. I felt the sacredness of this act and of being cleansed from the inside, cleaning away the residual energy from insensitive lovers, from my past.

Never had I felt such sacredness, a purity, even innocence. The meeting of our energies at that particular time was electric. It felt like silk, like water in the desert. We were both thirsty for knowledge and experience; we drank each other in and devoured each other.

I remember one time we made love before he returned to Israel. Challenges were waiting for him there, with his community. The priestess in me started to move. I was on top of him, and as I sensed he was in deep realms of openness and surrender, I started to envision his trip back as an empowered journey and whispered it into his ears, planting visions of trust and confidence in him as he went to face his challenges. Through the years, we developed and crystallized this method of sexual shamanism that showed itself from the depth of my intuitive knowing as ETP, empowerment through pleasure.

For the next two years, I commuted from the Upper East Side of Manhattan to his community in the Judean Desert. This was between Masada and Qumran, where the Dead Sea Scrolls were found and the Essenes lived. There were more camels than people.

I have a vivid memory of my first night after arriving. It was August 20, and Ohad Pele picked me up at the airport. His curls were wild like an image of Dionysus. As we drove back to his trailer or caravan, I looked out the window and saw date trees all around and a camel standing at the gas station as if it was the most normal thing in the whole world. I remember sticking my hand out the window and it was like thrusting it into an oven. We stopped to have the best falafel in Jerusalem, and the store closest to his caravan was down a long, dark, winding road that led to a nearby kibbutz—nothing like my Korean grocer on York Avenue! Everything was so different.

I arrived at his caravan to discover that only a paper-thin wall separated him from his ex-wife and three kids. They would go back and forth between the two sections. Next came the community—or rather I should say his lovers—eagerly awaiting my arrival and wanting to meet me. I remember the white mosquito netting blowing in the hot air as, one by one, the women came into the caravan and introduced themselves.

Who was the American girl who had captured their rabbi's heart? they wondered. Some were friendly, others less so. The good and the bad of Israelis is that they do not fake their feelings. All the while, I just wanted to curl up with my beloved and sleep.

Of course, I was challenged by his lifestyle, but I couldn't let go of his love and loyalty. He had an exceptional ability to accommodate all the new ideas and challenges I threw at him. Our lives were radically different on the surface, but at the core our souls transcended our differences. He embraced my wild, holistic parties, complete with free-love scenes in the "agave-licking lounge." He supported me being a part of his ashram, where they were just starting to look at ideas of relating freely outside marriage. They were years behind my friends and my own wild exploration but years ahead in their conscious awareness and dissection of philosophical minutiae. The new ideas and experiences we shared became integrated in our respective worlds. Walking the path of polyamory has always been for me a spiritual practice; without devotion to something higher—God, spirit, deep self-knowledge—I'm sure I would have bailed soon in the relationship.

∽

We traveled together in the Middle East. He took me to every historic site and festival, and slowly, slowly I became enchanted with this land, as I already was with him. I felt the palpable history and rich magic and wisdom of Israel. I longed to disappear and lose myself in it, and I did. Eventually, I found myself repeatedly participating in ceremonies that touched me and many others. A weekly ceremony called Kabbalat Shabbat, a prelude to Shabbat services, is a prayerful musical gathering dedicated to pleasure and being in the moment. One particular Kabbalat Shabbat swelled to one thousand people, all blissing out and singing songs that I initiated.

The Israeli spiritual community still resisted connecting love, sexuality, and consciousness. Sure, we had gatherings for hundreds of people, and festival culture thrived, yet I remember when I went to my first tantra gathering, there was very little open sexuality. I felt as if I had stepped back in time. I seriously wondered what it would take to liberate this tribe. They were primarily connected to the upper chakras, to the light, less so to the lower chakras. But to their credit, they had lots of heart. They would sing at any opportunity, which I loved.

Ohad Pele and I visited the red rock Sinai Desert in Egypt—where Israeli hippies go to leave civilization and chill with sea and sand, simple food, and lots of quiet. We wandered off into the mountains, taking artistic nude photographs of each other and making love in wild nature. I remember the moment I took his lingam—and it *was* a pillar of divine light—and put it on my third eye, to feel the transmission and connect to visioning.

At night we took LSD, and the mountains, lit by the moon, became members of this powerful journey. One day I started menstruating. This was a celebration. Completely ignoring the dangers of being caught by the Egyptian police, I started walking naked in the Sinai Desert. I saw the path.

I walked and sang, calling out for the women in my lineage,

invoking my "an-sisters" from the past and inviting the souls from my future community to join me. Along the way, I marked the rocks with my blood, sitting on them, opening my legs, and letting my blood make a path for others to follow.

When it came to eros and sexuality, the culture was repressed, hidden, and guarded. Our open relating was met with curiosity as well as with criticism, as if we were perverts or heretics. Back then, in 2003, it was hard to believe that we would ever see the love and sacred sexuality school we dreamed of come into existence during our lifetime. However, in my vision, I had seen such a school, a community, of spiritual sexuality. It took years, but it happened.

Some years after we started doing relationship workshops, I blended my dance and movement with his scholarship of kabbalah and community, and together we created a body of work called KabaLove. This has been our school since 2005.

In the beginning stages of our Temple of Love course, we felt that teaching about the feminine and the masculine was not enough. We needed something else, something that would allow women and men to feel beyond their little individual selves and stories. All of a sudden, I knew what to do: I took a low table, made it into a throne, and sat on it as the Goddess, opening my gates to pilgrims to come and be heard, forgiven, and blessed. Other women then took my seat and allowed the Goddess to move through them, taking them way beyond their little selves. This ritual grew and later became, in a more elaborate way, part of ISTA Level 2 shamanic inititation, where we let all the faces of the Goddess shine through.

In one ritual, I simply put my menstrual blood in a bowl by a tree and gathered women to talk about their bleeding times. Pretty soon, the idea of the red tent caught on in Israel. Reintroducing women to the red-tent gatherings was not difficult, as the bloodlines still run deep in the Holy Land. Instinctively, I guided them to remember their fullness and the ancient goddess traditions of this region, empowering and honoring the moon blood, making our blood holy again, and encouraging women to exchange menstrual blood for the bloodshed of war and destruction.

Some rituals took place in forests. Groups of women would undress, lie on the earth, and be guided into dreamtime while my two boa snakes, Kunda and Lini, would slide over and between them, calling them back into wild innocence. There, they began healing their own primal nature of sexuality and the duality between the good girl and the bad girl or primal temptation, the split between Eve and Lilith.

My work in sexual shamanism has moved me away from victim consciousness into real empowerment. We live in a world where sexual harassment and abuse are so common and the victims are so many. Yet, the way we deal with it in our society is usually by blaming the bad guys (usually men) and therefore keeping the victims stuck in victim consciousness. I too had an unfortunate initiation into sexuality through sexual abuse at an early age, which contributed to many years of disassociation and my need for self-medication and escape to other worlds. On the other hand, it also trained me, one might say, to travel in my mind, to vision, to feel deep into and beyond the body and become a sensitive empath to others. Though I was a victim myself, I refused to stay in the mind-set of victimhood. I know that if we want to reclaim our power, we need to be able to move beyond it.

The way of empowerment was what led me to move away from my family of origin. When I left, I knew that I needed my freedom and my space to make my own mistakes, to understand my place in the cosmos away from victimhood, much like the goddess Persephone, who needed to journey into the underworld for her realization.

My journey into the darkness of New York City, the underworld of Dionysian sexuality and nonmonogamous relationships, was entirely my choice. Persephone was not a victim! She chose the path of her empowerment, as did I. As time went on, my journey eventually provided the map I now use to guide women and men around the world toward sexual healing.

The life of the sex shaman is not always sweet and definitely not always easy. Loving one and many so deeply at the same time brings personal stories of victimhood to the surface. Lack of confidence, fear, anger, and low self-esteem—the bitter cocktail that people used to call jealousy—doesn't spare anyone, especially someone like me who has the good fortune of carrying, in spades, both the passion and the jealousy of Scorpio. I have felt the dagger of pain in my heart, but the learning happens when we pull it out and turn it into a sword of freedom, growth, and victory. I have sometimes wondered, *How much suffering and learning must I go through to get these life lessons?*

The most recent chapter of my life has presented new, tender challenges: traveling the world and teaching has taken me far away from my family, especially my mother. Like the fabled goddesses, I have an indescribably deep psychic connection to her. Even though the bonds run so deep—and maybe because of them—I needed to leave in my early days. I had to work hard to overcome and release her fear-based overprotective ways. Remember how Persephone was granted six months aboveground with her mother and six underground with her lover? Well, much like her, I too found a suitable arrangement for years, sharing my time among Israel and Ohad Pele, New York and my mother, and the world, traveling and teaching my workshops. Like Persephone, who shared her energy, giving her much-needed gifts to both realms, I found my own formula.

But now, in my mother's golden years, things are changing. Even though the connection between us transcends realms and even the illusion of time, my soul feels pulled to my mother during her last stages of life. After leaving New York for my first descent at age nineteen, I have returned and taken a place near her, some thirty years later. Sex and death are the two sacred doors through which we enter and exit this plane of existence, and escorting my beloved mother to the other side might be one of the greatest initiations of my life. I am harnessing the gifts of the underworld and living as love to play this supporting role. My prayer is to take the embodied wisdom of sexual shamanism into this next stage as well.

Dawn Cherie is an American performance artist, dancer, singer, and lead facilitator with ISTA. She is the cofounder of KabaLove and teaches spiritual growth and the way of sacred relationships internationally. After having helped establish a sacred sexuality community in Israel, Dawn lives part-time in New York State.

Sexual Divination

PURPOSE: Divination is the art of seeking hidden knowledge by the aid of supernatural powers. Sacred objects are used to gain answers to questions or to foretell the future. In this exercise, your eros is used as a divination tool in place of a crystal ball, dowsing rod, or tea leaves. The symbols and signs that arise from your erotic trance are interpreted like dreams to vision future events, gain answers to difficult questions, or attain guidance. This exercise requires a lot of practice and becomes easier with experience. The more you release sexual guilt, fear, and shame, the more open you become as a sexual oracle.

PREPARATION: Drink plenty of water to be hydrated for channeling energy. Set a sacred space with candles, incense, flowers, or any sacred objects that will aid your intuition, such as crystals or pictures or figurines of deities. Fruit or chocolate can be used as offerings or to eat after the ritual to help you ground. You may want to prepare an audio recorder or have a journal nearby to capture your insights afterward. Create a comfortable nest with blankets, pillows, lubrication, and your favorite sex toys. Take a ritual bath to prepare your body. You may choose to dress in special clothing if it helps remind you of your divinity. Play music that moves your spirit.

PROCESS: Start by shaking or stretching your physical body as well as your emotional body. Do any emotional clearing that may be needed so that you are centered. Meditate. Make prayers and ask for guidance on anything about which you wish to gain clarity. Set your intention and be sure it is for the highest good of all. Call in your spirit guides in whatever way is authentic and supportive to your soul. If you work with the seven directions, you may want to cast a circle.

Slowly begin the process of self-pleasuring. Start with slow, long caresses and then vary your touch. Use movement, sound, and breath to activate the body. If it pleases you, laugh, dance, moan. Touch yourself with the intention to connect to your higher self and source. Allow yourself to enter into an erotic trance and travel. Once consumed in pleasure, allow yourself to receive images, colors, and visions. Cry out to divinity; let your utterances be heard. Your visions are like dreams; they don't have to make sense. Let yourself flow.

When the journey is complete. You may want to record details about what you saw, heard, and sensed. Take your time to come back. Rest, ground, center. Eat lightly and drink water. It may take some time to interpret the message.

VARIATIONS: You can practice with a partner or partners, as long as everyone is in the purest state of surrender and service before engaging in this work. You can take turns, with one person going into a trance while the other holds space and offers pleasure, allowing the receiver to journey to other realms without losing presence. The giver is like a midwife, reassuring the receiver and reminding him or her to breathe.

RESOURCES: In the book *Sacred Sexual Healing,* Baba Dez Nichols teaches that "inside the womb there is truth. We can journey to anywhere in the universe. All of creation is in the womb. It is the hologram. This ritual is a way to source the magic." Thanks to Matooka MoonBear for coauthoring the above exercise. Dawn and Ohad Pele Ezrahi offer in-depth training in a similar practice called empowerment through pleasure.

6

FULLY EXPRESSED IN THE BODY

By Stephanie Phillips

Nabeel Khan

YEAR OF BIRTH: 1959

SUN SIGN: Capricorn

RESIDENCE: Melbourne, Australia

ARCHETYPE: Phoenix

SUPERPOWER: Energy clearing, conduit

LINEAGE/TEACHERS: Joanne Priest, Suzie St. George, Diane and Kerry Riley, Ray Stubbs, Deborah Anapol, and ISTA

EPITAPH/MOTTO: "Live! Live! Life is a banquet and most people are starving to death" (from the Broadway musical *Mame*).

SHAMANIC TOOLS: I have a supercharged crystal that goes with me everywhere and that I often use as a pendulum.

HOBBIES: Snow skiing, walking in the forest, adoring Australian birds, attending musical theater, and burlesque

I had settled down at last. My parents were relieved. Finally, at thirty, their daughter was in a stable second marriage, starting a family. Things were normal, comfortable; I was fitting in, being a conservative girl with a normal life. I loved our house in Melbourne. We were doing it up slowly when we had the funds. I was immersed in the duties of motherhood and growing our business, and we were planning our second baby. It must have seemed to everyone who knew me that my wild cabaret life and all those late-night performances were over after all. I'd hung up my sequins and feathers. And I was not looking back. It was a conservative life for me now. I was a corporate wife. Until . . .

One cold winter's night, we decided to curl up on the couch, cozy by the fire, and watch a grown-up film we had rented from the local video shop. A glass of wine and a movie was a treat for us as new parents with a toddler.

It was my turn to choose the movie, and out of curiosity, I was drawn to an X-rated flick titled *Sacred Sex*. We settled in for some titillation, but this video was different. It was a documentary that followed the sexual awakening of six couples as they attended a tantra retreat in Hawai'i.

I was mesmerized. The setting was lush and inviting. The photography was beautiful, and each scene was sensitively shot. The narrator took us on a poetic, beautiful journey as the participants unfolded from a normal everyday existence to an unveiling of depth, sweetness, and ecstatic vibrancy that was palpable to me, even watching it on the screen. Enthralled, I watched ordinary people surrender to whole-body orgasms while barely being touched. I had never seen this before but felt resonance in every cell of my body!

When the men and women were separated into different workshops for secret teachings, I watched the women dance in bliss, opening to their inner ecstasy, and it stirred something in me. It felt familiar, like a distant echo, a dormant remembering that hit my core. I witnessed all six couples blissfully reveal their essence as they connected with touch, breath, sound, and movement. It was natural, free, ecstatic, and intimate.

I could not believe my eyes. I had been touched by the raw truth. I had taught dance since I was seventeen years old and had never ignited this kind of expression in the people attending my classes. How could I learn to facilitate this? Did you have to have some kind of special gift? Where did these people come from? How do I participate? This was liberation on a whole new scale. I said to myself, *I want to facilitate that kind of energy in people. Imagine being able to wake that up for others!* It was a moment I will never forget.

Then reality snapped back. I was in my suburban house, totally committed to raising a family. Life was normal, and there was no room for this wild fantasy.

Watching that movie was like a tap on the shoulder, saying, "Wake up!" and it was going to rattle my cage with more and more intensity until I listened. How asleep I was back then—I was totally oblivious to the cost of not responding. There was more rattling to come, but that time I ignored the call. I buried the calling under my mundane tasks. It lay dormant for years, like an itch I never allowed myself to scratch.

My first husband was a Vietnam veteran. I was twenty-two. From a young age, I had studied ballet. After my classical ballet days ended in my early twenties, I entered the cabaret show scene and toured with a rock band with my husband. I was working for a top modeling agency doing shows, shoots, and magazine spreads. At the time, I enjoyed the momentum of constant work as a tits and feathers cabaret dancer, model, and TV performer. Sex sells, and I was onstage selling it. I sold everything from cars to margarine to Chanel by offering the dream, the fantasy, or whatever else could be packaged and sold.

For me, it was simple. I was just expressing what was running through my body. Nothing hides when the body moves. As a performer, I learned to connect with the audience through my body's energy. My ballet training had taught me how to move energy, transforming time and space, taking the audience on a journey and transcending reality by transfixing them in the moment. It was the sensual, sweet, raw, primal, honest expression of a soul in physical form. In the dance, I had found the ecstatic current, and I shared it, connecting with the audience from onstage.

It was great to ride this wave of consumer heaven when I was in my twenties, but the lifestyle didn't actually align with my deepest values and soul calling.

As a child, I always had a connection to spirit. My family wasn't religious, so I would take myself to the local church every Sunday, and when I turned twelve, I got myself confirmed. My parents came to my confirmation, but my father wouldn't kneel when it was time to pray. Clearly it was not their influence but my soul that brought me there. I was the one who wanted to be fully alive and expressed in this lifetime.

I knew that there was a deeper soul calling beyond the traveling for modeling and dancing gigs. I also longed for a stable family life. It was clear that this was not possible in my first marriage, so, after three years, we divorced. After the breakup, I continued on a US tour and met my second husband. Ah, sensible at last!

After our second child, a daughter, was born, I began a consulting business with my second husband. I had earned a degree in humanistic psychology and was skilled at changing belief patterns and reframing techniques. For me, we are, at our core, whole, fully alive vibrant beings. We vibrate a frequency of light and love at our essence; it is our society's conditioning that dims us. I sat in boardrooms with executives and multinational directors, and my job was to take them back to the part they had disowned, which had constricted their vibrant nature. It was so logical to me: we just peeled back the layers. Sexuality had no place in this work, but doing this work was invaluable training for me, learning how to hold space for the toughest men as they broke their hearts open and allowed themselves to feel again.

Personally, I felt my own sexuality start to shut down. The strain of being a wife, mother, and corporate consultant took its toll, and my second marriage inevitably collapsed.

Abruptly, I was in unknown territory, living a life I had never imagined for myself. I was a divorced single mum with two kids. When the marriage ended, so did my consulting work; ending one meant leaving the other. This marked the beginning of a twelve-year descent into the dark night of the soul. I was functioning day to day, but the battles kept coming, and life was tough.

I suffered excruciating physical back pain, a business collapse and accompanying financial ruin, heartbreak, disillusionment, broken friendships, and a day-to-day existence struggling to keep up with two kids whose needs grew more consuming every day. My son grew to be six foot five, passing my height on his fourteenth birthday.

I resurrected my remedial massage skills and gradually built a corporate massage business. I trained up my therapist team, and I also started seeing private clients at home. Eventually, by the time my daughter was in her late teens, I was running two successful businesses. Things were looking up. I could proudly buy my daughter the dress she wanted for the school dance. I could breathe again—and then it happened.

Playing table tennis at a carefree, fun barbecue with friends, I made a shot while dancing to Abba, tripped, and fell. Holding the table tennis paddle in one hand, I instinctively put my other hand out to break my fall. I went down, sliding my hand along a sharp, steel girder. It sliced through my palm and wrist like a fillet, as keenly as any knife. When I peeled my hand off the steel, I examined the damage with detached interest, fascinated at the inner workings of the human body. One centimeter more to the left and I would have severed a major artery. I knew in that moment that I was in serious trouble. Nerves and tendons were hanging out of my hand. It was all very surreal. In the years to follow, there were times that I wished I had bled to death right there.

The cage was rattling, and I still wasn't listening. I'd been ignoring the call, busying myself with the trifles of surviving in a dog-eat-dog world, and so my calling dealt me a blow that I could not ignore. It maimed me. It made me take notice once and for all. I was a hands-on massage therapist with thirty hours a week worth of clients. In a freak split-second accident, it was all over; I was never going to work again. I had two teenage kids at home, and they were relying on me. I spiraled down once again.

Over the next few years, I was consumed with trying to get the function and feeling back in my hand, the hand that won't let me forget. The nerve damage makes any touch painful, and yet the numbness persists; to this day, the function of my hand is limited. It was eight years before I relearned how to hold a knife and fork.

My massage business was no longer viable. I had to do something that didn't involve working with my hand. I started showing couples how to massage each other. At first, I only did it because some previous clients asked. I was surprised at how beautiful it was to witness two people with an intimate connection touch each other with loving presence. Guiding them with strokes that relaxed the other, they opened their bodies and authentically connected to each other with their eyes, often for the first time.

As they settled into my space, I'd say to them, "Everything is welcome here. Arousal is welcome. Pleasure is welcome. This is your time together, and I am honored to be your guide and witness." When they allowed orgasmic energy to run through from the sex center to the heart, that sweet intimacy felt, well, sacred. It seemed to be the most natural thing in the world. I realized that orgasmic flow was the life-force energy that moves through us all. In the couples I worked with, I witnessed that when love and presence were there, bliss opened up through the body. What I saw in these couples was that same look, that same vibrancy, that I remembered seeing in the *Sacred Sex* documentary all those years ago!

I realized this path is not one that you choose. It chooses you.

In fact, this innate energy had always been moving through me, but I never knew what it was until now. At age five, I felt it flowing naturally in my ballet classes, and it developed during my studies as a professional dancer. It continued onstage as a performer and in my twenty-five years as a model. It's stage presence, allure, charisma, or just "it." I now know it as the ecstatic current revealing itself.

Until now, I hadn't connected my sexuality with my spiritual longing. I shut it all down to be normal, to follow the rules, but I always knew something was missing. It's like the vital ingredient that's left out of a recipe, and that ingredient was sexuality in its pure form, in its sweet flow. Sexuality flows through the whole body, through the heart and the consciousness. It opens us to something beyond just ticking boxes and staying between the lines.

Around this time I started a relationship with a new beloved. After all of the hardship, I thought I'd finally found the man of my dreams, the love of my life. *Thank you universe!* I thought. There was a happy ending for me after all. I left my two kids, now grown, to make their own way in the world, and moved out of the city to start a new life with him. Still, there were more challenges to face.

I didn't understand what was happening when he disappeared for days at a time, coming home sapped of energy but also calmer. I learned he would go on "dope and porn benders." I stumbled on a huge porn collection that he said was not a problem.

My passion for opening sexual pathways was new for him. For me, sacred sexuality was an expression through my body, as natural as the flow of a stream. I was exploring opening to universal energies through an ecstatic current. He, however, seemed to be in some dark place that he could not share with me. I found his secret tastes extreme and often violent and cruel.

He was curious about my approaches and willing to learn, and we did some couples workshops together. He said that tantra helped him, but I didn't really understand his struggles. He said that I was the one with the issues; I was being narrow-minded. Sexually, I couldn't feel him with me. I didn't like being spat on or slapped, and when I told him what my boundaries were and tried to express my desire to be seen, he recoiled and then got angry.

One day, a girlfriend and I decided to visit a clairvoyant, just for fun. We waited our turn in the back of a hippie shop, squeezing ourselves onto wooden stools between hemp bags, velvet skirts, and an assorted array of giant dream catchers. The air was thick with the scent of sandalwood. My friend went first, while I amused myself trying on all the hats in the shop, and then got lost in the intriguing world of crystal wands.

When it was my turn, the clairvoyant told me to cut the deck, and midway through reading my cards, she stopped, sat back in her chair, and looked me square in the eyes.

"You've got all the elders from your family around you. They're telling me you're going to need all the help you can get. You're going to have to do your research and pull in some favors. You have to get out. Cut your losses and run." She leaned forward. "For anybody else, it would be fair enough to be resentful and bitter. But for you, however, more is required. You must open your heart in compassion. This is the frequency that is being asked of you in this lifetime." My world turned inside out and upside down. Spinning, I walked out of the reading with the feeling that my entire relationship was a lie.

I went home to my partner and recommitted to stick it out. I wanted to make this work.

A few months later, he turned to me calmly and said, "Porn has been a part of my life since I was twelve and is always going to be a part of my life. You have to go."

So there I was, again: no relationship, no home, no business, no income, no kids, and nowhere to go. I had no idea what to do next. The rug had been pulled out from under me. I stayed with different friends and drifted between houses for several months. I had nothing. There was nothing—no present, no future. I don't even have a pet, I lamented.

That's when I realized—I had nothing to lose! I was bound to nothing and no one. I had no mortgage, no loans, no encumbrances. I was free! I was free to choose my life. I could literally choose where in the world I wanted to live. If life was for living, fully expressed through the body, if I was here for some purpose, then I had no reason to hold back. I was fifty-two years old. If not now, then when? I had no excuses.

In a meditation, thirty years before, I'd had a vision. I was in a temple. The sun streamed through the glass-domed roof and sides and filled the space with light. I was collaborating with other healers, energy workers, and way-showers. We all had our own unique work, our own style, but we had a common purpose. We came together to offer something to the world, to show that cosmic energy is vibrantly alive in everybody, that sexuality—once the fear, guilt, and shame drops away—is the flow of life. We were here to show that together, when this truth is honored and harnessed with a clear intention for healing, we can create and manifest majesty, raising the vibrational frequency on the planet. This is reawakening the temples. Our bodies are the temples. Everything is alive in us already.

When I heard there was a mob of renegades doing amazing work in Sedona, California, I checked out Baba Dez Nichols and looked for his courses online. Synchronistically, he just happened to be coming to Australia for some workshops. I found ISTA and dove right in. I was home.

Stephanie Phillips is a transformation guide based in Australia. A dancer, shamanic dakini, and forest wanderer with a bachelor of education and a checkered history, she is the creator of the Body Whisperer and Orgasmic Alchemy retreats. Her clear energetic transmission supports sexual awakening and conscious embodiment. She's a global facilitator and ISTA faculty.

Sensate Focusing

PURPOSE: These simple but powerful techniques can help you increase sexual mindfulness and decrease sexual anxiety. You'll learn to shift from having a goal orientation in lovemaking to being in the moment. Individuals are empowered to take more responsibility for their own pleasure rather than assume responsibility for someone else's enjoyment. This practice builds trust and safety in a relationship. Sensate focusing can also be used therapeutically for restorative healing of sexual dysfunction.

PREPARATION: Create an explicit boundary with your practice partner. For the purpose of this exercise, sexual arousal may arise, but you are not to have intercourse. Decide who will be receiving and who will be giving. Set a timer for 10 to 30 minutes per person. The receiver disrobes and relaxes on a comfortable mat, first lying facedown then turning over.

PROCESS:
STAGE 1: The receiver lies with eyes closed and receives slow, light, nonsexual touch. In the first stage, you are not to touch breasts, nipples, or genitals.

If you are doing the touching, bring your awareness to the subtle textures and temperatures of your partner. Practice in complete silence so that both you and your partner can stay focused on the physical sensation of touch.

Feel free to repeat this stage as many times as it takes for both you and your partner to be completely relaxed before proceeding to the next phase.

STAGE 2: Breasts, yoni, and lingam are included in the touch, but intercourse and orgasm are still prohibited. Begin with light, feathery touches on the whole body before moving slowly, deliberately to the breasts and genitals.

The receiver can place one hand on top of the hand of the person doing the touching and gently indicate what is wanted, such as more or less pressure, a faster or slower pace, or guide the hand to a different body part. This nonverbal communication technique is called hand riding. The intention is to add direction. If you're touching, focus on exploration, not on trying to please the person being touched.

STAGE 3: Negotiate sexual boundaries for mutual touch. Intercourse is still off limits, no matter how sexually aroused you become. Examples of agreed-on parameters are woman-on-top position without penetration, or penis on clit, vulva, and breasts but not inside the vagina.

During all stages of sensate focusing, the focus is on sensations, and the exercise may be stopped or slowed down if either partner becomes anxious or orgasm focused.

If either person becomes tense or anxious during this exercise, it's time to slow down or stop to breathe. Do your best to experience the moment and not judge performance. When anyone is worried about doing it right, then it's not being done right. Relax, loosen up, and have more fun.

RESOURCES: Masters and Johnson introduced a series of sexual exercises that are widely used in the therapeutic community and in many tantra classes.

LOSING RELIGION AND FINDING GOD

By Patrik Olterman

Mio Olterman

TRANSPERSONAL NAME: Bhakti Aman

YEAR OF BIRTH: 1973

SUN SIGN: Sagittarius

HOMETOWN: Malmö, Sweden

ARCHETYPE: Trickster

SUPERPOWER: Pelvic sorcerer

LINEAGE/TEACHERS: Baba Dez Nichols, Bruce Lyon, Bonnie Bliss, Lin Lovely, Adinatha and Ananda of the Copenhagen Tantra Temple

MOTTO: If God stops telling jokes, I might act serious.

SHAMANIC TOOLS: Hands, heart, wand, and my connection to source

HOBBIES: Studying theology, swordfighting, reading, gaming, refereeing roller derby, and doing acro-yoga and martial arts

It was inevitable. The church leaders from the Salvation Army called for an emergency meeting, so I traveled six hours by train to attend. I was a pastor in their ranks and had just published a blog post about sexuality. This was the first line: "I guess it is one thing to talk about LGBTQ issues and theologize around the idea of alternate sexualities and queerness and another completely to come out and say: I am queer." In the closing paragraph, I wondered:

> Will writing a blog post like this make me a pariah, outcast from
> the Christian fellowship? Are we truly a redemptive, forgiving, grace
> community, where every prodigal is loved and cherished no matter
> how queer the secret? Or do we only want fellowship wearing masks,
> hiding our uniqueness, our queerness, pretending to all be straight,
> vanilla Christians who play by the rules and never cross any bound-
> aries? Let's find out!

When I looked into their worried faces, I realized that they were afraid.

"We feel like there has been an elephant in the china shop," said the Swedish national leader.

"Do we need to be worried about your marriage?" another one asked.

I knew what they really wanted to ask was: "Are you gay?" But Swedish labor law would not permit them to defrock me because of it. This meeting was the point of no return but by no means the beginning of my journey.

I have always been a sexual being; my oldest memories are of sensual dreams or sexual arousal. It seems that sex has always been a central driving force for me, the motor behind my decisions and my passion—not that I would have ever talked about it or, for that matter, let anyone know what was going on inside my mind. Even though popular culture jokes that men think about sex six times per minute, it is still not socially acceptable for a boy or man to admit that sex is always on his mind.

The Enneagram teaches that there are three basic instincts and that every person is driven by one primary instinct: sexual, social, or self-preserving. Maybe if I learned earlier that this was just my natu-ral basic programming asserting itself and that a third of the population of the planet functions just like me, I would have been able to accept the way I was wired. Instead, I thought that I was broken, and when I joined the church later on, this belief was only reinforced. I was told that I was perverted and sinful and that I had to resist my urges and suppress my sexuality.

In my early twenties, my pastor took me aside and told me I was not to talk to, or in any way associate with, any women so that I could "starve the pig." And starve the pig I did! I threw myself into fervent prayer and study of scripture, which reinforced my belief that I was a lost cause, a dirty sinner with no hope of redemption.

Outwardly, I was the perfect charismatic evangelical Christian, a young preacher with much promise. In my closet, I would look at porn and masturbate, disgusted with myself and my sexual drive. I married early because, as St. Paul says, "It is better to marry than to burn" (1 Corinthians 7:9).

In the beginning, the sexual energy crackled between us, but in compliance with the concept of "true love waits," we decided to delay sex until we were married. Naturally, we married fast. While we had been ready to rip the clothes off each other before, we found that on our wedding night neither of us had any desire. The few times that we actually connected, she could not get wet and I could not last for more than a couple of minutes, leaving her frustrated and unsatisfied. We spent a decade with a dysfunctional sex life, blaming the other for our lack of interest, desire, and sexual prowess. Like the singer-songwriter Butch Hancock, we were taught two things: One is that God loves you, and you're going to burn in hell. The other is that sex is the most awful, filthy thing on Earth, and you should save it for someone you love.

This paradox split me in two: my higher, spiritual self striving to connect with God and desperately win his approval and my lower, animal side sabotaging all my piety by being riddled with desire and lust.

Anatomically, I felt like I was cut off at the waist. The upper part of my body was appreciated and validated—I could sing, pray, formulate challenging theology, and preach the socks off my congregation—but the lower part of my body was to be suppressed and controlled, a wild and filthy animal. It was spirit versus flesh, and the battle raged every hour of every day. The only way to stay ahead of the battle was to take a firm stance of abstinence and piety, which drove me deeper and deeper into a very unforgiving legalistic fundamentalism, judging the people around me and judging myself even more harshly.

After fifteen years, my marriage was in shambles, held together by pure willpower and social pressure. Getting a divorce was not an option; it would end my career, and more importantly, it would prove to the world that all I had was a mask of holiness covering a rotten, worm-infested core of lustful perversion. I knew something had to shift, but I could not for my life imagine what could possibly save a wretch like me.

Church wasn't all bad. During this time, I had gotten a diploma of higher education in theology and mission, and my teachers taught me to question church dogma and tradition. My fundamentalism was slowly but surely eroded by a strict regimen of critical thinking and deconstruction.

I started questioning the church's stance on many social justice issues, especially in the realm of human rights and LGBTQ issues. When I was put in charge of a small congregation in my hometown of Malmö, which had a strong and vibrant LGBTQ community, I started theorizing how we as a church could be more welcoming and inclusive toward those with alternative sexualities. It was solely an academic endeavor concerning those others, however, and not me; I was not one of them. I worked my way through the alphabet of the LGBTQ acronym, quickly settling on the idea that as long as people are in long-term, committed, loving relationships, the postmodern church can bless them. After all, God is supposed to be a loving God, abundant with grace and forgiveness, and in the end, love wins, right?

The real trouble began with Q for queer. According to queer theologian Patrick S. Cheng, "'queer' refers to the erasing or deconstructing of boundaries with respect to these categories of sexuality and gender." He goes on to say that, "to 'queer' something is to turn convention and authority on its head. It is about seeing things in a different light and reclaiming voices and sources." This means that anyone who erases, deconstructs, questions, or crosses boundaries made up by societal or religious norms when it comes to sexuality or gender is in fact queer.

As I was slowly coming to grips with accepting and welcoming the LGBTQ community, there was a soft voice whispering inside my soul, gently reminding me that I may actually be one of them. However much my religious ego would protest, I might be queer. As it dawned on me that it wasn't us and them but only us, I felt like the ground under my feet had shifted and tilted and I was slowly sliding down a slippery slope. It wasn't I who had changed, but the rest of the world, or rather the way I saw the rest of the world. My religious glasses had been knocked askew, and I had woken up to a technicolor world; I was definitely not in Kansas anymore.

As I was on this intellectual and theological journey, I simultaneously watched all of my close friends' marriages fall apart, and though I was actively counseling many of them as their pastor or as their friend, I was powerless to help them. The tools of piety, prayer, and Bible reading were ineffectual to deal with their issues, which in almost every case was rooted in their sexuality, whether it was shame over hidden desires or disillusionment over a lack of desire due to suppressed sexuality. The couples I met had a near total lack of intimacy and openness concerning sex.

So, I went on a search for new tools to address this both for my friends and, more importantly, to save my own failing marriage. In this regard, the church failed me. There were no tools to work with sexuality within the context of the Evangelical church; the split between sexuality and spirituality is vigilantly guarded by the Pharisees of morality and ethics.

Instead, I started to look outside the confines of my own tradition for answers as well as tools to work with my sexuality. The only place I could find where one could even speak about sexuality and spirituality was in the world of tantra.

I went to my first tantra festival with fear and trembling. Was I compromising my faith? Was I selling my soul for cheap thrills and a quick fix?

I was met with a world of deep respect, loving light, and gentleness. I stayed in a corner of the room, listening carefully and soaking up the atmosphere, which was clearly saturated by the Divine. I was touched both physically and spiritually with pure and gentle love, drawn to the light like a moth to a flame, still fearing it would end me.

Intrigued, I wanted to know how deep the rabbit hole went. I danced and laughed; I was caressed and loved. The last night of the tantra festival, there was a wild dance party that lasted all night. In the end, we all fell to the floor, exhausted and happy. We were gently guided to close our eyes, bodies intertwined, breath synchronized like one big organism, ecstatic, bubbling with life force.

The gentle voice over the speakers told us to listen for messages from the Divine. I closed my eyes and saw a majestic elephant with glowing orange markings on its forehead coming through veils of mist toward me, touching my forehead with his. Tears streaming down my face and my heart racing, I shared with the group, although I had no idea what the vision meant. "Oh, that's simple," said the gorgeous woman leading the workshop. "That's Ganesha, the remover of obstacles, the god of new beginnings."

And a new beginning it was. That night, I went home and made love to my wife for two hours straight. When we were exhausted, she fell back on the duvet and exclaimed, "I love this new tantra stuff!" It was a brand-new world, a world in which spirituality and sexuality were no longer mutually exclusive but complementary.

Lovemaking had gone from being a chore and something disgustingly dirty to something beautiful and sacred. I started attending local "Sexibility" gatherings, which are sensual gatherings to explore and awaken one's sexuality. I gradually started to open to the possibility that perhaps I was not broken; maybe I was just human.

So many things changed during that first year, most of them very subtle changes in perception inside me. My marriage also transformed into a vibrant, living, open, and ever-changing relationship. Still, there was a glaring incongruence between who I now was on the inside and who I was in public.

I went to my first tantra massage, and though my dakini never touched my genitals, I came out of the room and exclaimed, "BEST SEX EVER!" It was a divine experience. The rising sexual or kundalini energy felt and manifested exactly like being baptized and filled with the Holy Spirit in church. What if it was the same spirit, the same energy? Encouraged, I started studying the sacred texts and found the Hebrew words and language for the divine spirit were both feminine and very similar to the tantric description of shakti and kundalini energy. As I Integrated and embodied this new knowledge and these experiences, my preaching slowly transformed from aloof, abstract spirituality to down-to-earth practical grace theology. I started blogging about my journey, working toward radical honesty and transparency.

This, of course, was rocking the boat or, as my superiors so elegantly put it, letting the elephant loose in the china shop. Not everyone was a fan of my transformation. When you tap into your life-force energy in a sexually repressive environment, you stick out like a sore thumb. The people around you are forced to face their own repressed sexual selves, and that is scary. More often than not, they will try to force you back into the pigeonhole.

One evening at a Sexability gathering not far from my home, the leaders were talking about how they had just returned from a one-week intensive workshop in Guatemala. They described what they had done at the course, and I remember thinking that there was no way I could ever do anything like that; it was too extreme, too hardcore. Little did I know that in just a few years I would be teaching that course!

At Bible college we had been taught to deconstruct and question everything, so we did. I started with my own sexuality, realizing that not only had I always fallen in love easily and loved more than one person at a time, but I also had a dark secret. I found myself drawn to the world of BDSM, not that I dared voice this to anyone, but slowly I was opening up within myself, daring to at least accept that I had wishes, desires, and dreams that I had in the past locked in a secure box deep inside my soul.

A year later, I was working in the coatroom of the Joyride Festival. The coatroom was a safe place to be, a place where I could retreat and hide if I got overwhelmed in the workshops offered at the festival. One of the workshop leaders was talking about the "inner marriage" and the process of becoming a whole person by affirming your inner masculine and your inner feminine. "You have the most beautiful man in the world and the most beautiful woman in the world living inside of you," he said with a warm and gentle smile. I had come to believe that the path to holiness was to truly become oneself. Though I had come quite a ways in becoming one with myself on the inside, I could also sense that I had only taken the first stumbling steps toward full integration, not to mention integrating my private and my public lives.

After speaking to the workshop leader, I was invited to a one-week intensive workshop in England. After a quick discussion with my wife, we decided that she would do the course first and I would find another one later that year. She left the next day, and I was left at home hoping that we had made the right choice. She called me several times during that week, checking in and asking if it really was going to be okay if she connected with somebody else sexually. I assured her that it was okay and encouraged her to follow her heart and dive deep, as we had already decided to open our marriage and live polyamorously.

A week later she came back healthier, stronger, and transformed. I was looking forward to my turn! I went on the website to find my own workshop and was immediately drawn to Israel and the fact that the leader of the Israeli community was a rabbi. I signed up, and shortly thereafter I was on my way to the ISTA Level 1 training, Spiritual Sexual Shamanic Experience, in Israel.

I thought that by going to Israel, the land of Jesus, I would get a deep but gentle initiation into this world of sacred sexuality. Boy, was I wrong!

I landed in Tel Aviv in the middle of the night and found myself sitting on a rooftop under a full moon, wondering what strange adventure I had gotten myself into. The morning after, I was off to the ISTA conference before the training. I was totally unprepared for the unashamed openness and directness of the Israelis, who start at 100 percent and then work their way higher. It was full throttle, all the way. On day one, I was thrust into a guided meditation of the underworld with fire, smoke, and snakes. It was a ritual, if symbolic, sacrifice of my own heart to revitalize the land, and I created erotic art in a beautiful workshop where I used my entire naked body as a brush. I tumbled out of this wonderland onto the rooftop where I was staying and fell deeply asleep, only to wake up to people making love all around me. In a matter of minutes, I found myself surrounded by beautiful people and their naked bodies. Scared witless, I ran and locked myself in the tiny bathroom, took a shower, and got ready for the real challenge: a one-week intensive workshop, working with myself, my sexuality, my spirituality, and these crazy people!

The workshop started with three days of experiencing only your own sexuality and your own life force. I went deep into myself and confronted my past, my shame, and my fears. Slowly, little by little, welcoming back my wild man, my inner animal, I made connections between the deep, dark earth and the spiritual light. I was broken down and reconstructed. It was only on the second day that I realized, *Oh, shit! I am at the same workshop—the one that my friends had gone to in Guatemala, the one I would never go to!*

I came to Israel full of fears, shame, and guilt, and slowly I was shedding these layers that hid who I truly was. I discovered that deep inside was not rottenness and worms but rather an infinite well of love and divine light spreading through my being, longing to reach out and touch others with affection and grace. I truly felt that for the first time since I was a small child I was completely myself.

Toward the end of the week, I remember writing in my journal that, yes, they are completely crazy, but they are my kind of crazy; they are my tribe.

The next Sunday, I was standing at the front of my congregation, playing my guitar and leading the congregation in worship. My body hummed with the music, feeling the energy of the entire church body, vibrant, alive, and free. The drums were thundering behind me as I sang the song "I Will Become Even More Undignified Than This." The song is about King David, who goes to meet with God on a mountaintop. He gets so into his worship that he rips off his clothes and dances naked, wild, and free before the Divine. When he walks back into town, the priests are presumably livid. How dare he, the king, be naked, and on top of that, claim that he was in worship?!

I sang David's response to the priests' anger: "I will dance, I will sing / To be mad for my king. . . . Some may say it's foolishness / But I will become even more undignified than this!" I had a big grin on my face as the drums thundered on. This was my calling to dance wildly, naked for God, a dancing elephant in the china shop disturbing the status quo, disturbing the peace and allowing my life-force energy, my sexual energy, to be seen by all, free from guilt, shame, and fear!

I vowed to myself never again to hide behind any mask or conform to any norm that made me smaller on the outside than I really am on the inside. Ultimately, my wife and I were asked to resign. The official reason: allowing yoga in the church. The real reason: daring to question the restrictive status quo that had been forcing people to stay small and repress their inner sexual selves. It was a hard blow, but in the end, I have only gratitude for the people who set me free from the church's chains so that I could finally live a full expression of my powerful, sexual self, giving to others the gift of freedom that I have been given.

Today, although no longer married, I live in an open, polyamorous relationship. I coach singles and couples in all sorts of relationship constellations; I teach tantra, conscious kink, and spiritual, sexual shamanism all over the world; and I also give tantric sessions to help people along the journey that I have lived. I am by no means a master, but I get to teach what I have lived, and I get to see people break out of their prisons and live freely with no shame, no guilt, and no fear.

I had spent so much time looking for God in the church, trying to fit in, making myself small and powerless in the process. When I finally found God, I realized that God had been with me all along, alive and well in the divine source of love that came rushing out from within once I dared to open the locks and allow myself to be who I really am—powerful, wild, and free.

Patrik Olterman is a pastor, preacher, poet, and public speaker. With formal training in theology, counseling, and social work. He is an Enneagram practitioner, life coach, and daka who can speak on many subjects including tantric Christianity, sexuality in the Bible, relationships, martial arts, and conscious kink.

Ecstatic Dance

PURPOSE: Ecstatic dance is a worldwide spiritual movement with boundless multidimensional benefits. In a modern culture that has lost its value for community, this is an important tribal experience. Although this is specifically not a sexual practice or a place to pick up potential partners, it is very effective for opening erotic channels throughout your body that lead to greater embodied awareness. Ultimately, ecstatic dance will put you in touch with your humanity by getting you out of your head and into your heart.

PREPARATION: Locate an ecstatic dance in your area by looking online. There are dance temples, jams, and churches in most major metropolis cities around the world. (If you can't find a local event to attend, you may consider creating one by following basic collective community guidelines.) Dress in comfortable, loose-fitting clothes, and bring water, a towel, and a contribution to help pay for the venue and DJ. This space is not polluted by drugs or alcohol, photography, judgments, or conversation. These rules allow people to move into meditation.

PROCESS: This is a free-form musical journey with no single format or specific steps. The arc of the event begins with a slow warm-up. Sometimes the dance begins with an opening circle and invocation, followed by self-directed dance. Typically, the dance builds slowly, comes to a peak, and then calms down. The group may then gather back together in a closing circle.

To help you get the most out of your journey, warm up your body by stretching and connecting to your breath. Breathe all the way down to your pelvic floor. Start by shaking or spinning. Use your whole body in the dance, including your face and your fingertips. Vary your movements. If you feel called to approach someone, do it with a smile and a nonverbal gesture and don't get attached. If someone approaches you and you are uncomfortable, move away. Express your personal boundaries with a namaste gesture or by saying no, thank you. Keep expanding into your own pleasure. Lie on the floor. Feel your feelings. Try closing your eyes. Don't stop breathing; keep moving. You may come to a point of resistance when you don't feel like dancing. Keep moving. Push through your limitations and be curious about what is on the other side. Allow the energy to move through your throat by humming, growling, hooting, laughing, or wailing. If your body needs air or water, take care of yourself, but don't stop moving to escape your emotions. Dance your fears and frustrations. Dance your longing and your lust. Dance yourself back into love. Observe everything that is arising in your inner realms.

VARIATIONS: Trance dance can also be done blindfolded.

RESOURCES: Gabrielle Roth popularized ecstatic dance in the '70s with her book *Maps to Ecstasy.*

8

DANCING BETWEEN DIMENSIONS

By KamalaDevi McClure

Pien Holdijk

TRANSPERSONAL NAME: Moksha
YEAR OF BIRTH: 1975
HOMETOWN: Mission Viejo, California
RESIDENCE: San Diego, California
ARCHETYPE: Muse
SUPERPOWER: Empathy
LINEAGE/TEACHERS: Sivananda yoga, Julia Cameron, Dieter Duhm, Greg Clowminzer, Yoah Wexler, Charles Muir, Daniel Schmachtenberger, and the spirit of Shekinah
EPITAPH: Wake up and dream
SHAMANIC TOOLS: Prayer, rope, latex, and tarot cards
HOBBIES: Soaking in hot springs, engaging in deep conversation, snuggling, vegan food, performance art, ecstatic dance, and watching *Star Trek*

The family cat, Kabuki, is an exotic breed who has a wild side as well as a domestic disposition. He lives with me, Michael, and our twelve-year-old son in a laid-back beach town in San Diego. Our home is surrounded by vegetable gardens and fruit trees. We've built a treehouse in the backyard. We're friendly to our neighbors, who probably think we're a bit eccentric because of the loud lovemaking. Once in a while, when running errands at the bank or natural foods store, we are recognized from our TV show or public speaking events; otherwise, we go about our daily business like everyone else.

We bought our house when I was pregnant, just in time for the home birth. Michael tells the story of me in labor, growling and panting like an untamed beast. But my memory was euphoric: I felt my spirit flying through nonphysical realms, communing with my unborn son, and bringing his soul down to earth. In truth, I am part animal and part god/goddess. All humans are.

A shaman is someone who straddles worlds, accessing dreamtime dimensions and guiding others with otherworldly wisdom while keeping one foot firmly grounded on earth.

My first memory of connecting to the other side came around age eight. I woke up and found my dad in the kitchen making breakfast. I asked, "What happened to the baby who died before I was born?"

A cloud came over his face, as he slowly recounted the time my mother was four months pregnant, cramping and bleeding in the bathroom. Before he took her to the hospital, he returned to the toilet to find the fetus fully intact. He scooped the tiny body into his hand; it was no bigger than his palm. But when he took a closer look, he could see that it had developed a little penis—it was a boy. His son. He felt its soul sort of lingering around, so he said good-bye. Then he put the barely formed body in a mason jar and took it to the UCLA Medical Center. When he looked up from telling his story, he asked why I was crying.

"I was there. I remember," I said.

My dad dismissed it. "Maybe you just overheard the story before."

"No. That baby was supposed to be me. I was supposed to be a boy."

"Nonsense," he said and went back to making sandwiches for our school lunches. We never spoke of it again.

My father was a professor of psychology. He was raised in Beverly Hills, with a rich Russian Jewish heritage. With all his book smarts, it's no wonder he was immediately drawn to my mother's natural intuitive wisdom. She is a *curandera* with a natural understanding of plants, animals, babies, and elders that goes well beyond reason.

My mother emigrated from Mexico at age twenty-one, with only a third-grade education. She worked as a maid and sent money back to her mother's pueblo to help raise her thirteen brothers and sisters. My parents met on the beach in Malibu, in the summer, and immediately fell in love. They had a deep spiritual bond. Together, they practiced yoga and transcendental meditation, but that couldn't mend their bitter intercultural differences.

My father's Jewish family objected to him marrying a Catholic woman, and my mother's father refused to walk her down the aisle. Despite their parents' disapproval, they took their vows and had two healthy boys. The third pregnancy ended in a tragic miscarriage, with my mother nearly hemorrhaging to death. About a year after that, I was born, followed by my little brother.

As the only girl in a family with three boys, I spent most of my summers playing in the mud by the river on a ranch in Mexico or studying the Torah at a prestigious Jewish camp in Malibu. My most cherished memories were by the campfire. Songs, stories, and silence all stirred something in me.

I especially loved ghost stories because I grew up in a haunted house. Our two-story home was formerly owned by a ballet dancer who allegedly died in our kitchen. Whenever anyone slept over, they'd report hearing the click-clack of high heels coming from the staircase around midnight. When I retold this story to people, they almost always experienced goosebumps and had strange dreams that night.

Storytelling is one of my shamanic superpowers. It may sound like a simple skill, but it can play an enormous part in the rescripting of reality for individuals as well as for the collective. My life's work has been about writing books, directing Tantra Theater, performing a one-woman show, and starring in a reality TV series. I believe storytelling, through these various media, is needed not only for entertainment and education but also because our future requires a new narrative. It's time we become the authors of our own love story.

Good storytelling starts with listening. A shaman listens not only to what is being said but also for what is withheld. It is a skill that takes practice, which can be messy.

Growing up, I was always eavesdropping and inappropriately retelling other people's stories, which amounted to gossiping. Once I was actually sent home from the first grade for standing up during show-and-tell and recounting a joke I had overheard one of my brothers say at the dinner table:

"What's the difference between snowmen and snowwomen?"

[Pregnant pause.]

"Snowballs."

After the humiliation of being sent home wore off, my innocent mind remained tortured by the underlying reality of this wisecrack. Why did boys have balls and I didn't? What was the real difference between the sexes?

I looked for clues everywhere. I overheard my three brothers talking about their spontaneous boners. And there were the occasions when my mom bathed us all together in the same bathtub, and they would tease me: "Yours broke off." I would feel left out as the only child without a penis, secretly praying that my clit would someday grow into a full phallus.

I felt like an amputee with a phantom limb. I spent most of my childhood with a vague sense that I was supposed to be a boy, or at least that some part of me was. Being stuck in a girl's body felt like some kind of cruel punishment. I would rage against all the restrictions of my female conditioning, especially when my mother, influenced by her Latin culture, insisted that a woman's place was in the kitchen and not outdoors. Studying was also considered man's work. These notions triggered many tumultuous fights with my mother at a time when she was already devastated by the painful process of divorcing my dad after more than twenty years in a dysfunctional marriage.

Around age fifteen, when my family was preparing for my Quinceañera, a traditional Mexican coming-of-age ceremony, I started experimenting sexually with girls—in particular, my best friend. And then my mother found out. To this day, we still can't agree on whether she kicked me out (my version) or I abandoned her (her version); regardless, I moved into an apartment with my father in another city, and we spent my last two years of high school helping ease each other's broken hearts.

My coming-out process was miserable. When I got the courage to tell my dad that I was a lesbian, he recalled his clinical studies in Freudian psychology and hypothesized that I was underdeveloped, still seeking the love that my mother wasn't able to give me because of her bipolar mood swings. He insisted I see a professional who happened to practice conversion therapy. For the next six months I actively trained to adjust my female fantasies with heterosexual scripts. When that didn't work, I was prescribed antidepressants. After several years, my psychoanalyst admitted that all efforts to make me straight had failed, and she diagnosed me with massive depressive disorder.

In the '90s, there was not much acceptance of bisexuals, much less trans or queer identities. (Tantra, polyamory, and shamanism were not even on my radar!) In college, when my first roommate found out I was gay, she complained to the management, and they transferred me to a single dorm room with no roommates. Desperate for connection, I began the first lesbian and bisexual women's discussion group at my school, self-medicated with recreational drugs, and escaped into casual sex—which kept leading to spontaneous transcendental spiritual experiences.

During this confusing time, I found sanctuary in studying performing arts, which provided any number of alternate realities, and this is where I learned to shape-shift. There existed a new movement called color-blind casting, where an actor could play any gender, race, age, or ethnicity. (I especially delighted in seeing women read for male roles.)

I started playwriting as a mode of healing my childhood wounds. Stories poured forth. I wrote about my malpracticing gynecologist, my incestuous feelings toward my mother, and lesbian domination fantasies, and I even got a scholarship for a stage production called *Honeysuckle,* which challenged identity politics altogether.

Although it felt like a betrayal to my lesbian community, I found myself falling in love with a male yoga teacher. When people asked me what I saw in him, I told them, "He was more of a goddess than any woman I ever met." I understand now that this was because he cultivated his inner feminine. After college, I followed him to Hawai'i, where we lived in a free-love drumming commune. My days were wild, experimental, and filled with magic.

That first summer, I took a job directing Honolulu's LGBT pride festival of '97. One of the performers was a professional dominatrix named Mistress Bleu, who invited me to become her submissive. At first, I was apprehensive about the ethics of sex work, but she described it as "performance art for one." I justified that I had a college degree in performance art and didn't get many opportunities to use it. I moved in with Mistress Bleu and played her submissive for about nine months. Together, we offered sessions in a commercial warehouse that she redecorated as a dungeon.

Our clients were mostly wealthy businessmen from overseas. They'd arrive dressed in expensive suits. I'd slowly undress them and then, kneeling before them, fold their clothing. After we had explored and enacted their personal erotic fantasies or stories from the collective consciousness, I was surprised to see them leaving the dungeon lighter and more liberated.

One Tuesday evening, during our weekly community drumming circle, I was dancing under the summer sky and felt a bolt of energy shoot through my spine, carrying my consciousness into the cosmos. I lost myself in the stars and saw my limitless soul connected to everything in existence. This timeless trance continued for weeks, where I experienced such bliss I could hardly eat or sleep. During this time, I had a profound sense of freedom that allowed me to strip off layers of social and sexual conditioning with no regard for what others thought of me. It no longer mattered if you called me lesbian, bisexual, poly, tantric, kinky, queer—I knew my true nature: I was love.

In order to reconcile my radical sexual awakening with my classical yogic training, I left the islands. The Sivananda Vedanta school has ashrams all around the world. I immersed myself in meditation and wrestled with the belief that celibacy was the only way to realize God. My teachers frowned upon anything that wasn't *brahmacharya,* or "spotless chastity." During my teacher training, we were taught to practice strict abstinence, which, according to Swami Sivananda, was "not merely from sexual intercourse but also from auto-erotic manifestations, homosexual acts, and all perverse sexual practices." I even shaved off all my long brown hair.

When I was initiated into the order, I was issued a new name, with an ironic caution. The orange-clad swami said they considered my astrological chart and the numerology of my birth name and decided on KamalaDevi. Officially, it means lotus goddess. But he cautiously leaned toward me and said it has a deeper tantric meaning: "She who worships the Divine with her body."

When I returned from my travels and told my family over dinner that I was changing my name, my now one-hundred-year-old grandmother slammed her fist on the table and declared, "Well, it's about time! I never liked your old name anyway."

From then on, everyone in my family treated me as if I was a new person, and my childhood trauma seemed a million miles away, as if it belonged to someone else.

As a yoga teacher, I felt intuitively guided to incorporate sexual healing methods into my private sessions. Many clients, who originally hired me to help with their flexibility or fitness, spontaneously started asking about how to increase their libido, control their ejaculation, reduce numbness in their genitals, or bring their spiritual practice off the yoga mat and into the bedroom.

Occult teachings seemed to naturally flow through me. It was as if I had instant access to a library's worth of wisdom, literally at my fingertips. The main character in my life story seemed to have suddenly shifted. She was no longer conflicted and confused but fearless and free.

I didn't know how to explain my sudden transformation until I came upon the theory of a walk-in—a new soul that takes up residence in a body. At times it happens because that person has unbearable life circumstances, but instead of committing suicide, the soul decides to make an exchange with a new soul with a greater purpose on earth. Or sometimes two or more souls walk along together like companions. I resonated with this notion because I had a strange sense that my soul was not singular. In any case, I knew it was not solely feminine. I've since come to accept that my soul is hermaphroditic.

For the next few years, I went on a sojourn to get to know my new self. I backpacked through Europe and Southeast Asia, studying everything I could about sex and spirituality. I stayed in monasteries and yoga ashrams and sometimes I crashed on the couches of lesbians I had met at a local gay bar the night before.

As romantic as my travels may sound, I was lost.

Depression struck, and I ran back to my mother's arms. She offered me work as the live-in property manager of the house where I was raised—the same house where I had struggled with my sexual identity for so many years. The haunted house.

I rented it out to young women who were artists, and it became a house of healing. My mother would join our weekly practice of yoga, meditation, and forgiveness. She learned to accept my lesbian lover at the time, and I learned to appreciate her power as a healer. She taught me about herbs and spells that she had learned from her grandmother, and, eventually, we found a connection that went well beyond our past and our personalities. We didn't have a context for the work that happened in that house, but in hindsight, I recognize it as shamanic soul retrieval.

Meanwhile, Michael, my soon-to-be husband, was living in San

Diego studying shamanism and supporting his grandmother Edith as she prepared to cross over to the other side. On St. Valentine's Day, after she transitioned, he volunteered to be a greeter at a modern tantra puja, led by my mentor at the time, Francoise Ginsberg. This is where our paths first crossed. We both felt an immediate multidimensional connection, and I like to think that his grandma's spirit had something to do with our finding each other.

When he tells the story, he says he saw the future in my eyes. But honestly, what I remember most was being mesmerized by his muscles. At the end of the night, when he walked me to the temple door and asked for my phone number, I immediately told him that if we were going to date, he'd have to accept the fact that I was bisexual and polyamorous.

"Even better!" he exclaimed.

So, I had a sexy first night with Michael, but I didn't yet tell him I had started seeing Viraja, the blond woman whose phone number I acquired in the bathroom that very same night. I had no idea that the two of them had also exchanged numbers and arranged their own date.

On our second date, Michael drove me to a hot spring in Mexico for a tantric retreat. Guess who was the first person we ran into? Viraja! She was cooking at the campfire, and instead of being awkward, we delighted in discovering that we were mutually attracted to one another. We enjoyed group sensuality in the healing waters under the full moon that night.

This was the perfect bohemian beginning to our lifelong partnership, which includes an intimate network of about a dozen long-term lovers, like Viraja, who are all deeply bonded through the heart, mind, and sometimes sex.

After several years of living with Michael, a strange man in orange robes started visiting me in my dreams. He had dark skin and a silver beard. He spoke of the goddess Kali. He was transmitting secret teachings through sounds I did not understand.

I found him, or someone who looked like him, on the internet, and we began an online connection. We discussed the possibility of my coming to India to visit his ashram. When I told Michael, he asked, "Who is this guy? How do you know he is safe?"

I told Michael my soul felt called to go. Although it didn't make sense, it felt like something I had to do. Michael said he wanted to come with me, but when I wrote my new guru asking if Michael could join us, he told me that he only worked directly with the goddess and he would not teach men. Further, he told me I didn't need to bring any clothing, as he would have my robes made for me when I arrived and that no further preparation was required, except to wire him money.

Michael was skeptical and unwilling to wait around at home while the woman he loved went off on a dangerous trip with a strange man. We argued. Bothered by the sexism that I felt from both men, I yelled at Michael, telling him that my spiritual pilgrimage was between me and God!

With love in his eyes, he pleaded: "I may not be called to India, but you are my goddess, and I'm called to be with you."

That moment brought me to my knees. I realized that as long as I sought an outside god, separate from myself or my beloved, I would forever be stuck in the illusion of duality. This was the beginning of another awakening.

Together we went on a tantric pilgrimage to South India. We traveled through various ancient temples and did puja to the planets, especially to the Moon, since she is the ruler of romance and our open marriage needed as much help as it could get. We did daily fire rituals and practiced prostrations at each other's feet. My guru revealed deep transmissions that included sound healing on sixty-four marma points on my yoni and within the womb. But as promised, he refused to teach Michael. Michael thought he was a fraud. I assured him that many enlightened masters still have wounded human personalities, and I remained devoted to his teachings until the day he lost his temper and slapped his senior disciple across the face. Michael insisted that we leave. That's when we fled the ashram with his disciple, who invited us to come with her to Sri Lanka, and we almost did, but Michael had seen enough and insisted we head home.

During our layover in Thailand, we learned that at the exact moment our airplane lifted off, the deadliest tsunami in history struck the very beaches where we had just stood, and devastated Sri Lanka. It killed more than 230,000 people. I had survivor's guilt. And it compelled me to start writing.

I channeled all my grief into an erotic novel called *Don't Drink the Punch: An Adventure in Tantra.* It was about a disembodied guru who teaches the left-hand path of tantra by speaking through various disciples, including the main character, who represented me (but happened to be male).

Shortly after the book launched, I got a call from my friend Baba Dez Nichols, who resonated with the leaderless model of group initiation. He had always been fascinated by the capacity of spiritual seekers to share power. He felt this aligned with his vision for the Sedona School of Temple Arts (the precursor to today's International School of Temple Arts). He was working on a book based on his own life's work, but the project was not flowing. He heard about a course I was leading called "How to Write a Book in 90 Days" and wondered if I could help him do so before the upcoming Daka/Dakini Conference.

(For about a decade, these annual gatherings would fall on my birthday weekend. This is where I would meet my most influential mentors, coconspirators, and lovers, such as Charles Muir, Annie Sprinkle, Betty Dodson, Mare Simon, Barbara Carrellas, Reid Mihalko, Betty Martin, Shawn Roop, David Cates, Kenneth Ray Stubbs, and Tracey Elise.)

As such, I felt I already had a soul contract with Baba Dez, and coauthoring a book felt preordained. We consummated our new partnership with a sex magic ritual, which opened a channel to all the allies, seen and unseen, that would support the manifestation of *Sacred Sexual Healing: The SHAMAN Method of Sex Magic.* The writing process felt supernatural; I heard voices and had visions. It only took five months to write and publish the book, from beginning to having the book in hand!

We even went away on a spontaneous writing retreat to Hawaiʻi, during the filming of his documentary *Sex Magic*. Michael, my new-born son, and a handful of lovers were also a part of the movie. When the movie premiered, I was bombarded with questions about polyamory. Isn't that cheating? Are you Mormon? How do you handle jealousy?

I looked around to see who would answer all these questions and realized I was the person for the job. I began talking to various news-casters and journalists and enrolled my intimate network to go on cam-era with me. We wanted the world to know that monogamy was not the only option.

One day, Deborah Taj Anapol invited me to do a reality show. We spent several years putting together pitches for Hollywood. When it didn't work out with Taj, I attempted with Reid Mihalko, then Hollywood actor William McNamara. Eventually, we were discovered by Natalia Garcia, who created *Polyamory: Married & Dating* and directed it for Showtime.

Before completing the legal contracts, we underwent a half-day psych evaluation. I was concerned about this because it required me to disclose my history of mental illness. I had been prescribed a laundry list of designer drugs with the letters *x* or *z* in their names—Prozac, Zoloft, Paxil, Celexa—but I never stuck with them. Even after intense postpartum depression, I chose to cycle off the meds as soon as I sta-bilized. Antidepressants numbed my authentic emotions, impacted my libido, and made it hard to orgasm. I'd much prefer to endure the occa-sional panic attack or teary outburst and feel fully alive. Whenever my demons surfaced, the best medicine for me was a combination of talk therapy, performance art, and being of service to those in greater need. During the evaluation, I chose not to tell the psychologist that I see spirits and hear voices in my head. So, I passed the test.

Another potential obstacle arose when the lawyers of Showtime advised against putting our then four-year-old son in front of the camera. That's when one of the voices in my head got really loud: "No! The world needs to know that polyamory isn't just something for young people to try before they settle down but a sustainable family model for generations to come!"

That was the voice of my art activist, the one whose purpose is to make the world more beautiful. I collected myself and calmly told the production team that my son's participation was nonnegotiable: "I want my son to grow up in a world where someday he could turn on the TV and see a nonmonogamous family like ours."

The show ran for two seasons and is still available online, making a positive impact on mainstream cultural acceptance of ethical nonmonogamy. After the season finale, our extended family was undergoing a series of painful breakups, in part because of the stress of the show, but we were still living with our girlfriend Rachel, and ABC's *Nightline* aired a segment about our triad, which went viral online. The responses were unmanageable and so were my emotions. I started receiving a daily dose of hate mail, while still wrestling with fits of jealousy. I stopped sleeping. I was haunted by violent images and became paranoid.

These irrational bouts were sometimes spontaneously accompanied by seizures. I'd fly into a blind rage, and my body wouldn't stop thrashing, falling and sometimes smashing into concrete. These epileptic-like events could happen anywhere: walking to the beach, sitting in the dentist's chair. One time I nearly jumped out of the passenger seat of my girlfriend Roxanne's car while it was still moving.

My deteriorating health contributed to the bitter loss of our relationship with Rachel, breaking all of our hearts and nearly destroying my marriage to Michael.

Embarrassed and out of control, I decided to take a year off work. How could I continue as a role model for alternative relationships when I was stuck in my own dysfunctional drama? During my mental health sabbatical, Michael and I attempted to save our family with marriage counseling, along with my own private trauma therapy. While mourning the loss of our triad, I repeatedly threatened suicide and divorce.

Michael froze and felt hopeless, desperately trying to help me out of my dire condition.

One of our therapists said, "Just imagine that your wife has survived a horrible car accident. It doesn't mean she'll never drive again, it just means you have to slow down. You can't jump back on the freeway; you have to let her sit still in the car and get comfortable putting the seatbelt on again."

That's when a lightbulb went on. I had experienced something like a horrible car accident: my childhood. Everything about my current circumstances reminded me of the agony of my upbringing. I didn't have to recall all the details to realize I was a hermaphroditic soul helplessly trapped in a little girl's body, surrounded by insensitive brothers and emotionally unavailable parents who were always fighting. Now, I was suffering from the symptoms of complex post-traumatic stress disorder (C-PTSD).

This diagnosis allowed me to look at myself through an empowering new lens. In my field, I've come to know trauma. I've worked with hundreds of survivors of rape, incest, molestation, and even religious or ritual cult abuse. What I've learned is that sexual trauma is a multidimensional disease. As a lover, I've seen people dissociate. As a coach, I've witnessed how the mind makes logical leaps. As a dancer, I've felt the somatic symptoms in the body. And as a shaman, I've seen the soul go away when it doesn't feel safe.

Since this is a complex problem, there is no simple cure. I had to accept there would be no quick fix. I vowed to heal. And not partial healing but all the way up and all the way down. I had been doing therapy for the mind and meditation for the spirit, but what about the body? Because the seizures had brought me to my knees, I was ready to face what I was made of. I needed to nurture my nerves and organs and dive all the way down to the bone marrow within my weary flesh.

Fortunately, my soul tribe happens to include many world-class healers. One of my lovers, Daniel, is an encyclopedic wizard who supported me through a series of scientific tests. The results revealed that my body was malnourished and carried dangerous neurochemical toxins (a side effect of extreme stress). I went through an intense time of detoxification and upgraded to a brain-boosting diet. Morning exercise, infrared saunas, cold plunges, protein smoothies, organic vegetables, and quality supplements all helped lower my center of gravity to include my anatomical structure. Finally, I could relax and resume listening to my soul.

Mysteriously, three years earlier, I had had a vision of leading a sexual ceremony in Jerusalem; it was a sexual oracle with my good friend Ohad Pele. He was a tantric rabbi who was now approaching his fiftieth birthday, and I was invited to visit. During my current healing sabbatical, however, I was rigorous about saying no to every invitation to teach, but when he and his beloved Dawn called me, the calling was bigger than I. My soul had already said *yes!*

Israel was like coming home—not so much to the Holy Land but back to my family of choice. I reunited with ISTA and Bruce Lyon who showed me that my seizures were a sign of my body reaching for more soul. Through a series of ceremonies and intimate encounters with the land, I stripped off layers of trauma, like layers of an old costume that didn't fit. Then I unlocked dormant spaces within my cells and welcomed all my disowned aspects to find sanctuary inside my newly renovated body-temple.

The masculine side of my soul finally landed deeply into this feminine form and is learning to share power and live on purpose. I am finally embracing my wild emotions, calling forth the wisdom of my womb and the brilliance of my wand in order to step naked into the mystery—which continues to unfold.

I admit it's far more fun to navigate dreamtime and ritual spaces than corporeal obligations, but to mend my fractured body-mind, I needed to show up for the whole spectrum. Sacred sexual healing is not just about surrendering to ecstasy; it's also about inhabiting earthbound structures. This includes self-care, deadlines, parent-teacher meetings, travel itineraries, and even vitamins. The further I journey into the inner worlds, the more I must anchor myself in the outer world. To dance between dimensions, one must embrace all parts, collapse the opposites, and allow the mystery to flow through. As such, I am no longer a mere collection of partial identities such as bisexual, poly, depressed, wife, mother, whore, Mexican, Jew, teacher, student, or even shaman. We are each more than the sum of all our parts.

KamalaDevi McClure is best known for starring in Showtime's docu-series *Polyamory: Married & Dating*. She is the author of five books, director of Tantra Theater, and cofounder of Poly Palooza. She lives with her husband and son by the beach in San Diego and travels the world as lead facilitator for ISTA.

Shakti Shake

PURPOSE: This simple but powerful practice offers deep somatic benefits such as discharging stagnant energy, stimulating lymphatic circulation, reducing stress, releasing trauma, and increasing an overall sense of well-being.

PREPARATION: Wear loose-fitting clothes or none at all. Dance or drum music is optional. The time for this practice can range from 5 to 15 minutes.

PROCESS: Stand up and shake. Shake your body. Don't worry about looking silly, just pretend your whole body is a pond and there are ripples moving through it. Shake. Shake. Shake! Put all your weight on one foot and shake the other foot and leg. Switch. Shake your calves. Shake your knees. Shake your thighs, hamstrings, hips. Really shake your hips. Shake your hips some more. Shake your entire pelvis, shake your buttocks, shake your yoni/lingam, and shake your reproductive system. Breathe lots of juicy energy into your sex center. Shake here as long as you can. Now shake your belly, twist your torso, shake your chest, shake your shoulders, lift your arms into the air and shake your armpits, biceps, elbows, forearms, wrists, hands, and fingertips. Shake your arms like crazy! Let your arms down and shake your head. Shake your jaw, lips, tongue, nose, eyes, cheeks, ears, forehead, and hair. Shake your entire body. Shake the space around your body. Now stop.

Freeze! Close your eyes and breathe. Notice the energy moving through your entire system. Where do you feel open? Where do you feel closed? Where is your body still? Where is it still moving? Notice the subtle energy moving.

VARIATIONS: This sequence can be done with a partner as a way to raise your energy before making love. Or you can use it in conjunction with a variety of emotional-release tools, or simply use it to change your state.

An alternate position is lying on your back with your knees bent and your feet on the floor. In this position, shaking can reverberate from the sacrum to the cranium.

NOTES: The intention is to create a vent or valve for stagnant energy, not to stimulate mental stories from the past. If done unconsciously, shaking and trembling can reactivate the wounding. If you have PTSD or tend to dissociate, be extra mindful that this practice is done with a felt sense of the body and present awareness.

RESOURCES: We recommend deeper study into Tension & Trauma Releasing Exercises (or TRE), which is designed to evoke natural neurogenic tremors in a controlled and sustained way. Online instructional videos can be found at the TraumaPrevention website.

9
FROM FROZEN TO FLOWING

By Sean O'Faolain

Arion Light

TRANSPERSONAL NAME: Dragon Dancer
YEAR OF BIRTH: 1971
SUN SIGN: Aquarius
HOMETOWN: Dublin, Ireland
RESIDENCE: Melbourne, Australia
ARCHETYPE: Dragon
SUPERPOWER: Vulnerability
LINEAGE/TEACHERS: Siddha yoga, ISTA, sexological body-work, gestalt psychotherapy, and the ManKind Project
EPITAPH/ MOTTO: Live life fully.
SHAMANIC TOOLS: Hands, heart, Tibetan singing bowl, rattle from Africa, medicine drum, oracle cards, and feathers
HOBBIES: Skydiving, bushwalking, camping, and tantra workshops

I grew up in a traditional household surrounded by four sisters, a loving mother, and a father who worked really hard to support the family. I knew from a very young age that my country, Ireland, was a land of mysticism and magic, an ancient land steeped in history—and a land where culture had been quashed, lands stolen, villages pillaged, and people raped. Local traditions had been wiped out, and the native language had been banned. Its people were impoverished, not just financially but emotionally, and the land had been devastated by famine.

I didn't know this from studying history at school; I knew it as deeply embodied grief, anger, pain, shame, fear, love, and joy all at once. It was a deep inner knowing. On the surface, I was confused; I was a sensitive child who couldn't understand why everyone seemed dead around me. I constantly wondered: What was wrong with everyone? Couldn't they feel? I sensed that something was very wrong. Why were they so closed? Why did each village have so many pubs? Maybe people simply couldn't bear to deal with such a challenging history. And maybe I didn't belong here.

At age eleven, I came across a book in a garage sale about yoga and meditation, and I started a daily practice. I emptied my room of all furniture and slept on the floor, and my life after school became a spiritual practice. I somehow understood this place of peace—it felt like home, and I felt alive. Although I was alone much of the time, I never felt lonely. My parents were concerned; they thought I was going mad. What was that strange smell of incense coming from my room? What was that weird music I played? Why would I no longer eat meat? This was in Ireland in the early 1980s, when yoga was practically nonexistent.

I lived this way for a couple of years until hormones kicked in. The church, my teachers, and society had force-fed me the idea that sex was wrong, dirty, immoral, shameful, and sinful. And so I repressed all my feelings and desires and became a sheep. As I grew into young adulthood, I did all the usual things—jobs, money, relationships, sex, travel—and, like most people today, became a cog in the industrial machine.

I was torn. I knew all this moralizing about sex was rubbish, but a big part of me also still believed it. My only way to engage sexually was to be drunk or stoned or completely emotionally detached, disembodied, and not present. My body felt unbearable shame whenever I engaged sexually, so I disconnected and checked out. The only pleasure I got was from one-night stands, where there was no love, no emotional connection, no real satisfaction. How could love and sex possibly coexist when sex out of wedlock was so sinful? I remembered saying once to a sexual healer, "How could you do that to someone you love?"

So I repressed my vital life-force energy—until one day, in my mid-thirties, I cracked.

My reawakening happened at a powerful festival called ConFest in my new home of Australia. One of my first workshops was a didgeridoo sound healing held by an indigenous Australian man called Eshua. I was lying on the ground in a group of maybe fifty people who all started moaning and groaning, crying and wailing, screaming and shouting around me. My first thought was, *What are all these crazy hippies up to?!*

My mind couldn't relax or let go. I was about to leave when the didge crossed over my body. Eshua moved the didgeridoo slowly up from my genitals to my heart, and then I cracked. I felt a surge of grief wash over me, then anger, then rage—the flood of a lifetime of repressed feelings.

As the ceremony came to a close, I stumbled around, unable to walk. I could see that all the other participants were standing in a circle around me, chanting, and I could see the three powerful trees outside the circle and remembered Eshua thanking the trees and the land for holding us. I felt the land speak to me, now. I couldn't get up. I was like a newborn baby. I couldn't walk or talk; I could only crawl to the edge of the circle, where a friend supported me like a child. I cried and wailed for hours as my friends watched over me.

From that day on, I could no longer live a lie. I was no longer able to repress, as most Irish people do, my emotions and sexuality. I had had a taste of something powerful. I remembered what I knew when I was eleven and started meditating. I heard a call from inside, and I responded again with passion. Many of my old friends fell away because I could no longer be around people who were emotionally shut down. So I found myself alone again.

I pursued many paths. Beyond spirituality, meditation, and yoga, I spent many years studying shamanism, tantra, and sexuality. I studied under anyone I could find, going from workshop to workshop, devouring books and trying out a variety of personal practices. I got involved with classical tantric practices—awakening life-force and kundalini energies, separating orgasm from ejaculation (still a work in progress), and sublimating gross energies into refined energies.

I knew that the root cause of much of the suffering in my life was my severely repressed sexuality and my frozen emotional body. I began the hunt for what people called an orgasm. I had never had one, or at least not something that I could actually feel in my body very much. I had had plenty of "genital sneezes," as spiritual teacher David Deida so aptly describes them, but I knew there must be more.

Not surprisingly, my relationships were wracked with tension. I had had some beautiful women in my life, but I rarely wanted to engage with them sexually because of my shame. Whenever one of these relationships ended, my heart hurt deeply over the loss of yet another good friend, but I never grieved the loss of a lover because I was never really lovers with any of my partners. They were best friends, companions with whom I had occasional unsatisfying sex.

Tantra offered a glimmer of hope. I started to feel more. I cleared some shame. I felt kundalini surge through my body—and yet I knew there was more. I would do practices to sublimate these feelings, but I felt that this was yet another form of repression, a spiritual bypass.

I met a woman named Karen who helped me commence my sacred sexual journey. She was a beautiful, powerful, and sexually open woman. Our relationship was sweet and loving but also chaotic, dramatic, toxic, and highly codependent. I always had one foot in and one foot out. Whenever things became emotionally charged, I'd break it off. Whenever I went to a sexuality workshop—and I went to a lot—I wanted to explore open relationships and work with all the women I was attracted to. I had little concern for how this affected Karen. I had found something that made me feel alive, and I wasn't going to let the church or my family or even a woman shut me down! Naturally, Karen felt abandoned and betrayed as I dragged her through the mud, kicking and screaming, from workshop to workshop, festival to festival. In her anger, she shamed me and my sexuality and regularly called me a predator. I would leave her again and again, and yet we always got back together.

One cold, wintry night, we were camping in a tepee together, warmed only by the fire and our desire for each other. For the first time ever, at thirty-nine years of age, I made love. Something shifted when I was inside her, gazing into her eyes. I became present and felt layers of shame dissolve. I glimpsed beauty and truth, a possibility of something greater, and broke down in tears. I felt how beautiful it was to be intimate with another, to share eros, to make love. I just watched her in awe.

In the three years that followed, there were a few more moments like this, where I allowed my body to guide me rather than my head. The rest of the time, sex simply did not work for us, no matter how hard we tried. Although I had done much, I still had a long way to go. There was still so much emotional clearing to do, and no amount of sublimation was helping.

During this time, I completed a men's initiation training through the ManKind Project and found guidance among my newfound brothers. One in particular, an older, wise, and humble man named Grant, became my mentor. One day, while we were talking, I told him how Karen had called me a predator. I was hoping Grant would support me, but he simply said, "She's probably right about you being a predator." He guided me through an embodied practice and helped me feel my predator inside. I realized that I often engaged in predatory behavior when I was frozen emotionally, and I froze most often when I was angry. Unconsciously, I was driven to engage sexually with women so they would help me open again. I was searching for "mommy" by using my sexuality. Grant challenged me to use the emotional tools I had learned at the ManKind Project every time I became aware of this predatory behavior. He challenged me to grow up and be a man—take responsibility for my frozen emotional state, release my anger, grief, and shame, and stop manipulating women.

Shortly after this, I discovered the International School of Temple Arts (ISTA). I was at ConFest again. I had just broken up with Karen, and we were both at the festival at the same time. I was exploring connections with other women. At one workshop, Baba Dez Nichols from ISTA gave a powerful talk about relationship choices and then, a day later, held a workshop with his lovers about sex magic. I was impressed and triggered at the same time. Baba Dez was charismatic, alive, and powerful. He was there with two or maybe even three beautiful lovers, equally powerful and sexually open!

There was something very different about these teachers, something I resonated with and yet held so much judgment against. My soul signed me on for an ISTA conference in Sydney right after the festival.

My first challenge was that Karen was also there. As usual, she seemed to fit in well. It appeared she was being intimate with someone else. I wanted to do the same, and yet I felt I needed permission from "mommy"—Karen—or, at the very least, needed her to stop shaming me for being with others, particularly when we were no longer together. I wondered how this guy Baba Dez could have three lovers in the same place, at the same time, and they all seemed to get along. I had heard of polyamory and had even tried it briefly, but I couldn't even handle being with one woman—how could I possibly handle more?

Luckily, I knew a few people at the conference, and I gravitated toward them. I began to notice my longtime pattern of searching for women whom I found attractive to feel safer. Somehow, a one-to-one connection with a woman in social gatherings helped me feel safer while in a large group. However, it was as if women could smell my neediness, and I found myself alone. I felt comfortable in the workshop during the guided practices, but during the break times, I felt the need to hide.

On Saturday evening there was a snuggle party led by one of the ISTA facilitators. I was nervous to join in but tried, at least for a short while, until it became all too much, and I fled to my room. I longed to be part of this world, and yet I knew I was so far away from feeling comfortable in these spaces.

I stayed for the rest of the festival, but it was very challenging. It took everything I had to simply survive in this free and open environment. I felt like an outsider, a dead, emotionally unavailable person, among these open, empowered beings. I yearned to belong and even wanted to continue on after ConFest ended and attend a weeklong ISTA training, but I had way too much fear and went home.

It would be another year before I found the courage to go to ISTA's Spiritual Sexual Shamanic Experience. In the meantime, I got back together with Karen and even traveled to India, but we soon broke up again, and the drama continued. Our pattern was generally that I would find another woman, often younger, and reject Karen. She, in turn, got angry and shamed me. I was doing all I could to let go of my guilt and claim my sexuality, desires, and power, but she would scorn me. It felt like that, despite all the work I had done, I was taking one step forward and two steps back. I blamed her, of course, because I could not imagine how I could be co-creating all this drama.

As I was registering for ISTA, for the second time, I heard that Karen would be there and that she and Baba Dez had been hanging out. I almost pulled out, but I was stubborn, masochistic even, and determined not to let Karen hinder my growth, even if it meant suffering along the way.

The training began. It was unlike many of the tantra trainings I had done before. There was a large focus on welcoming all emotions in the space, and the participants learned tools to help release emotions that were trapped in the body. I felt a lot of resistance to using the tools.

I was inspired by Baba Dez's facilitation and by many of the other people at the training. I noticed how they were able to be both powerful and vulnerable at the same time. As I moved through the training, I learned about boundaries and consent and how to release much of my emotional baggage. As I participated in powerful ritual after powerful ritual, I had my first taste of a freedom I had only heard people talk about. I began to access something dormant from deep inside, and I allowed myself to share my feelings with the group. By opening more, I connected with people and finally felt safe to simply be me. I explored new ways of being, asking for what I wanted and saying no when I didn't want something.

One morning after a very powerful ceremony, the whole group was ecstatic. They had been dancing and building energy. Most participants had gone to lunch, but a few stayed behind and kept dancing. I was surprised that I could dance in a small group while Karen was there. The room was charged, the sexual life-force energy was flowing freely, and I had never felt so open and ecstatic.

All of a sudden, a hot young man named Derek grabbed Karen, drew her close, and started dancing very sexually with her. He lifted her up, wrapped her legs around his waist, and pressed her into the wall. This was all too much for me. I could feel my whole body contract; I was paralyzed, frozen. I spotted Grace, a woman I had had a beautiful connection with the day before, and started dancing with her. She ignored me, so I tried harder, and she completely rejected me. I tried dancing with another woman. Another rejection. Then I heard Grant's voice loudly in my mind: "Take responsibility for your frozen emotional state. Stop manipulating women."

I realized that, even though I couldn't feel it, I must be angry. I ran out of the room, jumped in the river, and yelled as loud as I could under the water, thrashing about like a wild animal, diving my head under the water over and over until the anger I felt frozen inside finally thawed. I was angry that Karen was allowed to do that in front of me, but I couldn't in front of her. I was angry that I had given away my power to her, that I had cut off my balls and handed them to her on a platter. I was angry that everyone in Ireland was so shut down. I was angry that no one had taught me how to be a man, how to be vulnerable and open, how to relate to others. I was so fucking angry inside.

I now felt guilty and apologized to Grace soon after, telling her all that had happened. She honored me for being honest and real. Finally, I had caught myself in the act. I finally saw my predator, and it didn't want sex. It wanted support and love; it wanted a way for me to release the anger that was frozen inside me, weighing me down like a ton of bricks. Karen was right after all, even though I could never hear her. Now that I had the awareness that I could support this predator inside, I could free myself of the need to sexually manipulate a woman in order to support myself emotionally.

This was very powerful stuff that I was learning. It was deeply embodied work. This was my key to freedom. I needed to release and befriend my anger and eventually learn to channel it into power. I had a beautiful, loving heart, but I was weak. I had spent my whole life using so much energy to suppress all my feelings inside and was completely exhausted from carrying all this weight around. With my emotions flowing freely, I could finally find my power.

On day five, the group did a very powerful sexual-healing ritual, and I was paired up with the woman in the room whom I desired the most. In the past, I wouldn't have had the courage to work with her, unable to cope with my desire for her and the knowledge that she was in a relationship with another man in the room. My new-found power gave me a new freedom. I shared with her from the start my desire for her and how I would normally feel awkward with her partner and Karen in the room. Like Grace did before, this woman honored me for being open, real, and honest. She also told me that she was attracted to me.

In this ritual, she was holding space for me, with love and presence, to release my anger. I was yelling and roaring like never before. I felt a space open inside that soon filled with more energy than I had ever experienced in my life. I was flooded with pleasure, so much deep feeling and power that tears were streaming down my cheeks. I couldn't believe that I had allowed myself to be fully present and allowed all of that feeling to move through me while Karen and this woman's partner were in the room. I finally understood Baba Dez's catch phrase: "Totally present, totally aware, and totally out of control." I was on top of the world. I was free.

Naked, I ran outside and went down to the river. I jumped in the water again and blessed myself the way the Indians do in the Ganges, by bobbing up and down and immersing myself in water, baptizing myself. I was born again. I felt pure ecstasy flow out of every pore of my being. I sobbed and laughed at the same time, moved deeper than I had ever thought possible. The sky had been cloudy and gray for days, and in that moment the sun broke through, the birds sang sweetly, and the wind whistled through the trees. The sound of the river flowing was so sweet to my ears. I couldn't feel any separation between myself and everything that surrounded me; I was one with all. I felt like I had been touched by God. I knew beyond a shadow of a doubt that I had found my path. I knew I would have a long, long way to go, and yet I committed, in that river in that moment, to do all the work I needed to do to become part of the ISTA tribe. I knew I would need lots of support to get there.

I knew that one day I would become a healer, a facilitator of this work, and a sexual shaman too. I had found my path. I had planted the seed that would take many years to sprout. I deeply understood and felt on an embodied level what they talk about in this work—about bringing more love, power, and freedom into your life. Now I was truly on my journey back home.

Sean O'Faolain is a Gestalt psychotherapist with a background in meditation, ecstatic dance, transpersonal counseling, sexological bodywork, massage therapy, and is a certified yoga teacher. Passionate about empowering individuals, he co-created Pulse, a workshop venue in Melbourne, Australia, that promotes and hosts sex-positive events, and he travels as an ISTA facilitator.

Sex Chakra Sound Bath

PURPOSE: Sound healing is known to rejuvenate the body at the cellular level. Even the scientific community recommends sound healing for the treatment of various conditions and diseases. It has been proved to promote relaxation and pain relief and to release emotional blockages. More specifically, sound can activate the function and flow of both the physical and energetic sex center.

PREPARATION: Use your intuition to select an instrument. Bells, gongs, and bowls can all be powerful tools for activation. Singing bowls can be made of crystal or metal and are often manufactured to resonate with the vibration of a specific chakra. Your instrument does not have to be tuned to the sex chakra for you to get the benefits of this practice.

Take your time acquainting yourself with the instrument, without pressure. Get comfortable playing it. Notice the best position for your body type in relationship to the instrument size. Are you more comfortable sitting, standing, or lying down?

You may want to create a comfortable nest with mats, pillows, and/or blankets for deeper relaxation afterward.

PROCESS: Begin your session by visualizing radiant sexual health. Set your intention to clear any performance anxiety, guilt, fear, shame, or other energetic imbalances from your sex center.

Start by holding your instrument at your heart chakra and slowly allowing the vibrations to radiate through your being. If your instrument is stationary, visualize the vibration slowly penetrating each body part until you are fully relaxed. If your instrument is easy to move around, circulate it clockwise, slowly up and down your limbs. Continue playing the instrument at different places around your body. Allow the sound to gently wash over you and resonate throughout the body. Notice the sensations and the distance that resonate best. Play with the space above your head and around the body.

Once you have been cleared from head to toe, you can focus on the sex center. You can either meditate and allow the music to take you into a state of no-mind or practice active visualization. The sex chakra is vibrant orange or a golden glow. Imagine your life-force energy increasing. Allow yourself to become aroused as any residue from any past unconscious touch melts into love and light.

VARIATIONS: You can practice with a partner. This is especially effective with larger instruments such as stationary gongs or didgeridoos. We suggest you take turns for at least 20 minutes each. If you are receiving, simply close your eyes and surrender to the sound. Allow yourself to visualize or drift off and dream.

If you do not have instruments, you can use your voice to tune in to your partner's chakras. What follows are suggested mantras for each chakra: the full note on the musical scale with its corresponding solfège syllable (do, re, mi, etc.), the vibration of that note in hertz, the vowel sound it makes, and the *bija* mantra associated with it.

> Root (first chakra): C or do/utt, 396 Hz, *uuh*, lam
> Sex (second chakra): D or re, 417 Hz, *ooo*, vam
> Power (third chakra): E or mi, 528 Hz, *oh*, ram
> Heart (fourth chakra): F or fa, 639 Hz, *ah*, yam
> Throat (fifth chakra): G or so/sol, 741 Hz, eye, ham
> Third Eye (sixth chakra): A or la, 852 Hz, *aye*, om
> Crown (seventh chakra): B or ti/si, 963 Hz, *eee*, aum

Alternatively, you can find a variety of recorded chakra meditations online, including binaural beat CDs, MP3s, and videos. There are also many public sound baths and gong meditations being held in most major cities. Whichever method you choose, we suggest you drink lots of water afterward and allow plenty of time to ground and integrate.

RESOURCES: Many free MP3s and YouTube videos online claim to boost your libido, intensify your erections, heal herpes, and expand your orgasm, but your mileage may vary. The editor's top pick for shamanic sound healing is Tom Kenyon, author of the Magdeline manuscript. He offers a full library of his CDs at the Tom Kenyon website.

10

MY SECOND PUBERTY

By Ria Bloom

Kenny Benavides

YEAR OF BIRTH: 1984

SUN SIGN: Taurus

HOMETOWN: Kawasaki, Japan

RESIDENCE: San Diego (but a New Yorker at heart!)

ARCHETYPE: Geisha

SUPERPOWER: Ability to pause time and experience it as infinite

LINEAGE/TEACHERS: Buddhism, Judaism, Ohad Pele Ezrahi, KamalaDevi McClure, and Laurie Handlers

EPITAPH/ MOTTO: World peace, one happy genital at a time!

SHAMANIC TOOLS: Essential oils, diffuser, sage, palo santo, and Tibetan singing bowl

HOBBIES: Climbing, crafting, cleaning, cooking, and creating comics

I sat with an erect spine on the king-size mattress with Sara's bare legs draped over my thighs. With soft eyes I watched her delicate flower open as if it were springtime. I listened to the juxtaposition of my slow, steady breaths in between her sobbing and gasping for air until the next release as she wept, going deeper into her trance. She was at the crux, and my heart was pounding. I pressed my thumb next to the entrance of her glistening vulva, my first finger petting the contours of her clitoris, and asked, "What's here?"

After an undeniable pause, she said sternly, "My parents." I was captivated.

"What do you want to say to your parents?" I asked her and immediately questioned if that was the right thing to ask.

I forced myself to breathe painstakingly longer inhales and exhales, knowing that how I felt in my body could instantly penetrate and color her experience. I noticed the string of doubt tugging on my focus in that familiar, nagging voice, *Am I doing this right?*

In the flickering candlelight, I saw Sara's eyes shut tight. It was all up to her now. I was just her guide, in service to her body's healing in this sacred spot session. Tension filled the room like an airlock of a spaceship headed for deep space. The only choice was to surrender to the unknown mystery of human life. In my existential moment, she threw me a lifesaver and broke the deafening silence. "Get out!" she exclaimed.

My eyes widened, and my chest filled with hope. I expelled, "Yes, get out! Tell them to get out!" An avalanche of magic came full force from within as we chanted together, "Get out! Get out! You don't belong in here!"

"It's my body! It's my life! Get out!" she cried.

I was so proud of her. Sara found her voice to address the monsters of her childhood. Although the candles were almost burned out, the room felt much lighter from the heaviness we had just vanquished. We were in a timeless vortex. I guided Sara into a fetal position as I cocooned her head to toe in a soft cloth. It was time for integration, to gather insights, and return to center after an arduous journey.

Sara was one of those brave souls who didn't know who to turn to about her vaginal pain during intercourse. After consulting doctor after doctor, therapist after therapist, she finally turned to me because I offer something they can't.

Sara was the youngest of two; her sister, Maggie, was ten years older and was given a lot of freedom growing up. However, Maggie made a string of bad life choices as a teenager, and thus their well-meaning parents became extremely strict with Sara. The parental pendulum swung in the opposite direction. They gave Sara a dinnertime curfew. She could have no sleepovers or parties. She had to study on the weekends, and they wanted to know where she was at all times. This blanket of control during her childhood manifested as vaginal pain in Sara. Now in her mid-forties, Sara was recently separated and getting a divorce, caused by a cataclysmic combination of sexual and communication breakdowns. I listened with an open heart as this remarkable woman opened up to me. I knew her as an executive who could command any room with a single glance. She is a leader and activist, contributing many incredible gifts to the world, but she was silently suffering, abandoned by her most intimate partner, herself.

I reminded Sara to drink plenty of water, get grounded, and practice self-care because the following few days would be emotionally raw from her cellular exorcism. She thanked me and handed me a thick wad of cash. I expressed my gratitude, and after walking her out, I counted the money in disbelief. Sexual healing is holy work, and I am honored to do it. Every session, group, or ceremony I lead is completely unique; I never know what's going to happen.

This story is about how my false self needed to die so I could become a sex shaman. Or rather, how I die a little every day to become more fully alive.

Before I heard the call to shamanism, I was on the path to becoming a fashion designer. I was obsessed with name brands and appearances, wholly immersed in material possessions. I spent hours in front of the mirror, asphyxiated in my own vanity. Every lock of hair I moussed and sprayed with hardening chemicals represented a streak of sunken self-esteem I was desperately trying to hide—a far cry from my uncombed bed head I don't even blink twice about today.

Rewinding even further to my beginning, I was born to a Japanese Buddhist father and a Jewish American mother in Tokyo. My dad was devoted to his spiritual practices. To gain approval in our household, I felt I had to commune with God on a daily basis.

"God, why didn't you wake me up? My underwear is on backward!" I remember saying, as I ran to school late one morning, projecting my frustrations onto God.

I gained my father's affection by being his studious disciple. Curious, I'd ask: "Is God a man or a woman? Is it both?"

And then I would come to my own unique conclusions: "So then God is a transvestite and a cross-dresser! God must be gay because God loves everyone!"

These playful assumptions were natural for my young being. Although we joked about gender differences and sexual orientations, it was superficial and humorous. How fitting that these issues would later become human rights principles for which I would make a stand as an adult.

I remember masturbating from a young age. Late at night, I would lie in bed and ask God to give me privacy. I would fold my cotton panties alongside my inner labia and twist and turn in my bed, feeling the fabric against my genitals. I had a keen curiosity and yearned for pleasure.

Unmet in my stark reality, I submerged myself in anime and manga comic books. I would lose complete track of time drawing my favorite heroes and characters, who were much more alive to me than people. I just wanted a safe and happy place where I could explore my creativity, but the kids in the local Japanese public school never let me forget their prejudice.

"Freckle-faced foreign bitch," they would call me as I passed them in the hallways, a reference to my multiracial appearance.

For gym class, the boys and girls changed into uniforms. The girls were required to wear black bottoms barely five millimeters bigger than the white cotton panties underneath, which often poked out at the seams, whereas the boys got to wear loose shorts. Both genders pointed at and mocked my precociously developing breasts. I never auditioned for the class whore, but the spotlight became mine. I begged my mother to buy me training bras.

The kids in Japan tormented me, but the darkest and hardest years of my life were yet to come. When my mother separated from my dad and moved my sister and me to New Jersey, I felt as if my father had divorced me. I was his emotional mistress who was now without my master.

My grieving mother was busy going back to school, raising two daughters, and chasing cash. We moved to a neighborhood in the suburbs. Although the well-manicured suburban lawns were a lush green, they felt as lifeless as a desert. The suburbs had no creativity, no sexuality, no truth—just a thick layer of pretentious numbness.

The humility and self-deprecating behaviors that had worked well in my fatherland of Japan were not rewarded in America. I was a baby lamb stumbling into a starving lion's den, the defenseless rope in a tug of war between the violence in a New Jersey public school and the peaceful ways of my father's spiritual gospel. I had to quickly learn how to readjust my footing on the cultural slackline. *God, where the fuck am I? Where the fuck did you go?* I wondered. In this egoic mosh pit of chaos, I lost my faith.

"Fuck you. Suck a dick. Asshole. Whore bag. Stupid slut." Every insult hurled at me from my new American classmates was sexual and body shaming. I was unconsciously soaking up these patterns like a dry sponge plopped into a pool of water. Eventually, I waved a white flag of spiritual defeat and hopped onto the materialist bandwagon.

I confused sexual attention for love and became sexually active at age fourteen. By the time I was seventeen, I had had a miscarriage and an abortion. When the weight of my world became unbearable, I ate my feelings and purged them into the toilet. These survival mechanisms kept me going, but I was like an abused dog who wouldn't leave its open cage and stayed close to home for college. I applied to one school, New York City's Fashion Institute of Technology, less than forty miles away from my mother's house. I got accepted and majored in fashion design.

During my first winter semester I wore the same tracksuit every day. The buzzing New York City cars splashed through dirty puddles, as murky as my deep depression, and threw mud on my clothes. Alone, fucked up, and confused, I was at my emotional rock bottom. I knew that if I kept going, I would be met by death.

I packed my bags for Japan just six credits shy of graduating with my associate's degree. My pussy was completely shut down, zipped up and closed to the world. Beat up and numb, I spent the next year and a half horizontal on my father's floor. When I could muster the energy to wake up early enough, I'd ride into Tokyo with him to his holistic health clinic. In the hustling and bustling metropolis, this clinic was an oasis for the salarymen and office ladies to enjoy energetic bodywork. Here, I began to learn massage and the inner workings of the body.

New York City may have chewed me up and spat me out, but it sure did toughen me. I knew I couldn't stay defeated and had to get my mouth guard and gloves back on to get back into the ring. But how could I do that? Oddly enough, I leaned on my pride and refused to let anyone see my agony or pain. Damn Buddha, life is suffering.

Disaster relief took a few years, and a couple of relationships later, after I had returned to New York City. My care package arrived in Brooklyn in the form of a new beau who introduced me to psychedelics, and we struck oil opening our relationship to polyamory. I stumbled across the Burning Man scene, and I was in, hook, line, and sinker. We bonded at these burner-inspired raves. Smiling faces with MDMA-dilated eyes adorned in LED-lit colorful costumes dancing to the bass so loud words could only be made by shouting into each other's ears. Time melted since these parties often started at midnight and we'd stumble into a twenty-four-hour diner for a night cap in the morning hours waiting for the enhancement chemicals to evaporate from our systems.

This man became my hero, my messiah. I was saved! Or so I believed. I was simultaneously back in school, earning my master's degree in social-organizational psychology from Columbia University. All of a sudden, I was among the elite. A new wave of confidence flowed through me as I tried to scrub away the struggling-artist persona like a murderer washing the blood from his hands. I had something to prove—to my mother, to my father, to the world, but, mostly, to myself.

I engrossed myself in my studies, more poly and sex parties than academic. But my inexperience with polyamory eventually caught up with me. The fire of jealousy scorched my attempts to engage in a triad, and the relationship went into a tailspin, out of reach from my desperate need to control it. The agreements were simple—check in with me before having sex and wear a condom. Both were broken. I was so hurt but learned the most valuable of lessons: 1) do not invite his monogamous ex-girlfriend into my relationship as a third party, because she is clearly not polyamorous and is only seeking to get back together with him, and 2) do not trust his decision-making skills in love, sex, money, social etiquette, and so on. My trust for him dissipated as I woke up from the rosy fantasy fog I was living in.

When I dug deeper into my triggers, I realized I was still holding onto my baby blanket. My unconscious motivation for exploring complex relationships was an indirect way to heal the wounds I had with my mother, to gain her approval and love.

Questions of self-doubt inhabited the bottom of my soul: Do I even matter? Where do I belong in this vast universe? Heck, which country is my real home? My feeling of being an outsider was always a hair's breadth away from subverting my ability to maintain my sanity. My lizard brain, wired for survival, had taught me to become the best chameleon. My life was a circus, and I was a contortionist, bending above and beyond to fit the projections put on me from the eyes of beholders.

As I was developing, I unconsciously misused my voluptuous breasts and body to seduce, manipulate, and control. The sexual attention I garnered, starting from a young age, taught me these were power tools that could drill past any wall life presented. My flashy ego cleverly maneuvered social climbing to get further away from the scared little girl, frozen inside. I was hiding my vulnerabilities in a vault deep within, and I had thrown away the key.

After my relationship ended, I spent two weeks in a pool of my tears, unable to speak. A tornado engulfed me. As time passed, I felt a sliver of hope, and when I looked through the clouds of chaos into the eye of this storm, I found my soul, standing still. I became aware of the darkness in me. It was a bottomless pit, and I was terrified. In the West, people would call it a nervous breakdown, and in the East, a kundalini awakening.

The eureka moment that propelled me into this remarkable future happened in Palm Springs, California, at a festival for free lovers called Poly Palooza. I first met KamalaDevi in passing as she was getting ready to facilitate the orientation while I stood dumbstruck in front of my hotel room door. Her husband, Michael, followed, smiling flirtatiously, and we locked eyes. After a sensual hello, we had a heartfelt embrace. Little did I know that I would make love to this man, and he would be the first to teach me about sex magic for manifestation.

Michael and I first had sex in the Red Temple, a playroom for the participants. As we inched toward the peak of climax, Michael inquired if I knew about sex magic. I pleaded for him to tell me. Sex magic, he explained, is when we use the power of life-force energy, which is our orgasms, to manifest things we desire in life. *Now, this is the kind of prayer I could get down with!* I thought. That night, practicing sex magic for the first time, I infused my intention with orgasmic energy and planted the seeds for what is now my current life.

Poly Palooza was revolutionary. In five days, the rush of energy into my body unwired my Japanese repression. I learned how to breathe and understand my brain chemistry and attended workshops with titles like "How Not to Get Fucked Up in Relationships." Damn, I wish that course had been available during my first semester in college! I had been a bunch of discombobulated dots, and they were finally getting connected to create a picture that made sense.

About one calendar year later, KamalaDevi and Michael introduced me to the International School of Temple Arts. I joined them along with myriad global visionaries and leaders who gathered in the thick jungles of Hawai'i. The white waves crashed ferociously against the black rocks on the big island as did my old patterns. They were knocked into oblivion, and the core of my being was finally revealed. It was a real awakening.

The barefoot and clothing-optional landscape let me undress my hideous inner victim. I was holding myself hostage all of these years, and it was time to set her free, to unlock the internal doors and open the windows to my soul. I was in a new arena, no longer fighting the world, but my inner demons instead. In this transformational pressure cooker, I identified and shifted my emotions, uncovered my shadows, healed my parental wounds, and bonded with my soul tribe.

We traveled to beautiful remote places all over the big island. At the whirling natural pools, I met with death; in the underground volcanic yoni cave, I mourned my miscarriage and abortions; at the black-shelled cliff dangling off the edge of the world, I was reborn. The experience of meeting a group of sex shamans who were down to earth, relatable, and extraordinarily supportive of my growth touched me profoundly.

That winter, my overanalyzing head was guillotined on the chopping block and left to rot, and I had to learn how to surrender. I heard my true calling. *This is what I want to do with my life! I want to embody the great spirit, my true love, and transmit sexual healing!* I thought. The new opportunity was a prescription of profound clarity from my limited peripheral vision all of these years.

The medicine to my illness is a paradox. It's both expansion and death that shepherds my growth, over and over again. It's experiencing the mountain of love affairs and valleys of heartbreak.

Until I saw past the veil, I did not realize that I had been operating from a limited lens, seeing the world through a tiny keyhole. It's not that Life ever stopped being her untamable self; I just learned to become flexible enough to bend and not break. The saving grace was reintegrating the aspects of me that I dissociated from because I believed them to be unlovable. If I engulf the decrepit, the disgusting, and the gross to be comfortable in my insecurities and awkwardness, then what else could get me in life? When I face my death, I can live honestly.

I have learned that magic never shouts, it whispers, so we have to slow down and truly listen. I am lucky to have played it all out, to get to the bottom of my whims and rub my nose in desires. I strayed from my truth and supported illusion upon illusion. I fell flat on my face and was divinely guided back to reclaim my power. Every time I confront the intolerable, I am shaking in my boots. I am the salmon who swims upstream to spawn on gravel beds, each time meeting death and the beginning of a new life cycle of truth. I plug back in, my pussy pulsing, anus wide, recharging in shamanic sexual powers.

I am grateful for learning all my father has taught me from his spiritual gospel and bodywork, understanding the skeletal structure, muscles, and ligaments and how energy flows through it all. As I became more in tune with energy through my psycho-spiritual work, I started to unravel the depth to which I feel. The apex of my journey was bringing my genitals into my spiritual practice, while summoning a newfound sexual maturity. I'm not just reparenting but readulting, which is both awkward and thrilling, making my tantric awakening like a second spiritual puberty.

Ria Bloom is a sex educator, relationship coach, and author of the sex-positive comic strip *Welcome to my Riality*. She is apprentice faculty at ISTA and completed her MA in social-organizational psychology at Columbia University. Ria organized and seeded ISTA Japan and teaches in California, New York City, Washington, DC, Tokyo, and around the globe.

Death Meditation

PURPOSE: When we come to terms with our death before we die, we can become more fully alive. This age-old shamanic practice produces a deep meditative state to cultivate witness consciousness and detach from the ego, body, and other illusions.

PREPARATION: This visualization is best practiced on a dark moon or the early hours before sunrise. Create a completely quiet space where you will not be disturbed for 20 to 40 minutes. Read through the following instructions before you begin the visualization.

PROCESS: Lie naked in savasana or corpse pose on a hard surface with minimal padding. Close your eyes and relax each muscle group progressively from your toes to your crown by slowly stretching it on the inhale, holding your breath for a moment with the muscle tightened, and then exhaling and letting it all go. Extend the process to your internal organs as well as your extremities. The final step is to stretch the whole body at once, tensing everything on the inhale, holding, and then slowly releasing everything on the exhale.

Lie still. Imagine slowing your metabolism so that your internal organs fall into suspended animation. See your life-force energy draining out of every part of your being as you focus on each one. See your heart, lungs, stomach, liver, and kidneys stopping their activities. See your muscles, tendons, and even your bone marrow dying. Imagine the space inside each cell collapsing like a black hole and disappearing into the void.

If fear arises, remember it doesn't stand a chance against death. Imagine all of your emotions purging from your heart. If regret or lust or passion arise, let them dissolve back to the source from where they came.

Since imagination arises from the mind, free yourself from thoughts and allow your mind to die. Tell yourself that nothing matters in the face of death. Everything you care about is irrelevant. Death is the ultimate freedom. Let go of responsibilities, unfulfilled desires, and even your life's purpose.

Feel your entire being merging with the universe. Allow the essential elements—earth, air, fire, and water—to reclaim your corpse. Your body returns to the earth. Your breath merges with the atmosphere. The electric impulses from your cells are consumed by the sun. The water in your body drains out to the ocean. The space you inhabit dissolves into infinite space.

Lie still for at least 10 minutes longer.

What is left? After everything is dead and gone, what remains? What is the presence that is witnessing your death? Who is this witness consciousness?

After spending time dissolving into the void, take a deep breath and slowly return from death. Reanimate your being by filling empty space with your consciousness. Reverse all the steps of this visualization. Allow yourself to be reborn into the world of form. See all five elements coming alive. Allow your heart to awaken, your consciousness to animate your mind, and ultimately feel your body become active from the inside out. Visualize radiant energy filling each organ. Take your time to open your eyes and sit up. You can journal about your process, writing down who and what matters to you most in this life.

VARIATIONS: More detailed visualizations include the specific means of death, such as suffocation, drowning, being stabbed through the heart, beheaded, or eaten alive. There are as many variations on this visualization as there are ways to die.

RESOURCES: If you resonate with this exercise you may want to find a teacher who can initiate you in the Buddhist contemplation of death, or Maranānussati bhāvanā.

11

IF YOU WANT, YOU CAN

By Raffaello Manacorda

Tristan Gorski

YEAR OF BIRTH: 1977

SUN SIGN: Cancer

HOMETOWN: Rome, Italy

RESIDENCE: Barcelona, Spain

ARCHETYPE: Black Dragon

SUPERPOWER: Clear vision

LINEAGE/TEACHERS: The inner guru

EPITAPH/MOTTO: This too shall pass.

SHAMANIC TOOLS: My music playlists and presence

HOBBIES: Practicing yoga, collecting esoteric and rare books, learning new languages, taking photographs, exploring big cities, and cooking

Life for a suburban kid growing up in Rome in the '90s was pure adventure. Before my eighteenth birthday, I had already deejayed at techno parties with more than two thousand people, tried various kinds of illegal drugs, and traveled to a dozen countries on my own.

I was a student with stellar grades, despite the joints I smoked in the bathroom just before entering the classroom, savoring both the flavor of the melted hash and the thrill of the forbidden. There was only one thing that could instantly throw me off balance: girls.

Each September at the beginning of a new school year, I would daydream of the new beautiful girls I would meet in the coming semester. Their images, vague but nevertheless attractive, mixed in my awareness with the smell of new books and the early morning light as I walked to the brick-colored school building.

Reality, however, was much more difficult than my fantasies. Why was I tortured with sexual inadequacy and jealousy? Sometimes, waiting for a date, I would rejoice at receiving the phone call canceling the encounter. It felt so much cozier to just stay on my own.

When I did have a girlfriend, other obstacles and challenges loomed. Every time she looked at another boy, I would feel my stomach twist as my mind started furiously fabricating hypotheses regarding my impending betrayal. So many times throughout my teenage love life, I'd catch myself wishing that my fascination with the smell, the voice, the aura of women didn't haunt me day and night.

By age twenty-four, I had graduated with a degree in philosophy and I made a very philosophical decision: I would not live a normal life. I was determined to use my life-force energy to foster a revolution and create crazy, amazing projects rather than wasting it on a nine-to-five job.

I packed everything I had into a van that was older and in worse shape than me and moved to Barcelona, the European capital of an underground movement called squatting. Squatting, in case you haven't heard, is the practice of breaking into abandoned buildings and living there, outside the law and sometimes against it.

For the next twelve years, I lived on the fringes of society in abandoned buildings ranging from decadent to rotten, sharing a home with rebels, anarchists, poets, artists, troublemakers, and outright geniuses. We were motivated, uncompromising, righteous, and sexy. We partied hard, fought with the authorities, and made love, a lot. But we did not make life easy on ourselves.

We lived day by day, not knowing if we would wake up the next morning with a riot police squad kicking down our door and bursting into the house as we slept. Inevitably, that did happen. The local policemen knew us and didn't like us, just as we didn't like them. It was a low-intensity guerrilla war. I got beaten, harassed, and threatened on multiple occasions, had guns pointed at me, and even had my money stolen by both uniformed and undercover police. I was extremely alert, my senses sharpened by constant danger. I created a reality in which I got exactly what I needed: danger, presence, purpose, and lots of drama.

I learned about energies and auras in the most unusual ways. Once, I watched my petite girlfriend charge head down against a wall of policemen, big and armored and prepared for the impact of this tiny feminine projectile. I was witnessing energy in action. I didn't need to attend seminars on the power of manifestation and intention. Our motto was "If you want, you can." We could do anything we wanted if we wanted it bad enough. We climbed the tallest buildings just to hang a banner, created self-managed parks where the city council wanted to build a parking lot, stormed public buildings, and organized concerts in the middle of the street without a permit. It was magic at work, the capacity to project our will and intention onto the outside world in such a focused, emotionally charged way that the world had no choice but to yield.

During those years, while busy fighting the system, my comrades and I also worked on our relationships with ourselves and with one another. Our daily existence was like a twenty-four-hour workshop, which left very little space for integration, but if you could handle the pressure, you'd transform in a matter of months. We experimented with open relationships, sexuality, radical communication, and whole new ways of loving and living.

It was clear that we couldn't possess one another's bodies, let alone our souls. We were often the lovers of our best friends' partners. My jealous, insecure, and controlling self was shattered into pieces within the first couple of years. I had to adapt to a way of relating in which expressions such as "cheating" and "my girlfriend" had all but lost their meaning. It was such a different paradigm from the one I had grown up in, but it all made perfect sense! It was an intense, ongoing transformational process of accelerated growth.

Even though my relationship with the opposite sex was radically transformed, sex itself continued being pretty much the same, until the day one of my best friends lent me a book. It was a novel, *The Man Who Fell in Love with the Moon* by Tom Spanbauer. Among all the flamboyant adventures and quirky characters, I was especially fascinated with the character of Duivichi-un-Dui, a cross-gender Native American who could orgasm and send his ejaculation inward through his spine, until his own sperm flooded his brain and brought him into untold states of ecstasy. Okay, he was a fictional character, but *so what*! I wanted to do the same, and I wanted it so badly, I decided that I would get there no matter what.

I bought myself some books on tantra and became an experimental sex researcher. I was lucky to have a forbearing girlfriend. She had enough patience to handle all the twitching, screaming, and kicking that happened in our bedroom from then on! I embarked on the journey of "orgasm without ejaculation" with the eagerness of a six-month-old puppy on steroids. What a chaotic vortex of sexual energy I had summoned. I was sputtering my energy around like a spinning torpedo, and inevitably, I would pay the consequences.

Two years down the line, I ended up deflated, demotivated, and a little scared. I was ready to drop all of this "advanced sexuality" into the dustbin. I wanted my regular sex life back! Whatever states of higher consciousness I had dreamed of, I hadn't found them. I had also broken up with my girlfriend, and I was uncertain how much my sexual antics had to do with the sudden increase in emotional drama that had first shaken then shattered our relationship.

I spent the next year or so living in a dusty studio apartment in an abandoned warehouse, composing electronic music and playing video games. Light never seemed to shine into my room or into my life. In the midst of this thick fog, there was a faint but constant beacon, like a weak radio signal from a device abandoned before nuclear fallout. It kept emitting a message in my head: *Go to Thailand.*

It took me about two years to give in to that call, but when I bought my ticket to Thailand, it was as if the whole universe heaved a deep sigh of relief. I had no idea what I was looking for, but I felt I was being guided.

A few days after landing in Bangkok, I was visiting the golden reclining Buddha statue in Wat Pho temple, watching the serene face of the enlightened master, depicted in the position he assumed just before dying. Suddenly, I felt like I understood it all: life, death, the mystery of existence, everything that mattered—all was clear to me in one eternal instant. Tears started running down my face. I wandered about the temple for hours, kneeling in front of the tombs of dead monks, feeling that I was one of their kin and they were welcoming me home. In the afterglow of this experience, my entire inner world had to rearrange itself, like a puzzle that reveals a different image from the one on the box. I was alive. I was on my path.

In the following weeks, I roamed about the north of Thailand, where numerous adventures ensued, including my first silent meditation retreat and a visit to the hippie hangout of Pai, where I got trapped in a fire in the jungle. Of this latter experience, what I remember the most is my complete calmness in the face of the approaching fire. As branches wrapped in flames kept falling around me, I knew with absolute certainty that dying there, right after having entered a new chapter of my existence, was out of the question. I managed to escape the fire, but the same fire that chased me out of the jungle ended up chasing me out of Pai. In the aftermath of the fire, the air was so thick with smoke that I woke up every morning feeling as if I had been sleeping by a bonfire and smelling the same. I had to leave.

I decided to spend a couple of days in Koh Phangan, the "full moon party island" famous for its electronic music scene. Little did I know that it was there that I would find my spiritual school for the next seven years, fall in love repeatedly, become a yoga teacher, and see the last piece of my identity mercilessly shattered.

But let's not get ahead of ourselves. When I got to Koh Phangan, I did what I had come for: I partied and enjoyed life for a couple of days. I was just about to leave when a seemingly trivial encounter changed my life, again, forever.

It was a Sunday afternoon, and I was absorbed in reading a book at a cozy little teahouse made of wood, when one of the most beautiful women I had ever seen walked in. She looked Indian and Western at the same time. She had an aura of calmness and beauty around her that haunted me. I managed to find the guts to talk to her and learned that she was a yoga teacher. I had zero interest in yoga at that time; in fact, I thought it was just hippie stuff. I did have a big interest in meeting this fascinating creature again, however, so the next morning I went to the free yoga class she had invited me to. What a delicious disappointment!

Disappointing, I say, because she was not there. Looking back, I can see that she had accomplished her role in my life, and thus the universe had declared her free to go. Delicious, because what I found in yoga was infinitely deeper than a connection with an attractive woman. I had bumped into what I had been hoping to find many, many years before: a true tantric school! If I had any doubts about the infinite, all-knowing intelligence that was guiding my steps, those doubts were shattered then and there.

For the next seven years, I poured my heart, mind, body, and soul into the tantra yoga teachings, which were deep and powerful and made perfect sense to me. My daily practice consisted of a minimum of four hours, while the rest of my life, from meals to sleep to social life, arranged itself around my yoga schedule. I was fortunate enough to have an online job and could work from anywhere. Everything seemed perfectly arranged for me to delve deep into my tantric studies.

I learned to move sexual energy up into my higher centers and to do magic with it. Eventually, I learned to move other people's sexual energy too and to hold space and create healing. I was introduced to powerful tantric sexual rituals. I expanded my capacity to feel pleasure to heights that were inconceivable just a few months before. I learned to see the divine feminine in every woman and, eventually, to make love to it through her. I will be forever grateful for the depth of what I learned there, but not everything was harmony and joy.

The beauty of the teachings made a stark contrast with the power games, the secrecy of certain practices, and a vague feeling of backwardness that I perceived in some of the teachers. It was as if the whole school was looking back at a projected golden age rather than looking forward to the future. The headmaster's word seemed to be taken with a blind-eyed devotion. His antique way of conceiving of genders—men had to be fully masculine, while women had to be fully feminine—challenged my egalitarian, feminist beliefs. There was an absence of healthy internal criticism toward the policies of the school. Year after year, I grew uncomfortable with the contradiction between my love for the teachings and my repulsion for the power structure of the school. I was prepared to be a student, but I was not prepared to be a disciple.

Meanwhile, after a few years of steady practice, I had become a tantra yoga teacher. I was provided with a new, shiny identity. Always dressed in white, fit as never before, I reveled in my own magnetism. My success with women was overwhelming, and as I had become skilled in the tantric arts, I told myself I was helping the women I made love with. I am touching a delicate point here: conscious tantric lovemaking can be immensely helpful. Most, if not all, of the encounters I had were eye-opening, rewarding, and sometimes life-changing for me and the women I shared intimacy with. Yet, like weeds growing silently in the shade, my ego was growing stronger and stronger. I had found a new, powerful identity, and I was becoming attached to it.

This all came to an end when one of the main teachers of the school got involved in a murky situation with a student, one where boundaries were crossed, feelings were hurt, and explanations were demanded. Every teacher and most of the students in the school felt they had to take sides. For me, it was a no-brainer. I sided with the student. I campaigned for her and, in the process, lost my position and prestige within the school. Unable to wear the teacher's shirt anymore, I was left with no other option but to pack and leave the school I had once loved.

A few days after the scandal had blown up, I was sitting on a bench in the local food market, eating a snack. The market was bustling with people and filled with the smell of fried fish. I was shaken, confused, and angry. Suddenly, the noises and voices around me started to fade. All of my attention turned within, in a frantic attempt to find something to hold on to, some identity I could claim as me. I felt desperate to find a ground, a basis, a conviction, an idea—something. I didn't find anything. I was empty. No, not even that—there wasn't even an I to be empty or full. I was nothing. The mask had fallen. I shed tears of confusion, tears of desperation, and tears of loss. I felt as if I was falling down a bottomless pit. And the falling . . . just didn't stop.

Although at that time I didn't fully realize this, the scandal of the teacher and the student had delivered a mortal blow to my own image as a pure yoga teacher. I simply could not wear that mask anymore. I didn't know what other masks to wear. I was naked.

I ended up in a monastery in the north of Thailand and spent three weeks in total silence and meditation. I didn't know who I was anymore; I just knew I was falling. I tried to hold on to being a man, a sexual being, a human being, an animal, a creature, but when I grasped any of those concepts, it felt as if my hands were all soapy and slippery. I couldn't get a grip on anything. I was the falling itself.

I lost all hope that this falling would come to an end and I would hit solid ground, but then something unexpected happened: I started being comfortable in the falling. I noticed other things, other objects, were falling along with me. A cup of tea, falling . . . So why not grab it and have some tea? I started to realize the whole world was falling along with me. I still had a sense of nausea, a gripping, uncomfortable feeling in the pit of my stomach, but I got used to it.

During this process, I had all but sworn off sex. What was the purpose of going through all the motions of eroticism when they all were flickering images on a black, hopeless background? I felt as if I had been pretending all my life, no matter what I did: I was a cheap, crappy actor forced to act in a movie I didn't even like.

Then, a few weeks later, life crept back into the black hole at the center of my being, and with life, sex came back too. I found myself attending an ISTA training. Looking back, I can only marvel at the series of coincidences that brought me to that weeklong training. Desperate as I was, struggling with the utter loss of me, I felt as if I had nothing to lose. I flew all the way from Thailand to Guatemala, a remote country I knew almost nothing about, just to attend a seminar that I also knew almost nothing about. I invested the last money I had, and some I didn't have, without the faintest idea of how I would ever make my money back.

Among the many highlights of that eventful week, I made love again. Or, I should say, lovemaking happened. It was without any intention, without any agenda, with someone who I didn't even feel attracted to until the very moment we made love. I had dropped any expectations around sex, but as I relaxed into the present moment, not trying to control it, sex just happened to happen.

When I came back from the training, I realized that I was a survivor. Yes, my identity had died, along with all my ideas, opinions, tastes, and preferences, which had been burned on the stake with it. Something had survived though, because I continued breathing, eating, sleeping, and making love. In the process of falling and losing my identity, I had become hollow, and now the life force could move through me easier than ever before. I had become a shaman. Or rather, a sex shaman.

I didn't have any opinions about anything, so I made decisions on the spur of the moment. I decided I had to go back to Barcelona. I moved into a cozy little sunny attic.

Returning to a normal city life, I felt like a newborn, full of marvel and surprise and slightly goofy and insecure in its first steps. Magic seemed to happen like never before. I didn't even need to do much, just respond to the invitations.

I was invited to become a faculty apprentice and, eventually, an ISTA facilitator. ISTA is a mystery school, so there were no procedures involved, no exams, just pure magic and intuition. How different that was from the masculine, logical structure of my previous tantric school!

I felt blessed to have been through disciplined training, but also excited for this newfound field that embraced ease and freedom.

And now here I am, writing these lines, fifteen years after reading that book that started me onto the path of a sexual shaman.

The life I live feels both outrageous and normal. I spend about half of my time teaching workshops and seminars around the world. This usually involves flying to locations far or near, spending one to three weeks there being with a vibrant, authentic, raw group of participants and coteachers, learning, experimenting, and flying back home. There is a lot of airport time involved, but it's well worth it.

Another quarter of my time is dedicated to working one-on-one with people. When I'm in session, nothing else exists in the world but my seeker, the man or woman who came to me seeking transformation, release, counseling, healing. This is where I access my shaman archetype: I toss away my plain clothes, and I become a sacred priest. This transformation does not add to my identity as much as it subtracts from it. My main job is getting out of the way so that transformation can happen while holding a safe, loving space for whatever the seeker may go through. Often, there are tears, wild emotions, pleasure, pain—the whole spectrum of the human experience is activated by sexual energy, and the rawness of humanity shines through in all its glory.

In my session work, I especially love supporting women with medical conditions that affect their mobility to live more sexually and erotically fulfilling lives. The conditions of the women I work with range from multiple sclerosis to muscular dystrophy. These women have impaired motor skills, either because of a traumatic event like a car accident or because of a degenerative illness. I want to paint a picture to show you how touching this work can be.

Imagine a woman in her late thirties. She's smart, sensitive, and full of life. Let's call her Laura. Laura suffers from muscular dystrophy, which means that her muscles are weakened and impaired because of abnormal genetic mutations. She walks with a crutch, and most of her joints only bend to a small degree.

Can you envision growing up in this body, which is so different from the standard narrative of sexiness? Many of the women I work with have not had full sexual intercourse in their life. Not once. This was the case with Laura.

Growing up with a poverty of sexual attention, Laura developed deep negative beliefs around sex as a form of protection, something along the lines of "sex is not for me; I need to give it up." The pain and discomfort around sexuality were so intense that Laura had to shut off that part of her life just to gain some sort of peace of mind—but the life force cannot be denied! Laura had ended up living in a constant state of internal conflict between her natural desire for sexual intimacy and the belief that it was dangerous, unsafe, and painful.

When I work with women like Laura, we laugh, scream, move energy, cuddle, and sometimes, if it is within our boundaries and mutual consent, we make love.

Working with sexual energy is like walking a razor's edge. It is front-line work, thrilling and dangerous, and it exposes me to both gratitude and criticism, praise and projections. I accept that as part of my destiny. What really touches my heart though are those times like when, a few days after our last encounter, I received a voice message from Laura.

"Raffaello, I am sorry, but I have to cancel our next appointment. . . . Since our last session, something has shifted in me. I have met someone. I have a lover. I can't even believe it is true, but it is. I don't know what you did, but thank you."

There is nothing as satisfying for a shaman than realizing he is no longer necessary. The seeker can walk on his or her own now. And a shaman I am. Sure, I have a bag full of tricks and techniques under my belt, but that is not essential. What I have gained through my own self-destruction and death is something infinitely more powerful. I have awakened my magic by means of the utter sacrifice of my own identity and ego. My personal life has become simpler, more ordinary, without the need for too many frills and thrills and emotional ups and downs—just simple and powerful.

But a shaman can't work alone. By entering the field of ISTA, I found something I had once but lost: a community, a family, a tribe. I lived in a community during my squatter years, then I voluntarily stepped out of it, wandering around and finding my way outside the pack. Now, having done my solo journey, I felt ready to be in a tribe again. So here I am, embedded in a crazy gang of soulful sex shamans, each one coming from a different walk of life, all committed to supporting the life force in all of its manifestations.

As I write this final paragraph, sitting in a café in downtown Barcelona, I look at my calendar in awe and bewilderment. In the next twelve months, I will travel all around the world, sharing magic with hundreds of people on five continents. It feels as natural as drinking a cup of cold-brewed coffee, like the one I now hold in my hands. The complex has become simple. Life force runs through what's left of me— an empty vessel. And the play continues.

Raffaello Manacorda went from earning a doctorate in philosophy in Rome to being a squatter and radical activist in Barcelona. His relentless exploration of sex and spirit brought him to two decades of tantric practice and eventually into ISTA. Author of *Conscious Relationships* and creator of the Network of Love workshops, he is based in Barcelona.

Yoni Mudra

PURPOSE: *Yoni* means "womb space" and *mudra* means "seal"; thus this is the yogic practice of returning to the state of mind experienced in the womb. Yoni mudra is often used to awaken the kundalini, bringing about higher states of consciousness. It can also be used to contemplate the void. In shamanism it is used to detach from the outer world and activate inner reality. By closing off the gates to the external senses, we open more subtle channels.

PREPARATION: This exercise involves cutting off input from all the external sensory organs and withdrawing from the world by closing the eyes and mouth and plugging your ears and nostrils with your fingers.

PROCESS: Sit in a comfortable position with a straight spine. If you can, cross your legs and position one heel under your perineum to gently seal your root chakra (*mula bandha*).

Use your thumbs to close your ears. Index fingers gently rest at the corners of your closed eyes. The middle fingers plug your nostrils. Place your ring fingers above your upper lip and your pinky under your lower lip to keep the mouth closed.

Lock your root and direct your focus toward the point between your eyebrows. Now, breathe into your lungs from your lips, which you've formed into *kaki mudra,* or a crow's beak, similar to the shape you would make if you were to whistle.

Do not force this practice. Finish when you feel it is time. Release all the mudras and return to the natural breath.

VARIATIONS: Yoni mudra is also used in nada yoga to hear the inner sounds that arise when the ears are closed; these are also called mystic sounds.

NOTES: Depression or extreme introversion are contraindications for this mudra.

RESOURCES: A variation of this practice is taught in Source School of Tantra, created by Charles Muir.

12

BLISS OR BUST

By Ellie Wilde

Maijke DeJong

TRANSPERSONAL NAME: Golden Fire Dreamer

YEAR OF BIRTH: 1971

SUN SIGN: Pisces

HOMETOWN: Harlow, Essex, United Kingdom

RESIDENCE: Mount Maunganui, New Zealand

ARCHETYPE: Elf queen, mother of dragons

SUPERPOWER: High-voltage emotional body, sensitivity to unseen worlds, dark worker

LINEAGE/TEACHERS: Janine MacDonald, Bruce Lyon, Baba Dez, Deej and Uma, Shakti Malan, Betty Martin, Chuluaqui Quodoushka, Institute of vibrational Wellness, and Bernie Prior

EPITAPH/ MOTTO: Keep the wild in you.

SHAMANIC TOOLS: Frankincense, music playlists, and deep trust in the mystery

HOBBIES: Being naked in nature as much as possible, performance and visual art, and being a social provocateur

There I stood, in a hotel room in Auckland City, about to meet my first client, a gentleman I had spoken to earlier that morning. We would meet across the road first, and if need be, sit down in the café and chat face-to-face. *Fuck, what am I doing?* I thought to myself. *How did I get myself into this? What on earth was I thinking? What compelled me to get here?* Then my phone rang. I had no time to question things; he was in the foyer downstairs. I glanced in the mirror, looking into my blue eyes. I took a breath, answered the call, and went down in the elevator to meet with him.

That was 2011. My private practice as a sexual-healing and empowerment coach has since evolved beyond my wildest dreams. My early days were about helping liberate people from shame and guilt and supporting, accepting, and giving permission to them to open into their full expression, with self-acceptance and self-love. I was meeting them in ways they had never been met before, and in the process of giving myself to them, I was giving them back to themselves.

Back then I called myself Goldie, from a Native American name that was given to me at a Quodoushka retreat called American Indian Sacred Sexuality. It was short for Golden Fire-Dreamer (gosh, I sound like a cliché, don't I?). I advertised in the adult entertainment section of the *Auckland Herald*. My first advertisements read "intimacy and relationship coaching for personal development and transformation."

The early days in those hotel rooms, I attracted guys who were there for stress relief, connection, and intimacy. (Some of them were really just coming for happy endings.) I suspect they were intrigued as my advertisements sounded a little different from the usual adult entertainment ads.

Getting them to focus on their own bodies and experience and not get lost in me was, at times, futile—as was teaching them to relax into arousal. Most seemed to contort their bodies and hardly make a sound before releasing the tension in a sneeze of an orgasm that would leave them limp and exhausted but finally relaxed on the table. On occasion, however, I would get a goodie who would breathe the energy up into his heart, expand and relax his muscles as he became aroused, and have mind-shattering orgasms. By the looks on their faces, it was clear that they hadn't experienced that before.

What really blew me away was the number of men who sought and needed my services—often normal married men, mainly in their fifties or early sixties, with no sex life at home, or sometimes just lonely men who, because of their situation in life, had a lack of intimacy, connection, and physical love. They needed nurturing as well as sexual pleasure.

The first day my ad went out, I was totally overwhelmed and astounded by the nonstop ringing of my phone. I would go into my spiel explaining the massage sessions: "My sessions are about sexual empowerment and learning to focus on your own sensations and arousal rather than sourcing arousal from the outside. It's about relaxing into a more liberated and expansive expression of sexuality." The clients all seemed to say the same thing: "Can I um . . . you know, well, is there . . . um, relief at the end?" I had to chuckle, but soon it became tedious. I wanted to give sexual empowerment sessions; I didn't want to scratch people's itches.

Fast-forward a couple of months to a tantric temple a friend and I created in Auckland City. I was now offering intimacy coaching as well as tantric massage. I would offer two-way touch sessions and guide them to pleasure me. It was pretty amazing to get paid for this service. I was receiving so much pleasure and being paid handsomely for it; however, sometimes I struggled when someone crossed my boundaries.

My session offerings broadened to include kink and BDSM role play and also coaching around porn addiction, erectile dysfunction, and emotional issues linked with sexuality and interpersonal relations. With my sexological bodywork training, I also brought in other types of sessions, including anal massage and body de-armoring. It was a rollercoaster ride, with little supervision and no peer support. There were times when I felt out of my depth, but I trusted in my innate wisdom, intuition, and inner guidance to keep me on track and help me when I felt I was losing my original intention for working in this way.

This work could also be a lot of fun. One of the most hilarious sessions I ever gave was a double-domination (two women) session for a gay friend who came to the temple for a cup of tea one afternoon.

My domination and submission client hadn't shown up, so I asked this friend if he would like to take advantage of our services. He had never been dominated, and while I wasn't the right gender for his sexual preference, he agreed to have a new experience anyway.

I was adorned in my full dominatrix regalia—thigh-high boots, black latex corset—and I was also totally in the zone. One minute, he was drinking his cup of tea at the kitchen table. The next, he was blindfolded, spread-eagled, his pants around his ankles, head down, leaning against the massage table, his bare butt exposed and vulnerable, quivering under my whip.

My girlfriend played the bossy headmistress, while I was more of a seductive evil bitch. Between the two of us, we had this guy guessing about what would happen next. I think it was the sheer spontaneity that amplified the session and what would have otherwise been a very ordinary afternoon for him.

These early days were like a fast path to learning about boundaries and consent. This was a real-life training ground. I quickly saw all the ways I put other people's feelings and needs before my own. And simultaneously, these days were incredibly sexually empowering. I traversed so many incredible territories with people, such intimacy, rawness, exhilaration, and commiseration, all in one large exhale.

I have been blessed with many deep and mystical experiences in my life. I believe I have always been interested in unseen worlds.

As a child, I was haunted by these questions:

> *Who are we beyond this physical world?*
> *Where do we go when we die?*
> *Who were we before we came to be here?*
> *What would we be if this whole reality didn't exist?*
> *How did all of this come into creation?*

I would give myself headaches trying to figure it all out in my mind. Nobody around me had any believable answers. My family wasn't religious, but I remember longing to have some kind of faith, something that would make sense of it all.

When I was a really small child, my mother said I would often scream and cry and point at things as if I were seeing stuff nobody else saw. In fact, one time I put them off buying a house, as I wouldn't stop crying until they took me outside and away from that place.

One morning, I claimed to my mum that I had just been visited by Jesus. She shrugged it off, but I distinctly remember waking to the sun beaming into my room and a feeling of being surrounded by an angelic presence. I'm sure I even heard a chorus of angels singing in my still sleepy state. I remember thinking, *This is Jesus. He has come to see me.*

I have always been sensitive. When I was younger, I would curse my thin skin, wishing I could let things roll off easier and not feel so hurt and wounded by this world. I was also painfully shy and awkward. I have a distinct memory of being unable to go into the sweet shop and buy candy with my money because I didn't want to talk with the shop owner. I remember trying to convince my younger brother to do it for me.

My parents divorced when I was nine years old. It was a confusing time. My mum had not told us our dad had left, and I found out from a boy who lived down the road. I guess she just didn't know how to tell us that he had gone and was struggling with the reality of being alone with four small children.

Heartbroken and fearful to be alone, she quickly met my stepfather, Malcolm. She told me later that she picked him because he was ugly, and she thought, *No one is going to try to steal him off me.* Obviously, my mum was still hurting from my dad's infidelity, which is what broke up their marriage. Within six weeks, my stepdad and mum were married. I came home from school one day, and my mother had flowers in her hair. I looked at her, puzzled, and she told me she had gotten married today on her lunch break at work—for real!

My stepdad had met me and my brothers and sisters only a handful of times. Now he was living with us, and we were to call him Dad.

He was younger than my mum, a vacuum cleaner salesman with the gift of gab. He liked to tickle me, but then wouldn't stop when it hurt. He loved to touch me in any way, actually, and I quickly became his favorite. I accepted him; I just wanted Mum to be happy.

Looking back, I can see how he worked his magic on me. He saw that I was needy for attention, and he gave me all the attention I desired. If he was going anywhere, I'd go with him. We were often alone together.

He began to talk with me about boys and orgasms, which I had never heard about before, and asked me if I had ever touched myself sexually. I enjoyed the affection and love he showered on me. Being one of four, it was always difficult to get time with my mum, and my dad had pretty much gone AWOL at that time.

My stepfather became more and more interested in me. He would appear at nighttime in my bedroom naked, just looking at me. He took the door off the bathroom, some excuse about needing to see us all in the bath in case we drowned. He would ask me if I wanted to see my mum's vibrator. It was all a little overwhelming, but I trusted him; I loved him. At some point, he started talking with me about masturbating. I really don't remember everything, but I know that he got me to do it in front of him many times and also entered my yoni with his fingers. I was eleven years old, and I thought that's what dads did.

My innocence and naïveté protected me back then. It was later, as a teenager, after my mother and stepdad had split up and we had fled the house because of my stepdad's physical abuse of my mum, that it started to feel like some creepy story. I realized my stepdad had abused me mentally, emotionally, sexually, and physically. My teenage years were confusing as I tried to process the hurt that I felt.

The sexual abuse taught me that I am loveable only if I offer myself sexually, that I am not valued unless I am being sexual. I thought the only relationship you can have with a man is a sexual one. I had a very hard time with boundaries and as a consequence would often find myself in sexual situations I didn't want to be in, where I had no voice.

My training in sacred sexuality has helped me to find pathways to heal. My originally numb and frozen body is now alive and awake with the life force. I feel empowered in my sexuality and in my life. My relationships have improved immensely. Boundaries are much clearer, and so is my ability to recognize and communicate my needs and desires. It's like I am plugged back into the mainframe computer of the universe.

It's been a long journey for my body to fully open and trust, but it's this incredible transformation and healing I have received that inspires me to want to help others. My deep emotional processes have given me an unswerving ability to hold space for strong emotional charges in others.

I believe you can't take anyone through anything that you haven't been through yourself; you can't lead people through a territory you haven't traveled through yourself. For this reason, I am profoundly grateful for all of the struggles I have gone through. They have become my superpowers and expanded my capacity to hold strong voltages of energy and power in my being. Now, when I am standing naked holding a microphone in my hand facilitating a workshop, I am amazed at my transformation from the shy, awkward little girl—who is still in there, by the way—to this Amazonian woman commanding a group process.

What really got me keenly interested in tantra and sacred sexuality was an experience I had when I was about thirty; I had an incredible experience while making love. At the time, I was with a man who would later become the father of my child. I had always been interested in tantra, reading as many books as I could get my hands on. I instinctively knew that sex was powerful. I knew there was more to it than the physical; it went beyond even orgasms.

I wanted to experience God through it; I wanted it to take me to who we are beyond this realm. I had no idea if I could really achieve this, as I didn't meditate enough or do enough yoga or eat only lentils and vegetables. I felt that on some level I wasn't "spiritual" enough, but I spent hours reading about the possibilities. I began practicing some of the techniques with my partner at the time. He was just interested in the physical, I think, but he was also willing and interested enough to do these slightly odd practices of shaking the body and breathing in certain ways if it meant having sex.

One day, while we were in the middle of lovemaking, I began to visualize us as one body, like one of the tantra books had instructed. I didn't tell him; I just began to do it myself. I felt us as one being, with four arms, four legs, two heads, and two torsos. I started to see the shape of us, as if there was no separation between our bodies, and then I began to feel it, to get a sense of it at a kinesthetic level.

It was at this point of embodiment and feeling that things started to shift. I felt us merging, and then in one moment, we became one moving mass. I went right through the eye of a needle into a different level of reality. It's hard to explain in words, as the experience was so profound, but basically all of the existential questions I had my whole life were answered. I remember thinking: *Of course! How could I forget?* In that moment I remembered who I am, who we are, where we are from. I experienced reality as it really is. All I felt was incredible *love*: it felt so nurturing, so all-encompassing, and so safe. I knew that there was no separation. It went through everything, this love. I could hear my partner's thoughts; it was as if he were talking, but his lips weren't moving. I wanted to cry, to laugh out loud. It was so exquisitely blissful.

Eventually, we stopped making love and sat next to each other in bed, facing the wall in front of us. There were no words; a stillness permeated the room. To this day, I still don't know what his experience was, as we never spoke of it. It was as if the experience was too profound, too sacred to speak of, but judging by the stunned expression on his face at the end of our lovemaking, I sensed that he experienced something as well.

I couldn't comprehend why I had had this experience with this man in particular. I didn't really have a deep love for and understanding of him. He later became an important teacher by pushing my limits, pissing me off, and showing me where I needed to grow. Years later, he would help me see how far I had come; thus he was a pivotal part of my journey to empowerment.

Many questions remain unanswered.

One thing is certain: sex is a powerful gateway.
Sex is a portal, an opportunity to meet who we are on a spiritual level.
Sex is our highway to different levels consciousness.
Sex is a way to connect to our deepest being and to the deepest part of each other.
Sex is a way to journey back into love when we get lost.
Sex has the capacity to take us beyond where we are, to heal us on so many levels. It is also a way to reclaim unconscious parts of ourselves.
Sex is a healing balm of bliss and pleasure!

At thirty-three years old, when my son was just two and I had recently separated from his father, I was seeking my tribe, trying to find family and community. I decided to enroll in a weeklong retreat called Extreme Transformations, but when I arrived at the retreat center, my initial instinct was to get as far away from these people as possible. I took my concerns to the course facilitator, and she spoke to me in what I later found out was "light language." Afterward, she assured me that she had cleared the past-life trauma I was holding in my power center and said I should start to feel more relaxed.

I wasn't convinced but decided to stay. We were instructed to lie down on mattresses, and the course leader would bring in vortexes of energy channeled from Metatron, the galactic light network, and other such ascended higher frequencies. People were writhing and screaming and talking about being pierced by something. I lay there, feeling like they were all faking it, and then suddenly I started to shiver and feel very cold. Quickly, the course facilitator was over at my side like a shot. "Keep feeling into it," she said. "Go with the shivers and let your body go." I was soon writhing and shrieking like everybody else. I had no idea what was going on. I screamed and yelled as my body contorted and twisted. I saw and felt devas from Earth coming up into my body. I felt a huge anger, as if I was Earth being poisoned, raped, robbed, abused, and violated.

I ran screaming out of the workshop and flung myself onto the grass outside, sobbing and hugging the ground. I felt such a deep love and remorse for the planet. The week continued getting weirder; sometimes we experienced up to eleven vortexes a day. My body ached, I lost my voice, and I had no idea what was going on. To top it off, I was at the training with a very jealous and angry boyfriend who was convinced I was trying to have sex with other men enrolled in the course. On the last day, after no sleep and an exhausting argument with him, I started to feel very unbalanced. There was talk of one of the women being possessed, and we all went outside into a barn on the property to perform an exorcism.

Something in my consciousness snapped. All these vortexes were playing havoc with my nervous system. The next thing I knew, I was alone in the barn. A fire was burning in the fireplace, and I saw the devil appear in the smoke. I thought I had to face and overcome the devil, and to do this I had to sacrifice everything, to fully give my life away. I screamed, and it was as if I blew up. I next saw my boyfriend in front me. I yelled at him that I had a black serpent in me that he had fucking put in there and that he had to pull it out.

Afterward, I tried to calm down, but I felt dizzy and filled with fear. Every time my boyfriend came near me, I felt as though an evil energy was possessing me, an energy that wanted to kill him. It took all of my strength to control myself. The leader of the course told me to repeat my name and say out loud, "I am the owner of this vehicle. This is my body."

I left that retreat in deep fear; I was totally confused and barely able to function. I picked up my two-year-old son from a friend's house where he had been staying, drove home, and lay on my bed with my son next to me. When he put his little hand over my head and then my heart, it was if he was giving me a healing. I lay there weeping. I felt I had lost my mind. What if I died here alone with my son? Who would look after him? I felt trust. It was time to die.

In that moment, I felt myself leaving my body. A part of me died, and I was flooded with incredible healing power. I was taken on a journey through the universe. I met many beings and people and was showered with indescribable love. I felt tiny but important. I expanded out way beyond my body, up into the stars and galaxies beyond. Once the cosmic journey was complete, I returned to merge with Earth. I felt the dense heavy matter of Earth and my body become one; it was so heavy that I could not lift my head from the pillow.

I don't know how long I was unconscious, but when I awoke it was with a large jolt back into myself. "Thank God!" I said out loud. I was alive again! I was left with a profound energetic shift. I could hear people's thoughts. Even my plants were speaking to me. I was experiencing a very high vibrational state, but my physical body was very sore, especially around my heart. I imagine this is what it feels like to return from a heart attack. I'd run out of breath easily, from just walking, but I felt emotionally and energetically ecstatic.

This altered state lasted for about a week. The house was a complete mess. When I tried to cook I would burn the food. Yet I could spend hours playing with my son. There were no other thoughts in my mind. I was so incredibly present in the moment; I enjoyed having extrasensory perception. Eventually my energy settled, and I could carry on a normal conversation without hearing everyone's thoughts.

I was relieved, astounded, and amazed by the whole experience but also a bit scared. I vowed not to take the fast track anymore when seeking transformation. Slow and steady seemed like a safer option.

Many years later, at forty, I attended my first ever Level 1—Spiritual Sexual Shamanic Experience—and found a place to scream and sob and shed tears of laughter and pain. I was healing the sexual disempowerment that I hid deep inside. In all my previous attempts to connect to the Divine out of the body, I had never touched this. Now I started to feel the Divine within me, instead of searching for something outside. I began to have an embodied experience of love, the divine love I'd longed for my whole life. Finally, I found myself among a crazy family of like-minded beings just like me.

As I continue on this journey, I count my blessings every day to have found such an incredible pathway. I feel both humbled and privileged to journey into such intoxicatingly intimate work, and I thank the powers that be for helping me find it. It certainly took me through some interesting doors to get here, but now, looking back, I can see every sexual experience, every relationship, and even the sexual abuse I suffered at the hands of my stepfather was perfect preparation for this work.

I predominantly work now from the void. Working from the void means totally letting go of the need to know anything at all, being in a space of deep vulnerability, and just trusting the wisdom that comes through the body. It can be nerve-racking. To the best of my ability, I aim to be a hollow bone, allowing the Divine to work through me. I have developed an ability to trust and surrender. I regularly feel as if a higher power or a higher version of me comes through to facilitate the sessions.

Rather than using my body or energy to initiate healing, I aim to help people understand how to move energy through their bodies first, expressing sound and using breath to clear the lower chakras and sink deeper into their bodies. I help activate people by connecting to their own shamanic juice.

Who knows the master plan
that resides deep inside every soul,
the mysterious ways the intricate
web of life weaves its perfect lace?
Catching a glimpse of the real
truth by the mercy of grace.
Live within and also beyond,
this beautifully excruciating
illusion we call life.
One foot in each world.
One hand always
with the Divine.

Ellie Wilde is a certified sexological bodyworker and somatic sex coach who has trained with the Institute of Somatic Sexology, Chuluaqui Quodoushka, and the late world-renowned women's sexuality teacher, Shakti Malan. She is a faculty member with ISTA, artist, poet, and social provocateur and lives in New Zealand with her son.

Merging into Oneness

PURPOSE: The intention of this practice is to experience union, dissolve the ego, and realize our divinity, while making love.

PREPARATION: This is a sexual practice to be done with a partner whom you trust. You want to begin by sitting face-to-face and taking turns discussing your highest intention for this ritual. Give each other permission to temporarily lose yourself in this exercise, with the promise that you will take time afterward to ground and regain a sense of sovereignty. Name and release any obstacles you may have to oneness. State your boundaries, fears, and desires. Begin by meditating together and communing not just with your individual souls but your connection at the level of the oversoul as well.

PROCESS: Begin by gazing into each other's eyes. This will generate intimacy. Continue to intermittently gaze softly during foreplay and sexual play. Breathe together. By squeezing or adding pressure on the exhalation, you can coordinate your breath, especially as sexual excitement builds.

Continue conscious breathing even while kissing. You can play with sharing breath by taking alternate long, slow inhalations and exhalations while your lips are locked.

Imagine yourself as one being. As you touch your partner, imagine you are inside each other's bodies. When your partner feels sexual pleasure, imagine you are feeling the same thing. Notice if your partner has goosebumps or shivers and allow your body to do the same, as if it were a tuning fork. Shift your perception from the physical form to the energy between and around you. You can visualize an energy field that engulfs both your bodies. There is no separation. Even the highest power particle microscope cannot distinguish where you end and another body begins. Allow yourself to melt into an oceanic expanse, floating on waves of pleasure that carry you both. As you breathe together, imagine you can feel everything the other is feeling. As the excitement rises, allow your hearts to beat faster and in unison. Consciously move the orgasmic energy up the spine. Do not chase orgasm, but do not resist it either. If either one of you has an orgasm, experience it as if it came from you both.

Lying together in the afterglow is especially important. Don't separate too quickly; take your time to come down. Be sure to share your thoughts and feelings about this approach and allow yourself to laugh about any challenges that you may have experienced. You may want to share some dark chocolate or a light snack to help come more fully into your own body.

VARIATIONS: You can also visualize you and your partner joined inside a three-dimensional six-pointed star. If you are a sensitive empath, you may want to unravel or release cords together after this ritual.

NOTES: Oneness is a state of grace that can be cultivated or can occur spontaneously. Setting the intention and doing this ritual doesn't guarantee that you will have a mystical experience. As they say, you never know when lightning is going to strike, but practice will make you lightning prone.

RESOURCES: Margo Anand explains this experience in a number of her books, as it is similar to her spontaneous initiation into tantra.

CONNECTION WITH
PROFOUND MAGIC

By Stephen Soulove

Sarah Knox Photography

SUN SIGN: Cancer

RESIDENCE: California

ARCHETYPE: Wizard

SUPERPOWERS: Seeing into unseen worlds and through shadow dynamics

LINEAGE/TEACHERS: Birth and prenatal psychology, sexual trauma resolution, relational and sexual shamanism, myofacial unwinding, eye movement desensitization and reprocessing therapy (EMDR), brainspotting (BSP), somatic psychology, theater, dance, and sacred ritual alchemy

EPITAPH/MOTTO: Every action that you encounter in another is either an expression of love or a cry for love, although often convoluted.

SHAMANIC TOOLS: A pen and writing pad, fire, music, spoken word, pillows and chairs, the wind, ocean, earth, and stars

HOBBIES: Being in nature, caring for plants and creatures, attending transformational events, snuggling, personal growth, cooking, going to farmers' markets, biohacking, writing, and traveling

It was a hot afternoon in early autumn as I walked past the colorful vendor booths at one of the final West Coast music festivals of the season. Instead of lingering with the crowds of festival-goers, I was drawn to walk through the meadow and then into the forest where the new arrivals were setting up their campsites. *What attraction filter will I use today?* I thought.

It had been a few years since my teachers showed me how filters influence the world I see. Most people only use a small number of these perceptual lenses and never make conscious choices as to which ones they are using. For many people, the predator-prey filter is usually on constant autopilot, with men typically being seen as predators and women as prey. Other frequently used perceptual lenses include the selfish "what's in it for me" filter, the doomsday "worst case scenario" filter, the "I desperately want to rescue someone" filter, the judgmental "would my mother approve?" filter, and the romantic "looking for the one" filter.

My teachers showed me how easy it is to get stuck seeing the world through our habitual filters, especially the ones that we unconsciously took on early in life, causing us to collect more and more evidence to back up our distortions. If your filters create a world where you see yourself as a victim, you'll be more likely to feel unsafe and disempowered, and to find yourself as a victim. Even though you may be 100 percent certain that aspects of your world are unsafe or a threat, others may be experiencing the exact same situation completely differently, in a rainbow of other possibilities.

As I walked along the dusty forest trails, I decided to see what happened if I chose the "deep connection with profound magic" filter. The moment that this occurred to me, a big yes of contentment resonated through my belly, and I began to sense the infinite possibilities of connection and magic that awaited.

Of the hundreds of festival-goers that passed by, I sensed only light attractions to a few of them, but no one resonated strongly with this specific attraction filter. After about a half-hour of walking the forest trails, I began to recognize that I was being led somewhere, as if an invisible force was pulling me deeper into the woods for an unseen mystical purpose.

Arriving at a small campsite of tents underneath a canopy of large shade trees, I felt resonance with a woman in the final stages of setting up her campsite, so I stopped and said hello. She responded with a smile and a hi back in my direction.

I continued, "How's this day been for you?" She stopped, as if my question was a welcome interruption in the routine of her setting up her campsite. "My day has been interesting," she replied.

I held a soft gaze and silent presence. She continued, "It's been pretty challenging, if you want the truth."

As we stood there in front of her tent, her vulnerability met my vulnerability, and I replied, "I do want to know the truth."

After brief introductions, we sat on an old burgundy and gray rug that she had placed just at the entrance to her tent. She seemed proud and stroked the fabric as she told me, "This rug was handed down from my grandmother to my mother. I bring it with me whenever I am camping by myself."

"You said your day has been challenging. Please, tell me more."

As she opened her mouth to respond, her words got caught in midspeech, as if the response to my question was hijacked by something else that suddenly arose from her depths. The softness in her eyes was quickly replaced by a tension that seemed to be a mixture of fear and distrust. "What are your intentions?" she barked with an accusatory harshness in her voice.

I decided to speak into the core of the distrust that was sitting with us on the burgundy and gray carpet. Without flinching, I said, "I'm here to deceive you like all the rest of the guys in your life. All I'm interested in is taking advantage of you for sex, and really bad, disconnected sex, and as soon as I get what I want, I'll leave you for the next woman I see."

There was a tense silence. Then, her face shifted from disbelief into an amused relaxed smile. "Well, I'm glad I asked!" she laughed. "What made you say that?" she replied with intense curiosity.

"It seemed like what needed to be said. If I'd said anything else, those suspicions would have remained as a backdrop to everything else we would talk about."

"What you said about guys taking advantage of me, that's exactly what I'm upset about! How did you know that?" she asked.

"It was in the field of consciousness surrounding us," I replied.

For the next hour or so, she told me stories of men she'd dated and how it always turned out the same way. She'd meet a man and eventually he'd want to be sexual with her. At first, she would hesitate, refuse, or be confused, but then she'd be "talked into it." They would have sex, or even a relationship for a while, but confusion, doubt, guilt, or shame would eventually arise. Eventually, she'd start judging him and then would end up going through the motions of sex and being in a relationship with him. Soon, she'd find herself intensely attracted to another man and, rather than being forthright and open about it, she'd just stop communicating with the current guy, by avoiding him and not returning his calls or texts, as she'd get involved with the new man. Her confusion, doubt, guilt, or shame would eventually arise again, and the same thing would happen all over again. She didn't trust men and wasn't respectful to them because she could only see them as being interested in her for sex.

I listened intently to every word of her journey with men and, with as much love as possible, replied, "You're such a great sex and relationship victim, but I respect you too much to go along with it. Even though it might make you feel better in the short run, I'm not going to collude with your belief that all these men are only interested in you for sex. Do you want to continue seeing the world through this filter and having these experiences over and over again? Let me know if you'd be interested in clearing some of your victim beliefs and reclaiming your authentic sexual power."

She looked at me, confused and uncertain how to respond. I continued, "Taking full accountability for your life and your experiences with men and sex, please tell me *your* part in these experiences."

The confused look in her eyes then morphed into a "busted" look.

"I don't know what you mean," she said, playing coy.

I reached out with my right hand, and she placed her left hand in mine and looked into my eyes, as if to sense whether it was safe for her to tell me the secrets of her hidden worlds. I continued, "This experience you are having, if you are playing any part in it, tell me about your role. I have no judgments, just curiosity to understand and to unravel this pattern in your life."

She looked down to the rug and spoke with a sober voice that quivered with each word. "I've never told this to anyone before. When I'm attracted to a man, I cast my desire into his heart. I draw him to me with my eyes and my body. He sees me, notices me, and becomes interested in me, but I pretend I'm not too interested because I don't want to come across as being easy to get. Eventually, he initiates something with me, and I go along with it, but I make him do all the work. If he wants something sexual with me, I don't meet him there. I want him to want me, but I don't want him to get me. Eventually, I give in, have sex with him, but I end up resenting him and myself. If he is older than me, I turn him into some sort of creepy predator, and if he is younger than me, I dismiss him as being just a boy. Either way, I end up having sex with anyone I want to but feel bad afterward. Then I meet someone new and irresistible. I cast my heart into him and convince myself this new guy is somehow different, but the same thing happens over and over again. That's fucked up, isn't it?"

"It's actually perfect," I replied. "Your beliefs and strategy perfectly create the same painful outcomes over and over again."

Her voice crackled with frustration and sadness. "Do you have any ideas about how I can get out of this pattern?"

I allowed her words to dance within me for a moment and then asked, "Do you want to have kids someday?"

"Absolutely! At least a boy and a girl. Maybe more!"

I asked her to close her eyes and imagine her boy child. "How old is he? What do you see when you look into his eyes?" I asked.

She replied with a smile, "He's three years old and so cute. In his eyes, I see his innocence."

"Now, watch the innocence in his eyes as he grows from three years old to four to five to six to seven. What do you see as he grows up?"

"I still see him . . . he's such a beautiful boy and I still see his innocence."

"Observe his innocence and tell me what you see when he is in his early twenties." She watched her imaginary child grow through his life.

"He's become a young man, but he hasn't lost the beautiful qualities I saw within him when he was a boy."

I asked her to name a few of those qualities. Fun to be around, handsome, kindhearted, caring, generous, and trustworthy were some qualities she described.

"Now imagine him meeting a woman who wants him and casts her romantic desires into his heart. See her pretending that she's not that interested in him and making him do all the work, and then having sex with him but resenting him and blaming him for being interested in sex, and then cutting off communication with him when she meets another guy."

The softness in her smile melted, and her face became etched with a look of deep sadness.

"Imagine this happening to him over and over again with all the women he meets."

Tears began to stream down her face, and her forehead began to quiver as she spoke between sobs. "I see his heart breaking over and over again, and I don't see the innocence anymore."

"This loss of innocence and heartbreak is the relational legacy you leave in men's hearts. Your presence leaves a somatic imprint in men's emotional bodies in both conscious and unconscious ways and remains with them as your relational legacy. Men do this with women as well."

The look on her face spoke of sadness and sincere regret for what she had done. With a spark of determination, she replied, "I don't want my son to grow up in a world filled with women like me! How do I change myself and help other women change their experiences with men?"

"Traumatized people traumatize people. If you aren't able to meet men in their innocence, and if your actions leave them with a loss of innocence, it may mean that you need to reclaim your innocence."

"How do I do that?" she asked.

"I don't know yet," I replied. "I never know until you choose to begin the journey and we open that portal of possibility. There's a guidance system within you that can guide you there. Are you open to taking that journey?"

"What do I have to do?" she replied.

"Nothing," I responded. "You have 100 percent choice. You can leave this conversation whenever you wish. All I will ask you to do is feel your feelings and sense into your body. Are you down for that?"

"Yes, of course!"

I took a moment to sense into her yes. It felt authentic, something that she was doing for herself and not just for me. I also sensed into myself to see if there was resonance within me to continue this journey with her. When I connected with both her and my authenticity to move forward, I began to speak.

"The innocence that you saw in your male child, can you find that quality within yourself with respect to your relationships with men?" She paused to look within and softly replied no.

"That's okay. We can do some interdimensional journeying to find and reclaim your innocence. Are you down for doing that?"

"Fuck yes," she replied, with fearless determination beaming from her eyes.

I took her on a journey back to her three-year-old self. "Can you find that quality of innocence within her?"

A disappointed look came over her face, and she replied, "Sort of yes and sort of no. I find some innocence but not the purity and full innocence that I saw in my son."

I guided her to travel back further, to imagine herself as a baby.

After a few minutes, she replied, "I still can't find that pure innocence within myself."

As she curled up on the rug with her knees close to her chest, I guided her to time travel into her mother's emotional body and to sense into the field of consciousness of her mother's body while she was pregnant with her and even earlier in her mother's life.

"It's the same mix everywhere within her. It's something other than pure innocence, but I don't know exactly what it is yet."

We continued to time travel and seek that quality of pure innocence. We journeyed through her mother's life, and her grandmother's pregnancy, and even into her grandmother's childhood, until tears began to fall down her face.

"I see my grandmother when she's about seventeen years old, and she still has her innocence, but she knows nothing about men or sex. She was protected like a porcelain doll sitting in a cabinet, praised for her looks but too beautiful to touch. She's curious about the mysteries of her body, but she can't talk openly about it with her family. I see her being attracted to someone, but she doesn't know how to engage with him in a healthy way or how to say no or yes or even know what she wants. No one ever taught her how to know her body and speak its desires."

Then she let out an anguished cry. "I see her in her first interaction with a guy. He desires her, and she goes along with it, but then she feels guilty and blames herself and him too. The innocence is gone and replaced by shame. She ignores him, pushes all her feelings down, and smiles like everything is okay, but all I can see in her eyes now is fear and shame."

"Follow her life as she becomes older and tell me what you see," I requested.

"I see her a few years later. She is pregnant with her first child, my mother. I feel the fear and shame buried within her womb."

I listened and encouraged her to keep following this shamanic thread that was connecting her to her maternal lineage.

"I see her loving her child, but I also see her passing down her fear to my mother, and then my mother passes it down to me."

She sat up, opened her teary eyes, and said, "My mother used to tell me to be careful, that guys are just trying to get something from me and I shouldn't give it to them. All the girls and women in my life spoke about men in the same way."

Her sobbing quickly passed and was replaced with a tenacity for understanding herself better.

"I can see now how the expectations I learned from my family and the fears I carried within me led me to doubt my desires and to demonize men for their desires. I blamed them and myself for participating in the story that I created around their agenda!"

"It seems like you dehumanized men into being sex-seeking predators and dehumanized yourself into being their prey, who was being sought only for sex. Is that right?"

"I never thought of it that way before, but yes, that's exactly what happened. I was the one who treated men like objects because it was the way that I saw myself and the way that both my parents taught me to see men."

"Help me to better understand how you do it," I asked. "Would you cast your desire into my heart?"

She gazed at me with some resistance and shame, then softly spoke a tentative sounding, "Okay." The look in her eyes shifted as she locked them into mine with a quality I hadn't yet seen.

As we sat together at her campsite, bathed in the late afternoon sun that trickled through the trees, my lingam grew hard. It took about two seconds from when she spoke "okay" for me to feel my body respond in a sexual way. Almost immediately, I had a rock-hard boner buried within my dark-blue cut-off shorts, and I felt an intense attraction I hadn't felt previously.

"Okay, pull your desire out of my heart," I asked. Within ten seconds, my lingam lost all of its hardness, and the irresistible attraction I felt for her was gone.

"You have undeveloped shamanic powers," I replied. "It's time to stop playing games and learn how to use them for sacred purposes."

That moment reminded me of when my teachers taught me the difference between attraction that is authentic for me and what it is like to feel someone else's attraction within me. Knowing how to tell the difference is essential for connecting in love without hooking each other.

On the journey of sexual shamanism, we come to know that our attractions are primarily about ourselves and not the other person. The same is also true about our suspicions and doubts. We learn how to claim both our own authentic attractions and also our shadow projections upon another and to relinquish the tendency to always make it about the other person.

"How many men have you done this attraction-rejection dance with?" I asked.

"About fifteen or twenty," she replied.

I asked her if she was ready to clear this pattern and stop the manipulation, shame, and blame.

"Yes, *fuck* yes!" she replied.

I wrapped a scarf around her head as a blindfold and placed my hands on the front of her shoulders so that I was able to direct her to walk backward through the woods. We walked this way together in silence, step by conscious step. At first, she stumbled quite a bit and seemed unable to trust my guidance. I encouraged her to breathe into her belly and to trust her own innate guidance system, and then her steps became smoother, as if she were dancing backward through the forest.

I guided her to speak each man's name out loud, take accountability, and offer an apology. While stepping backward in trust, through a maze of rocks, sticks, logs, and plants, she spoke.

"Daniel, I apologize for making your sexual desires wrong when I was the one who called you to me in the first place. I apologize for blaming you for my own sexual insecurities and shame, and I apologize for getting what I wanted from you, making myself into a victim, and then rejecting you as not being right for me.

"Matt, I take responsibility for casting my desire into your heart and not clearly telling you no but instead giving in to you and then blaming you when you wanted to have sex with me the first night we were together. I apologize for spreading a rumor at college that you raped me when I got jealous after I found out you were seeing Emily and Madison at the same time as when we were hooking up.

"Ryan, we went deep into such a lovely beautiful connection with each other. I apologize for suddenly closing my heart to you after Andrew gave me the ultimatum of it being him or you. I apologize for blaming you for my confusion and making it about you not being right for me. I apologize for not being 100 percent truthful with you when I first met Andrew and for cheating on our sweet love with Andrew.

"Ethan, I take accountability for using you to fill the void of my own loneliness and romantic cravings. I made you the source of my happiness and then blamed you for when I wasn't happy. I apologize to you for this."

As the early evening shadows fell over the forest, she continued, man after man, speaking their names, taking responsibility, and releasing them from being the source of her pain.

After a couple of hours, her voice grew silent. "That's all of them," she said.

As we paused for integration, she fell forward into my embrace and released a deep wail of pain. She pulled the tear-soaked scarf from her face, and I held her as she wept in my arms. In that moment, it felt like we were lovers who were grieving together for the loss of sweetness and innocence that had been destroyed by these painful relationship dynamics. After a few moments, she looked up into my eyes and whispered, "I hardly know you, but I feel like you know me better than I know myself. Who are you? Where do you come from?"

I knew that if she made this about me, she couldn't come into her own power. When your shamanic skills are first seen by those who are also on the shamanic path, it's easy for them to default to making it about you being someone special. You can become their Disney prince, their knight in shining armor, the father or mother they never had, or the one who will rescue them from all of their pain and suffering. They fall in love with you, but it's an unequal love where you're destined to fall from the admiration pedestal when all aspects of your humanity are expressed and your shadows emerge. Yes, even shamans have their shadow worlds.

My teachers had encouraged me not to take the bait. I learned that if I persist in holding presence for someone's greatness to emerge, they eventually fall in love with themselves.

I took her questions into my heart and responded, "I have come from the same star system as you do. I am you. Our atoms have met and left each other a billion times already. There is nothing you have felt that I haven't felt or experienced at some time or another. I know you through knowing myself. We have come together today for deep connection and magic, to shed our illusions and to awaken into truth."

I gazed up into the vastness of evening sky and then looked deeply into the same vastness within her eyes and spoke softly, "We have more work to do, dear one."

I asked her what a healthy interaction with a man would be like if there was no suspicion, sexual shame, or guilt. "I don't know. I guess that I'd have to let down my guard and be vulnerable," she replied with a lost look in her eyes.

I motioned her to again place the wet scarf over her eyes and I encouraged her to sense into the wisdom and innocence within her belly rather than listening to the familiar chatter of her mind. I began to again walk her through the forest and asked her to address the men from her past from a place of her pure innocence.

Like a young girl on her first date, she spoke with a mix of words and giggles. "Brandon, I like your smile. It's cute. I want to kiss you. Is that okay?" Streams of tears dripped from beneath her blindfold.

"I can't just say that! Is it really okay to be that honest?" she exclaimed.

The many layers of her game playing, manipulation, and emotional posturing began to dissolve, and the innocent sexual young woman began to emerge. "Brandon, I want to kiss you, is that okay? It *is* okay? How can it be that easy?" she asked me.

"Keep going," I replied. "Who's next?"

She continued, "Zack, your eyes are beautiful. I just want to look into them for hours. Is that okay? I'd love to cuddle with you and kiss you." We walked through the forest again together, step by step, in a consciously chosen way, but this time, instead of walking her backward, I got behind her and guided her to move forward, as if she were stepping into her future as an authentic, emotionally present woman. We went through every one of her men. As we dialogued back and forth, I responded as the men she was talking about, holding the same innocence and tenderness that she offered.

"Jonathan," she said, "ever since we first met at the dance party, I've wanted to get to know everything about you and to make love with you."

I replied as Jonathan, "Thank you for expressing your desires. I've felt the same way. Let's get to know everything about each other and create a sacred sexual experience together!"

Hearing Jonathan's words, she became choked up with emotion. "That's what I've always wanted," she replied as another wave of tears streamed down from beneath the scarf and onto her cheeks.

By the time we finished dialoging, the stars were glistening and campfires were dancing in the distance. We walked back toward her campsite in silence, holding hands and savoring the sweetness of the past eight or nine hours we had spent together. Stopping for a moment at a small campfire where several people were sitting on logs and playing acoustic guitar, we sat together enjoying the music and taking in the vast tapestry of stars above us.

Through the sweetness of the music and the majesty of the stars above, I began to sense the penetrating presence of the wounded masculine somewhere in the field of consciousness that surrounded us. A few men approached the fire that I had never seen before, but their righteousness was quite familiar to me. One sat between us, the other to her right, and the third to my left. One man began chatting with her, and the others seemed to form a protective shield around her. Feeling awkward with the sudden change of circumstances, I suggested that we continue walking.

As she stood up to join me, the older man who was sitting between us also stood and exclaimed, "Stay here with us, sister; the fire is warm and cozy. You don't have to go with him if you don't want to."

The other two men then stood up in a confrontational manner. The older, more vocal man turned to me and said, "We've been watching you walking around this festival picking up women, blindfolding them, and taking them into the woods with you. The jig is up, brother. You have to leave. She's staying here with us."

I saw it as a spiritual challenge. Their projections and fears offered me the opportunity to test my own sexual shame. With a dark smile, I replied, "Your suspicions are the perfect reflection of your own shadow. Take accountability for your own sexual integrity, brother, and I'll take care of mine. Being the self-appointed hero that saves women from other men isn't going to repair your sexual shame or make up for the times you've been out of integrity or hurt by someone. That's your inner work, my friend. Enjoy the cozy campfire, brothers!"

As I turned and headed up the small hill that led toward the campsites, I heard her footsteps racing to catch up with me.

"What happened there?" she asked between breaths.

I replied, "In the same way that you objectified men's desires, men also do this with other men and with themselves. It's internalized oppression. What we saw at the campfire was an outward reflection of the deep sexual mistrust that men have for each other."

As we approached her campsite, her voice was filled with a strong quality of determination. "I know that pain and distrust very well. I've carried it for most my life, and it almost killed me. Today, you helped me to see it and release it, but I'm not sure what to do with these new perspectives."

"In every challenge, there's a gift," I responded. "What is the gift you received from all your past painful experiences with men?"

She thought for a moment and then spoke with certainty. "I lost my innocence because I grew up in a family that didn't teach me about the sacredness of my desires and the desires of others. That caused me to live a life of self-doubt, protection, fear, and depression. I binged with food. I drank and got high in order to try to get out of this pain. The gift I've received from these traumas with men is finding my desire to help others discover new ways of living and loving. I want to remind girls and women of their sexual innocence. I want to help transform the pain that men carry within themselves, which gets expressed outwardly as violence, jealousy, and wars. I want to be for them what you were for me today."

I smiled, "A lot can happen when you go for a blindfolded walk in the woods with a strange guy you only met an hour before."

"Yes," she replied. "I need to meet more of them . . . and become one of them too!" She smiled back at me. "Can I kiss you?"

As our lips slowly moved closer to each other, I thanked her for her request. "I'm sure that a kiss from you would be luscious, but I'll have to gracefully decline. Our time together has been sacred; let's not romanticize it. Instead of casting your desire into my heart and having me lust after you, consider using your newly found shamanic powers to nourish your own heart and those of the men in your life. Find me again, and we'll create more magic together. Good night, dear one."

I turned and walked into the darkness.

Stephen Soulove is a transformational facilitator and ISTA faculty member. He draws on a lifetime of study in bodywork, tantra, somatic and birth psychology, consciousness research, systems thinking, and sexual shamanism to catalyze the transformation of trauma, leaving people reunited with their soul fire and reconnected to their self-worth.

Cord-Cutting Ceremony

PURPOSE: This practice can help you regain lost power by setting you free from unhealthy relationship patterns. By clearing old attachments, you create space to relate in the present moment. This does not mean that you are cutting people out of your life.

PREPARATION: Make sure you are well rested and fed. This ritual should come from a loving intention as opposed to a state of hurt or revenge. Unplug from all distractions. Optional: Have meditation music cued up and/or sage ready to light for afterward.

PROCESS: Throughout the practice, you'll be taking long, full breaths without retention. Use the exhalation to release tension and the inhalation to experience more freedom. Relax your pelvic floor and feel your connection to Mother Earth.

Once grounded, you can invoke your higher self, guides, or gurus. If it's appropriate to your belief system, you may call on Archangel Michael, who is particularly skilled at cutting cords with his mythical sword.

When you are ready, visualize the person with whom you want to detatch.

Locate on your own body where the cords are concentrated. Romantic cords may be centered around the heart, the navel, or sex center, depending on whether this energetic connection was about sex, power, or love. Spiritual and mental relationships tend to bundle around the top three chakras. Notice if the cords feel like delicate filaments or thick cables.

If you have a healthy, conscious relationship, you may simply imagine returning someone's cords and retrieving any of your own attachments. You may feel and see your power returning. You can bless the person and say, "I now release you in love and light."

If the relationship was unconscious, toxic, or karmic, you can cut attachments by visualizing the cords being severed in the present and for the future. You may also move one of your hands with an up-and-down motion.

Don't forget to cut above your head and below your feet, as well.

Ultimately, some cords may refuse to be severed because they are still serving a purpose.

After all the cords have been released or cut, you may feel around your auric field for holes or scars. You can heal them by visualizing a golden light. Allow the healing to fill the room, enter your body, and guide you into healthy relationships in the future. Complete the ritual with a visualization of yourself as a whole, strong and sovereign.

It's important to rest afterward. You can turn on relaxing music or smudge your area with incense or sage. Even though the ceremony is complete, the energetic ripples are still in motion. Relationship attachments take time to dissolve and heal.

Afterward bathe in sea salt, Epsom salt, or Himalayan salt. Negative, toxic cords of energy cannot hold a charge when you bathe your aura in sea salt.

VARIATIONS: Cutting cords can be like pulling weeds: you have to get the root out or the cord will grow back. Repeat this exercise as needed until you are free and clear from emotional enmeshment. Some teachers practice this ritual on a daily basis, while others don't recommend it more than once a month because they feel time is needed to help assimilate.

RESOURCES: *Sacred Sexual Healing* by Baba Dez Nichols and Kamala Devi

14
BIRTHING A NEW REALITY

By Crystal Dawn Morris

Heather Kadar

TRANSPERSONAL NAME: Shamimi
YEAR OF BIRTH: 1955
SUN SIGN: Capricorn
RESIDENCE: Sedona, Arizona
ARCHETYPE: Priestess
SUPERPOWER: Resonating unconditional love
LINEAGE/TEACHERS: Shamanism: Michael Harner and Linda Star Wolf. Tantra: Margot Anand and Lama Yeshe.
Bon Buddhism: Tenzin Wangyal Rinpoche. Self-realization: Bentinho Massaro.
EPITAPH/MOTTO: Awaken love and freedom now!
SHAMANIC TOOLS: Rattle, Tibetan singing bowl, drum, and a variety of Young Living essential oils
HOBBIES: Making art, dancing, and taking nature walks

My mother fell in love with the name Crystal Dawn when she was eighteen. A couple of years later she joined the air force and met my dad. They had a whirlwind six-week romance and were married on Good Friday. I wanted that name, and I was conceived by Easter Sunday. When she reported her pregnancy, my mother was honorably discharged. My father was shipped off to Germany when I was only one week old.

My earliest memory was nursing at my mother's breast, looking into her sad eyes, and feeling the pain she felt at having my father so far away. As a small child, I could read people's energy and realized I was on this planet to help stop suffering. Intuitively, I knew how to shine love light out of my heart and into the hearts of others.

I decided to drop out of high school on my sixteenth birthday. I knew something more profound than clothes, boys, and good grades were in my future. I announced my decision to my psychologist mother, and she shrugged her shoulders and said, "I trust your inner guidance."

Upon hearing the news, my absent electrical engineer father came to our house. He told me that if I quit high school, I would end up on welfare. I told him it was a bit late to be offering me fatherly advice—he had been noticeably absent most of my life. After he left the house, I felt surprisingly confident. I didn't need to know what was going to happen next. I saw a world in need of a radical makeover, and I was going to do my part to make it better.

Now free of my school schedule, I spent time reading books on philosophy, consciousness, and Eastern spirituality. I was especially intrigued by Carlos Castaneda's *The Teachings of Don Juan: A Yaqui Way of Knowledge*. Don Juan's teachings reminded me of the joyful experiences I'd known as a child, when summer days were spent playing away from the prying eyes of adults. They seemed incapable of recognizing the magic that was obvious to me. When I was in the woods, I talked with the trees, listened to the birds, and felt the presence of the angels as they shined unconditional love on me.

One Friday night, a friend came by with a surprise. He had scored two tabs of mescaline and asked me if I'd like to spend the night tripping with him. Mescaline is the psychedelic ingredient in peyote, the same plant medicine Don Juan had given to Carlos Castaneda. I was excited to rediscover the magical world described by Don Juan's teachings.

The evening was chilly, so we built a fire in the fireplace. We talked until the mescaline took effect. I had recently been given a pair of mahogany click sticks. I began to play with them, and I soon found a rapid, repetitive beat that was hypnotic. We stared at the burning logs. Eventually, the walls of the house faded into the background and the sounds of LA went silent.

Suddenly, we were no longer in my mother's living room but in the desert. It was nighttime, and the stars were so close they caressed my hair. I was dancing around a roaring fire with my spirit tribe. A power song was given to me in a language I didn't know but that sounded familiar. The song wove into the sounds of the click sticks. Twenty years later, I would learn that playing a repetitive rhythm of three to four beats per second causes the brain to enter a shamanic state of consciousness, or SSC. I began to communicate with the fire. It changed colors, blue to green, purple to red, and orange to yellow. We made love under the Milky Way. When dawn arrived the fireplace in my mother's living room reappeared. The flames were now a pile of amber coals. My friend was asleep on the sofa.

I felt called to go outside. As I stepped out the door, I noticed that the world, or my perception of it, had radically shifted. There was no me as a separate subject or as the thing called an object. Everything was made of light. Giggles emerged; tears flowed. I arrived at the park and saw that the pond, the ducks, and the trees were all energy in motion. I was seeing through the cosmic kaleidoscope. The Divine was dreaming the world into existence. How did this apparent truth stay hidden from view most of the time?

I went home to sleep. Several hours later, I woke up, and the mescaline was no longer in my system. I went into the backyard, curious to see if things had returned to "normal." I climbed onto the trampoline and looked up into the branches of a large oak tree. I closed my eyes, became still, and felt aliveness all around me.

The next few days were spent exploring the world through the lens of no-self. I was making love with life. The people around me didn't seem to notice the change. Day slipped into night, sleep came, and a new day began. The song I learned continued to play in the background of my awareness. Occasionally, when I'd feel a slight sense of separation arising, the song effortlessly played in my mind, and the feeling was replaced with a blaze of bliss.

When Friday rolled around, I was certain that I would be spending the rest of my life vibrating as *satchitananda,* a Sanskrit word for being-conscious-bliss. But everything changed. The bliss that had been so clear for the past week was nowhere to be found. Previously, all I had had to do was remember the song and the bliss returned, but the song had also disappeared. I felt abandoned. How could something so clear and profound be lost?

I asked myself, *What's the purpose of realizing bliss only to have it disappear?* The answer came: I wasn't meant to focus on what had faded away. I needed to be curious about the next step on my path. I spent several days asking what I was meant to do next. The answer was: "Go forth, find a man, and start a family."

This was not the answer I had expected. I was in my teens. I sat with this possibility and felt my whole body say, *Yes!* No matter what twists and turns life had in store for me, I knew I'd never forget the connection and bliss that had been shown to me. I knew this experience would be my guiding light.

So, in the summer of 1971, I left LA with a car and three thousand dollars given to me by my mother, along with a list I had created of qualities I wanted in the man who would be the father of my children. He would be smart, handsome, responsible, family oriented, and from a diverse gene pool, to avoid risk of genetic anomalies. I also wanted someone whose company I enjoyed.

I was guided to a budding commune forming in Applegate, Oregon. The founder, whose name was Roger, had a vision of creating a sustainable community on a 160-acre farm. He and his wife had recently opened their marriage. She had another lover, and he was exploring being lovers with women other than his wife. I observed him from a distance and noticed that he had many of the qualities on my list.

The Farm, as it was called, consisted of between twenty and thirty people depending on the day. They ranged in age from sixteen to thirty-two, but most were in their midtwenties. Roger had planted a garden, was working on plans for a communal house, and intended to create some kind of business that could support his hippie commune. His parents owned a shoe factory in LA, and Roger was working as a shoe salesman to helped him finance the commune.

In order to build a cost-efficient communal house, Roger decided to purchase a huge barn in town. It had to be dismantled by mid-August. Roger, just five feet eight and weighing 135 pounds, was a hard worker and had enormous stamina. He put in twelve-hour days and expected others to follow his example. When they didn't, he tried army tactics to rally his hippie troops. At 6:00 a.m., he rang a gong made from an old brake drum. This was the signal to wake up and head for work. Hippies don't respond well to being given orders, and tension started to mount.

Once the barn dismantling was under way, Roger left on a shoe-selling trip. He needed to make money to complete the house by winter. With him gone, hippie values soon prevailed. The next few weeks taught me a lot about people and power and how egos are determined to get their own way.

That August was unusually hot and dry. The men came home complaining they were tired of dismantling the barn. The group had only ten days before the barn needed to be completely torn down. We had a long discussion, and everyone agreed that we would keep reclaiming the wood until the deadline, at which point we would simply knock it down and leave what was left.

The very next day, however, a handful of guys decided to ignore the group's decision and drove a flatbed truck into the wall of the barn until it collapsed into a heap of rubble. When Roger returned, he made no comment about the size of the wood pile. He just turned his attention toward building the house.

One afternoon, he approached me and asked if I'd like to sleep with him in his refurbished Metro Van. I was surprised and curious. I remembered my list and responded with a yes. We enjoyed getting to know each other and had many things in common, including a desire to have children. A few days later, we became lovers.

Roger's leadership style and work ethic were soon a point of contention again. After several weeks of struggling, he'd reached his limit. He headed back to LA while I stayed behind, until one day it became clear to me that it didn't matter how well intentioned people were, egos are doomed to continuously create one drama after another. If I wanted to create a better world, I would have to learn to move beyond my ego and help others move beyond theirs.

I returned to LA and visited Roger in Hollywood. One night, he started telling stories about being a Green Beret in Vietnam. He shared things he had never told anyone, not even his wife. I held him in my arms as he wept. I was touched by his vulnerability. This was a turning point in our relationship.

A few days later, while making love, magic happened. I was straddling him, and as I began to orgasm, I experienced everything—including me disappearing. Infinite and eternal awareness remained, appearing as the universe. I was not a body or a mind. I was the Divine, pretending to be a person, living in a world. I was everything that existed and simultaneously nothing at all. When the room reappeared, we were orgasming together.

Afterward, I lay in Roger's arms, wondering silently why I had never heard anyone talk about sex being a path to God. The fact that no one was talking about this, even as a possibility, made no sense to me! Why was sex only being touted as recreation or procreation? I had only recently lost my virginity; surely, I wasn't the first person to discover that sex was a sacrament, a way to commune with the Divine.

Roger's marriage ended in an amicable divorce. I wanted our relationship to be based on something stronger and longer lasting than romantic attraction. I wanted to build a life together of mutual respect and a shared vision. Just before Thanksgiving, Roger and I rented a house together in North Hollywood.

In January, a week after my seventeenth birthday, I had a miscarriage. My periods had been irregular since I'd quit taking the pill, so I hadn't realized I was pregnant. The pregnancy was over before I even knew it had begun. Still, there was grief. This reality check caused Roger and me to reconsider if we were ready to be parents. After many discussions, we decided we wanted to go ahead and start our family. Birth and death apparently walk hand in hand.

By March, I was pregnant again. I hadn't realized pregnancy was such a taboo subject. Women rarely shared their birth experiences, and when they did, it was mostly to say how bad it had been. When the fetus began to quicken after twenty weeks of gestation, I was elated. It felt as if butterflies were dancing inside my belly. My boyish figure had begun to change: I was developing breasts, hips, and a rounded belly. I hit one hundred pounds for the first time in my life. I had a human growing inside me!

Pregnancy made me feel like a goddess. It troubled me that I lived in a culture that treated something this miraculous as a somewhat shameful medical condition. I began reading everything I could find on natural childbirth. I realized that every pregnant woman was an embodiment of the goddess of creation.

Our son, Elijah, was born in November 1972. We hadn't been able to find a doctor or midwife willing to attend a home birth in Southern California, so we attempted to do the birth at home on our own. My labor was extremely long and exhausting but not particularly painful.

We eventually ended up going to the hospital because I was unable to urinate and my bladder was preventing me from being able to push the baby out. Once the doctor drained my bladder, the baby was out in one push. Holding my son and looking into his eyes had a profound effect on me.

I had a new respect for the sacredness of life. I was a mother with the responsibility to love and protect this child. I wanted to make the world a better place for him to live. Now, as a grandmother of five, I feel even more devoted to shifting global consciousness.

In April of 1975, Roger and I bought 160 acres in the Ouachita Mountains from my grandfather. Our plan was to live on top of this mountain, ten miles from nowhere, and create a sustainable off-the-grid lifestyle. The first year, we lived in a sixteen-foot-by-sixteen-foot army tent and created an incredible garden in the middle of a dense forest. The process of creating a homestead was extraordinarily rewarding.

In September 1976, our son Joshua was born in his great-grandfather's house. This was across the street from the house where my mother had been born. This labor was very different, and it only lasted a few hours. The experience following his birth was serene, with no hospital procedures to follow. It was a family affair.

Moments after the birth, Elijah came into the room with his grandparents and met his baby brother. An hour later, we were all having a hearty breakfast. I now understood that every birth is unique. I know that when a woman is allowed to trust herself, birth is an empowering initiation that intimately connects her to the source of creation.

After Joshua's birth, my calling was confirmed: I was to become a midwife. When Joshua began kindergarten, I started nursing school in Palm Desert. Three years later, I started the Nurse-Midwifery Program at San Francisco General Hospital. For the first time in my adult life, I would be living on my own.

Being five hundred miles away from my husband also helped me see that my marriage was beyond repair. For several years, I had been doing 90 percent of the work to keep it viable in an effort to avoid putting my sons through a divorce. I shut down sexually and convinced myself that I preferred cuddling to sex. I went home on Labor Day weekend for a visit. My husband had come to a similar conclusion. We both agreed it was time to end our sixteen-year relationship.

A few weeks later, I found a new lover. He helped me rediscover what I had learned at sixteen, that sacred sex was a way to merge with God. My body began to open and surrendered into bliss again. My sexual energy was reignited. One morning, while making love, a bolt of lightning shot up my spine and out the crown of my head. I was that which existed before the big bang, the infinite and eternal source, beyond the beyond. When I returned, I was back in bed with my lover. His experience was simply being in bed, making love to me. He was unaware of my cosmic journey.

I had read a book called *The Kundalini Experience: Psychosis or Transcendence* by Lee Sannella, so I knew that I had just been blessed with a kundalini awakening. Over the next few years, I taught myself tantra. The universe put two more formative books into my hands, *Conscious Loving* and *The Art of Sexual Ecstasy.*

After graduating from midwifery school and passing my board exam, I decided to start a home birth practice in San Francisco. A few months later, my lover and I decided to move in together, but after a year I realized that cosmic sex was no guarantee of manifesting a conscious relationship.

The very thought of asking him to move out made me freeze like a rabbit. I had spent thirty years perfecting the art of being a good girl and had difficulty saying no. I knew I needed professional help. A friend told me about a woman offering a new type of therapy that was body centered. During the first session, she explained that "intimacy happens where two people's healthy boundaries meet."

After a month, I asked him to move out. Over the next several years, I jettisoned a lot of emotional baggage. A major shift happened when I finally got in touch with anger. Body-centered somatic therapy taught me to listen to my emotional guidance system. I began to create more ease and flow in my life. I realized I didn't want to live in San Francisco any longer. Since I was sixteen I had wanted to live in Sonoma County.

In January 1991, I moved to Sonoma County and joined a private nurse-midwifery practice. The first Gulf War began, and I soon felt called to do something to bring more peace to the planet. I started a shamanic drumming circle with a friend. Later, another friend introduced me to Michael Harner and core shamanism. He used repetitive drumming and rattles to create sonic driving, which helps shamanic practitioners go into a trance state and journey.

This approach allowed me to access an SSC for guidance, healing, and transformation. For the next fifteen years, shamanism was the heart of my spiritual practice. Through doing sweat lodges, going on vision quests, creating sacred art, and journeying with the drum, I receive support from the spirit realm. I was blessed to learn from a variety of native and non-native teachers.

In 1995, I felt the call to start a part-time shamanic coaching practice called Wise Ways Healing. This prompted me to take the Two-Week Shamanic Healing Intensive at the Foundation for Shamanic Studies (FSS), held at the Esalen Institute, Big Sur, California. We journeyed eight or more hours a day.

At night, I soaked in the sacred water of the hot springs where, within days, I was listening to the vibrations of each rock, tree, plant, animal, and element. My body became like a crystal bowl vibrating and amplifying the sounds of life in and around me. I literally heard the whole world singing. This continued for the next two months. I learned how to be simultaneously in nonordinary reality while navigating ordinary reality. Later that year, I started the FSS Three Year Program of Advanced Initiations in Shamanism and Shamanic Healing.

The day I attended my one-thousandth birth was the day I finally understood what it felt like to be a real midwife. The veil between the worlds is thin at the gateways of birth and death. The art of midwifery is to be a "hollow bone," to hold space for the divine creatrix in each woman to move through her, unmolested. The hands of a midwife worship at the altar of the yoni. I trusted women and birth. I saw the Goddess in every woman and the divine child in every baby.

Over a period of twenty-two years, I welcomed more than 2,500 divine beings into the world. Each birth, no matter what it looked like, was a miraculous and humbling experience. The last birth I attended as a nurse-midwife was the birth of my granddaughter, who was born in January 2007.

In August of 2001, I journeyed to the ancestors to ask what I could do to honor them. Three ancient grandmothers appeared and told me to do a specific kind of vision quest. They shook their fingers in my face, saying, "Three days. No food. No water. Just do it!"

After three months of preparation, I was ready to go inside the sweat lodge where the Inipi purification ceremony is done. I found myself sitting in the darkness with my pipe and a rattle. I had sat in the womb of the unknown. I prayed and asked how I could serve the ancestors. Slowly, over the next three days, I was given detailed instructions. My life was changing course.

Earth was undergoing a major shift, and the ancestors wanted me to actively midwife a new vibration into being. When the third afternoon arrived, the flap was raised, and sun pierced my eyes like tiny shards of glass. I stepped out of the lodge and felt as if I was just learning to walk for the first time. I was reborn; who I had been was no more. I was beginning a new life.

A life-changing initiation occurred when I attended my first SkyDancing Tantra weekend in 2003. Less than one hour into it, my whole body was vibrating with bliss. I knew this was the path the ancestors wanted me to follow. I fell in love with SkyDancing Tantra and knew it was the next step on my spiritual journey. Tantra blessed me with many powerful spiritual transmissions.

One powerful experience happened after the first week of Margot Anand's Love & Ecstasy Training. I was doing a meditation with a new lover. The practice involved circulating energy through the chakras. As we did this, we both became the timeless space of awareness. Then, at the same instant, we raised our arms and sent out love to the world. When we checked, more than ninety minutes had passed. At that time, I usually found meditation challenging because my mind was constantly full of mental chatter. In this meditation, we both effortlessly ceased thinking. As I devoted myself to the path of tantra, I saw how it wove all aspects of my life seamlessly together.

I went to Sedona, Arizona, to visit a friend, and as I came around a bend in the road, I saw the Verde River, the red rocks of Sedona, and the snow-covered peaks. The sheer beauty and power of the scene penetrated my heart, causing my whole body to vibrate with joy. A voice in my head said, *It's time to move to Sedona.* Within months, everything fell into place!

By August 2005, I was living in Sedona. It seemed a good time to take a midlife break. For the next six months, I explored being, and gradually the doer began to relax. I meditated, hiked, and slept. A month later, while meditating, I realized I wouldn't be returning to the practice of midwifery, at least not in the way I had been doing it for the past two decades. If I was going to transform the world, I needed to find a new way to help people wake up. I was curious about the next phase of my life.

Within days of this insight, I learned Margot Anand would soon be offering her tantra teacher training course. Halfway through the training, Margot suggested that I present at a sexuality conference. Weeks later, I attended the Daka/Dakini Conference in Sedona. I ended up becoming friends with the founder, Baba Dez Nichols. I presented at his next conference and got involved in his school. Eventually, I became one of the lead facilitators of ISTA's Spiritual Sexual Shamanic Experience (Level 1 training). As a master facilitator, I knew I wanted to be a clear channel so that wisdom could transmit through me unimpeded.

In 2010, my mother moved to Sedona. One year later she was diagnosed with an aggressive form of brain cancer. I supported her through her end-of-life transition, and she died painlessly in my home four months later.

The next several months, I felt like I was drowning in a tsunami of grief. One night, I grabbed my throat. I couldn't breathe. I blacked out. At that moment, I had to choose: Would it be death or life? Every fiber of my being wanted to live! My lungs filled with air. I was back in my body again.

The next morning, the sun was shining, and the emotional seas were calm and clear. I was ready to reengage in life. Grief helped dissolve the sludge of delusion related to my earliest life experiences with my mother. After this, I felt even more compassion for other people's suffering.

In 2014, I began practicing Tibetan sleep yoga. This practice went beyond the lucid dreaming that I had explored for several years in the mid-1990s. It is a meditation practice focused on being lucid in deep sleep as a way to realize the true self, the clear light of awareness that never comes and goes. While doing this practice I became acutely aware of a luminosity that is present before, during, and beyond my dreams. I realized that I am this continuity of awareness that is infinite and eternal. It is literally all that ultimately exists.

The beauty of sleep yoga is that in deep sleep this luminosity is not masked by content. However, this luminosity is also present in the dream state as well as when we wake up in the morning. It's always here and yet difficult to recognize because it is so subtle and ever present that we don't even notice its existence. Because is it beyond form it is difficult to explain.

Through the practice of sleep yoga, I realized that enlightenment is not about bells and whistles or entering into ecstatic states. It is simply knowing without a doubt that I exist beyond the body, mind, and world. I am inseparable from the One Absolute Source that creates the flow of life. Life unfolds in an infinite variety of ways. Sex, birth, and death are portals through which the Divine transforms emptiness into form and then dissolves back into emptiness again.

As a sex shaman, I know I am one with the absolute. I am able to help others to consciously align with the true self so they can freely shine their love light and give their gifts. When the true self is realized, life becomes a conscious creative experience; instead of feeling controlled by life, people can begin making love to life.

My commitment as a sacred sexual shamanic midwife is to support the birth of a new consciousness on Earth. Rather than birthing babies, I am now birthing a new paradigm on the planet.

Crystal Dawn Morris is a tantra teacher, shamanic minister, and spiritual midwife. Her life is dedicated to creating a world of love and freedom. She is on the ISTA faculty and teaches around the globe. Crystal lives in Sedona, Arizona, where she offers personal retreats and online coaching and events.

Energetic Sex

PURPOSE: Energetic sex can be a doorway to increased sexual chemistry and can expand pleasure and heighten awareness. It can also help integrate healthy masculine and feminine energies within.

PREPARATION: Find a partner who is open to allowing their energy body to communicate with your energy body. If this is your first time, we recommend that you keep a layer of clothing on so you can experience how energetic penetration contrasts with the physical. Decide who will be receiving and who will be giving. Since this does not have to do with genitals, gender, or sexual identity, it can be very powerful to switch and take turns playing both roles. Next, drop any skepticism and give yourself permission to use your imagination and your intuition.

PROCESS: Start with one hand on your heart. Tune in to your breath, not just the inhalation and exhalation but also the space in between. Notice all the sensations arising in your body. Deepen your breath and notice your heart chakras expand.

The receiver can imagine a lotus blossoming in the heart. The giver can imagine getting an energetic heart-on. Notice the strong magnetic force between your hearts. Breath, sound, and movement will amplify the experience. It's natural to feel a range of emotions, physical sensations, and bioelectric impulses.

The penetrating partner may choose to initiate energetic penetration by asking, "May I enter you energetically?" If the receiving partner is not ready, the receiver can say, "Not yet." Both partners can continue teasing each other with their energy, creating an intense experience. If the answer is yes, you can allow yourselves to make love, even without physical touch.

After playing heart to heart, you may choose to explore the connection between other chakras. Try connecting your third eyes in a tantric kiss or feel the electrical exchange between your power chakras.

If you're ready to go deeper, visualize your genitals lighting up and your energetic yoni and/or lingam drawing closer together, perhaps the lingam teasing the outside of the yoni temple.

Allow the energy to guide you, listen to your body's intuition but don't fall into habit. If you feel called to add touch, go slowly. The lighter the touch, the more likely you are to feel the subtle electrical current.

Sometimes the energy gets really big and may even push you farther away from each other. Notice what is happening between your bodies. If the energy guides you closer, you can try sitting in *yab-yum,* in which the receiving partner sits on the lap of the penetrating partner and wraps their legs around the penetrator. Breathe together and rock your pelvis forward and back with each breath. You can boost the energy by squeezing or pumping the PC muscles.

Ride the ripples of pleasure. Allow yourself to vibrate, twitch, shake, and shudder. These energy jolts are called *kriyas,* and they can be seen as little energy orgasms. One of the great benefits of energetic sex is that you can continue riding one orgasmic wave after the other, you don't need an erection to have fulfilling sex, and there is no refractory period!

VARIATIONS: This can also be done as a solo practice. With visualization, movement, breath, and sound, you can grow your etheric genitals and commune with your own inner god/goddess or merge with the Divine.

RESOURCES: After many years of working with medicine people, Kenneth Ray Stubbs developed a working model of energy that transcends the current somatic and psychological modalities. In his documentary *Path of the Sexual Shaman,* he details how a shaman can radiate, expand, extend, and resonate his or her energy.

15

KINKY QUEER WITCH IN LOVE

By Matooka MoonBear

Jeff Larson

YEAR OF BIRTH: 1957

SUN SIGN: Leo

HOMETOWN: Manhattan, New York

RESIDENCE: Manchester, New Hampshire

ARCHETYPE: Priestess

SUPERPOWER: Seeing ancestral patterns and holding space

LINEAGE/TEACHERS: ISTA, priestess path, goddess school, witchcraft, and Native American spirituality

EPITAPH/ MOTTO: Love is love.

SHAMANIC TOOLS: Drum, rattle, smudge, flower essences, crystals, tuning forks, feathers— the possibilities are endless!

HOBBIES: Creating rituals and sacred temple space, painting, and making shamanic tools such as drums and rattles

I got curvy at age twelve. Older boys started noticing me. I had strange and wondrous feelings that I couldn't understand. I asked my mother what was happening to me, but she couldn't go there. We didn't speak of sex; she told me I wasn't ready and to wait. Before my first period, my mom gave me a book about the human body and reproduction. That was her talk.

What she didn't realize was that her husband had been molesting me since I was six years old. My childhood was spent with an abusive man who physically, mentally, emotionally, and sexually abused me. So, my sexual understanding was both naive and distorted.

By the time I was sixteen, I ended up living with my maternal grandmother. She criticized my expressions of dance, beauty, and sexuality and made every attempt to suppress me so that I would choose what she called a normal life. She said I was trying to be seductive and was looking for trouble, and she told me the story of John the Baptist and Salome. But I wasn't raised with organized religion; we didn't have any spiritual practices.

I was seeking myself in all the projections of the world. Once, my grandmother caught me gazing in a mirror and accused me of vanity. For me, it brought me to an altered state. She would tell me not to think much about myself and that I wasn't pretty. Clearly, her goal was to knock me down a few pegs.

Perhaps my grandmother's mother had passed these same messages to her as well. Perhaps this is a pattern from seven generations. It feels deeper than me, like an energy field—blood memories passed from mother to daughter for generations.

In my early twenties I married a man twenty-four years my senior and started a family. It never occurred to me that there was more to life than being a mother and raising a family. I had a normal monogamous marriage with three children and lived in a home in the country. I was content to give my family a better life than my mother and grandmother had given me. I chose to pass their father's religious upbringing along to my children. I have always been spiritual, so it didn't matter to me how it was expressed as long as it was love. I always made sure to tell my daughters how beautiful they were.

After my last child was born in 1986, I found the New Age: crystals, channeled books, and Native American spirituality. I was on fire, devouring new information, playing with crystals and transformative rituals. Shamanism was introduced to me by the work of Lynn Andrews and Sun Bear. I also explored alternative healing modalities that brought catharsis. I sought energy work through reiki studies and massage therapy at DoveStar Institute in New Hampshire. I dove into witchcraft from the '90s to now, leading me into deeper shamanic experiences.

One day, the metaphysical shop I used to frequent suddenly closed. This inspired me to open my own shop called MorningStar Loft, which was conveniently located just over my garage. It was primitive and earthy. I partnered in this venture with a friend, and it took me on a cathartic series of events from 1989 to 1996.

At that time, I could feel changes in the air and within me. When my husband became ill, my faith was shaken. Animal allies began to guide me to move forward, like a caterpillar drawn to create its cocoon. These changes within made it difficult to continue life as I knew it.

The portal opened on a full moon night, October 16, 1997, when a stag stepped in front of my car! I struck him, and he died. He was a graceful beast with long legs and jagged horns. To me, stag means love, compassion, protection, and sacrifice. When he gave his life on the full moon, I saw it as a gift from the Divine that opened my path to a new dimension. I have honored him as a gatekeeper ever since. From this moment, I shifted my soul's exploration and wholeheartedly dove into spirituality and sexuality.

As my fourth decade came to a close, I came out as a lesbian, leaving my eighteen-year marriage. It was a summer weekend when I decided to go off by myself and join a pagan camping event. There was a downpour on the first day, which confined me to my tent. I rested quietly for some time and must have dozed off. I awoke to the sound of a truck coming into camp with a camper in tow. Looking out my small screen to see the goings-on, a figure appeared to be systematically setting up camp in the rain.

Butch dyke alert! My gaydar was raging high on the Richter scale. I knew she was someone I had to meet. The next day was dry enough to gather in the field for a ritual, and I went out of my way to meet the newcomer, whose name was Wren.

She shyly welcomed me to sit and visit in her camp. I was excited and bold, asking questions about how she had found herself there. Before long, our visit took a turn, and my excitement sunk into disappointment when she told me her husband would be joining her soon. What? Was my gaydar off? Something didn't feel right, but I accepted her answer and decided that friendship was the next best pursuit.

My new friend was a fascinating conversationalist, spiritually minded and as committed to personal growth as I was. She was a druid priestess from Washington state, her rituals had already amassed some popularity. Wren had experience in shamanism. Nature was her true love, so every event she held was outdoors.

In December, I attended her big Yule gathering in a snowy meadow. It was very magickal! After six months of sharing rituals and workshops together, she came over to say good-bye. She was leaving for a job in Buffalo, New York. My heart sank. We never lost touch though; I made sure of that.

When Wren came back that August, I could tell something big was changing inside her, but I didn't know exactly what. I was not sure that she knew yet either. She invited me to do a Norse rune study series with her. During this time, things shifted between us. By November, she had moved out of her marriage and was sharing her deepening feelings for me. I allowed my heart to fully open to this woman. I fell in love. In fact, I went crazy over the top. I was ecstatic to have met my spiritual match. I felt we were on the same page about our pagan path, leadership, and community!

Then the unexpected happened: she came over to tell me that on the inside she was a man and planned to live that way. At first, I thought she meant that she intended to live out her masculine tendencies as a lesbian. This was not the case. She intended to totally transition into a male, leaving her female identity behind. My head began to swim— what was happening here? I couldn't wrap my mind around this information. I felt like she was leaving, and I didn't want to lose the woman I had come to know and love. Love demanded that I stay and support her. My heart was already given. How could I turn away now? My heart ached as if my girlfriend was leaving me for a man, a man who was locked away inside her!

Wren began counseling. I supported this process by attending often. These sessions continued until the therapist decided that Wren was ready to fully embody his new identity. In 2008, it was legal to have a civil union between same-sex couples, and so in June we were legally joined as a same-sex couple in the state of New Hampshire. Initially, Wren wanted to wait until he was legally a man, but I wanted to honor who we were and my lesbian journey, so he obliged me.

Later that summer, he was scheduled to have top surgery. I couldn't believe it. I was devastated. I felt that I was losing the woman I loved; Wren was dismantling her before my very eyes. Although nothing in my life experience had prepared me for this transition, I wanted to be strong and supportive for him, so I pushed my feelings aside and witnessed as this shaman shape-shifted from one gender to another. Body hair grew within a few months of taking testosterone; his muscle tone, his voice, and even his smell changed. Once Wren became legally male, we married again in September, in the state of Maine. Now we could slip by as a heterosexual couple, no one the wiser.

Within a year, Wren was a man and became Wrentek, quickly learning to navigate his new life. It took me longer because his changes were so continuous I could barely keep up. His sexual appetite grew, and how he expressed it changed as well. His consciousness also expanded. Upon reflection, I realize that I had been growing along with him. My lesbian identity had broadened to include my attraction to a man.

When Wrentek first wanted to explore BDSM, I was mortified! Why would any survivor of abuse do that? I tried to explore by reading information on the internet. I even talked to a friend who had an abusive past and chose to participate in impact play with floggers. She told me that this process shifted something for her. It was then I decided I'd give it a go but slowly: I first just wanted to observe impact play at parties, which I did.

Then one evening we attended a play party where I decided to have my first experience with impact play. Wrentek took me to the St. Andrew's Cross. My vision went black as someone tied a blindfold over my eyes. My clothing was stripped away, and I stood naked. I felt someone wrap smooth ropes around my wrists. My hands were hoisted upward, above my body, knotted firmly. Someone guided my hips to the cross. *Thump! Thump!* I felt the even rhythm of a flog thumping my back. I felt myself morphing as if I were on a medicine journey. At one point, my body collapsed, hanging there by my wrists. I felt Wren's warm hands releasing my bonds. Afterward, I felt drunk. I couldn't walk. I was helped to a soft seat with blankets to recover. That was my first experience of subspace. It was an extraordinary shamanic state. I realized this wasn't just kinky play but a shamanic healing practice.

My relationship style is also one of my spiritual practices. A few years into Wrentek's transition, someone came up to us at a community event and asked if we were monogamous. I answered yes, but Wrentek had a different answer: he was unsure. I was shaken by the response and felt a vibration in my core. I wondered what was true. We had talked about this before we got married, so why the change of heart? Over time, I came to realize that he was not only changing physically but also on every dimension of being. He was questioning everything! As he shape-shifted, Wrentek was reweaving his deepest beliefs and assumptions. I realized that when my partner changes, so do I. My assumptions about marriage and commitment were being challenged. I had to ask myself: Are these assumptions true for me or just ingrained from societal structures? Though difficult, this experience opened me, giving me permission to seek a deeper truth.

At first, we explored opening our relationship in controlled settings like play parties, where I could experiment with certain agreements. After he had some experiences with other people, we decided to open our marriage completely, although, I will admit, my heart and head were not always in alignment with this decision. In the end, I feel that it helped us to expand both our minds and our emotions.

In May of 2014, my beloved went to California to start his journey with ISTA. Every day, he'd call to check in with me. He was so clear and beautiful. I felt his energy opening and shifting in ways I had never known possible. All our prior work in shamanism didn't touch the sexual wound that was finally being challenged and healed. It became clear that I needed to take this journey myself.

I did Levels 1 and 2, back-to-back, in Ireland. It felt like my neurological system was being rewired, and I was downloading new ways of being and thinking, filling in gaps of missing information, shaking up and rearranging my identity on every level. ISTA has since taken me on adventures traveling to Costa Rica, Guatemala, Montreal, and Israel. Each training is new, and it is never the same experience, not only because the flavor of each container is different but also because every journey brings new insights and liberation. There is no match for my connection to this tribe and the life-changing work we do!

I continue to work hard on myself, taking the priestess path and apprenticeships to discover my blocks around sexuality so that I can become my truest self and help others.

Presently, I am immersed in the role of organizing for ISTA. I'm excited to be bringing it to New England, where I currently live and work as a massage therapist, seeing four to five clients a day, four days per week. When I align into the vibration of the land, I sense suppression from puritanical thought embedded in the stone. I believe that healing needs to happen here to clear the embedded pattern so that liberation may happen for all. The American pioneers started here in the Northeast, so perhaps true freedom can spring from this sacred work spreading coast to coast.

Sexual shamanism is about bringing in a different consciousness to one's relationship with sexuality. It requires rewiring and transforming the deeply seeded identification and returning to the original identity with sex as sacred. My witchcraft community doesn't say much; I think sexuality is taboo even among pagans. However, I have connections to tantric community and kink that allow space for exploration.

I also discovered that I love being sexually dominant. I use my power as a priestess to take people on a dark shamanic journey toward healing and transformation. I teach men that serving an actual goddess is much more fulfilling than their fantasies of serving a goddess. Service can come from a place of mindful presence. Having worked with me, some submissives become altogether different people. The changes can be profound. One man I worked with became free of a life of alcohol and continues to grow and heal. Another has developed his divine masculine by holding space and mindful presence for women. I'm honored to have helped to aid the transformation of others in small and large ways.

Through power play, I met a man who became my submissive for a good, long while. I was touched that such a powerful man would allow himself to be put under my control. During the time we shared, I embodied the goddess and priestess for him, while he helped me rewire my own experience of the healthy inner masculine. Our journey together was magickal, spiritual, and there was love. It surprised me that I could love with deep intimacy someone other than my husband. I could have another beloved. Our relationship transformed from dominance and submission into a different way of relating: companionship and mutual opening. Yet another transformative experience.

This lover saw there was something I was to bring forth into the world and thus chose to support me not only emotionally and mentally but also financially. He sent me to ISTA trainings and took me to HAI workshops and pujas. We had two lovely years during which we were both challenged and grew, but I couldn't give him enough time. He needed more and met another woman who was already polyamorous, but I wasn't able to adjust to this new arrangement, so I needed to love him enough to let him go.

Wrentek and I have since continued exploring shamanism, polyamory, and power play, both together and independently. I am forever grateful for his help in my awakening. Through the years of our journey, he held space and bore witness as I unpacked multiple layers of ancestral story and judgment imprinted in my psyche. Without his calling to spiritual sexual work, I may not have unraveled, rewired, and moved from my past into who I am now.

I am blessed with many gifts. I see and sense patterns particular to the ancestral tapestry. I bring awareness to what is being held in people's emotional, mental, physical, and spiritual bodies. I have the gift of empathic resonance. My ability to feel others, has been painful at times. Perhaps, I am a wounded healer, but I'm willing to spend time looking at my shadows and facing my darkest demons. I believe that our lives affect those yet to come, and this motivates me to repattern myself. I work with my ancestors to heal the future.

By calling upon the ancestors of flesh, blood, bone, and of the land, I ask for guidance to help restore balance. There are deep cellular imprints from the past seven generations. The intention is to bring these vibrational patterns into alignment now, in the present moment, for only in the present can we cast healing into future generations.

Matooka MoonBear is an initiated High Priestess in both the Feminine Mysteries and Temple of Witchcraft Traditions. The Temple is a center of magickal training and personal development in Salem, New Hampshire. She is a ritualist, intuitive, practitioner of alternative healing, and diviner. She lives in New Hampshire with her husband and is an organizer and faculty apprentice for ISTA.

Charging the Crystal Cavern

PURPOSE: Crystals can draw out negative energies that can get stored in soft tissue. Using crystals in your yoni and/or anus can increase libido, strengthen the pelvic floor, improve muscle control, heal trauma, and lead to more pleasurable sex.

PREPARATION: First, source your special crystal. You can find gemstone dildos, butt plugs, and jade eggs at gem shows, New Age crystal shops, or online. Choose the crystal and shape that is best for you. Rose quartz promotes self-love, and amethyst increases intuition. The Taoist traditionalists prefer jade eggs. It is less about the specific tool and more about your connection to it and the meaning you make of this ritual.

Cleanse your crystal by soaking it in a glass of hot water. (Be careful not to overheat and crack the crystal.) You can add three to five drops of either food-grade hydrogen peroxide, tea tree oil, or grapefruit seed extract or spray it with colloidal silver, but do not use soap. Rinse and air dry.

If you are using an egg with a drilled hole, thread about one meter or one yard of unwaxed dental floss through the hole and tie a knot so that you can pull it out like a tampon.

Next, massage your crystal wand or egg with your favorite lubricant.

PROCESS: There is a range of methods for crystal healing that spans traditional Taoist practices to modern celebrity day spas. As always, use your intuition and do what feels right for you. What follows are some best practices.

Connect your heart and your pelvis with breath. Allow yourself to connect with your yoni or anus. Massage your breasts and open your heart. You can massage your external genitals, inner thighs, and perineum.

When you're ready, massage your opening with the large end of the egg (or the small end of the wand) and find a comfortable angle. Exhale as you gently insert it into your cavern.

Relax and smile as you visualize healing energy rising toward your heart. Try undulating your hips and feel all the new sensations.

For yoni healing, gently contract your vaginal muscles at least nine times for three sets to help circulate heart energy and release negative energy that does not serve you.

If you climax, practice drawing that energy into your heart.

When you feel complete, push the egg downward with exhalations until it exits or can be pulled out easily.

If the crystal comes out early, that's okay. Listen to what your body is telling you. Laughing, sneezing, or coughing can unexpectedly eject an egg. Discontinue if you feel discomfort or any adverse effects.

VARIATIONS: Amara Charles recommends a dreamtime practice of inserting a jade egg before going to sleep and removing it in the morning. She recommends doing this for at least seven consecutive nights to stimulate your internal awareness. Other healers recommend inserting the crystal first thing in the morning and keeping it in for 20 minutes during the day.

NOTES: This practice is not recommended if you are pregnant or have an intrauterine device.

RESOURCES: Amara Charles offers sexual restoration courses and teaches yin way jade egg practices.

16

EMBODIED ENDARKENMENT

By Janine Ma-Ree

Wild Rose Photography

YEAR OF BIRTH: 1965

SUN SIGN: Virgo

HOMETOWN: Inverell, Australia

RESIDENCE: Gilgai, Australia

ARCHETYPE: Mystical womb witch

SUPERPOWER: Ritual magick

SHAMAN TOOLS: Breath, sound, and movement

LINEAGE/TEACHERS: Eclectic, many sources

EPITAPH/MOTTO: Follow the ecstatic current.

HOBBIES: Spending time in nature and experiencing wild innocence

Let me introduce myself
I am a wild lover of the Earth
I breathe the Earth in and I breathe myself out
I remember the wildness of my soul
In connection with the soul of the Earth
Open, alive, ecstatic, innocent, embodied
I ground in the web of life
My dark light vibrates

In sovereignty and synergy
I am but a small speck
And yet part of this powerful being of Gaia
As wild Earth lover
Where my soul being fully expressed
Breathes ecstasy into the web
And we breathe as one

As a born mystic, I've always been attracted to all that I saw as religious and spiritual. I remember lying on the grass at five years old, getting lost in the clouds and their morphing shapes, wondering about the meaning of life and noticing that as each second and minute passes, I would never experience this moment again, or this moment or this . . .

I briefly contemplated entering religious life, but I also longed to find "the one"—to marry and have children. Deep within, I had a soul longing for more. Knowing it was out there, I was seeking, questioning, wondering, and feeling frustrated in the search. This longing was relegated to the shadows, the unconscious, struggling to get to the surface.

I grew up in a conservative country town in Australia, attending a Catholic school and living a secure, stable life in a small community, with the traditional values of my lineage, which went back at least four generations. As far back as I can remember, I felt the cage of my conditioning and my desire to break free—but free from *what* I did not know.

My life followed a traditional path: falling in love, suffering heartbreak, riding the waves of romantic fantasies, marrying young, becoming pregnant, and having children. When my womb carried new life, growing within, I got my first glimpse of embodiment, a feeling of being deeply connected in my body, which would later become foundational to my life and my life's work. Loving the connection, opening, and awakening from within, I heard whispers of the primal, whispers from Earth.

Three weeks before I birthed my firstborn, my father unexpectedly died of a heart attack.

My father was a strong presence in my life, embodying sacred masculine qualities such as presence and protection. When he was around, I had the sense that everything would be all right. He held a stable, still point for me and my family, and he could lovingly cut through bullshit and penetrate chaos with clarity.

With him gone, I needed to ground myself. My life spun out of control, and my world fell apart. My beliefs shattered, my heart broke, and I was overwhelmed by confusion, grief, anger, fear, abandonment, and betrayal of all that I thought to be true and real. This existential crisis was a jarring crack in my reality that would ultimately lead me home.

I can see now that my life had always been leading me down the dark path of descent. I studied naturopathy and became a holistic practitioner. I threw out traditional religion and pursued New Age philosophies, thinking I was on a path of ascension going to the light, but all the while it was part of my path down.

After many years working in alternative medicine, I decided to write a "book about everything." I called it *The Clearing Generation* and included in it my perspectives and philosophies on many aspects of healthful living, topics such as meditation, emotions, healthy eating and lifestyle practices, ascendant New Age philosophies, how to shift limiting beliefs, and more. And of course, I even signed the last page "love and light."

A month after the official book launch, the universe gave me another swift kick. I met a man who oozed with animal and primal energy. He walked through my defenses, broke through my cage, and revealed to me that my book about everything had left out quite a large piece: sexuality. And so the dark path of descent gained momentum.

I started exploring embodiment. I learned about conscious self-pleasuring and connecting with my body, emotions, soul, and spirit. I immersed myself in the temple arts, sexual mysteries, emotional release, and body-based healing workshops and books, dearmoring my yoni and my heart with the assistance of various practitioners.

I met with like-minded pioneering explorers, and together we dissolved generations of conditioning and broke new territory in somatic, emotional, and sexual healing. We were down in the trenches getting dirty together, creating deep containers for exploration. With other warriors of love, I journeyed into the heart, riding the intensity of unburying a lifetime of emotional blockages, suppressions, and repressions.

Along the way, I discovered a frozen, frightened part of me buried under all the mud and grit—too scared to even breathe, contorted and constricted from trying to fit into a box of outer and inner expectations. Embedded in me was the belief that at my core I was flawed.

As I connected with myself, I learned to hold my tender vulnerability, to let my body shake and tremble. I learned to slow down and gently listen. Gradually, bit by bit, this frozen part of me started to thaw. My blood warmed, my heart opened, and ecstatic feelings started to bubble up and emerge. My life force, which had been so shut down by cultural and religious conditioning, began to awaken.

I attended the first ISTA Sex and Consciousness Conference ever held in Australia, more than a decade ago, at Warburton, Victoria. A global tribe of thirty-five pioneering spirits emerged from cities, towns, metaphorical caves, and the bush, unknown to one another. They were practitioners, facilitators, teachers, and others, coming together for the first time. The one thing we had in common was that we all felt the upwelling of the sexual life-force energy that was ready to move in the world, when it was still in the shadows, in the unknown. Opening to an integrated life and love, to an ecstatic current, we felt the joy of being part of something bigger than ourselves, the next wave of evolutionary change on the planet.

One of the most influential teachers in those earlier years was Baba Dez Nichols. I remember the first time I heard him speak at the Warburton conference. He spoke about masculine and feminine energy being inside each of us, regardless of gender. He spoke of the life force, sacred marriage within, and how guilt, shame, and fear block the flow of the life force in our body. I felt each word resonating in every cell in my body. I could feel the life-force energy he spoke of being transmitted into my body.

A year before that, I had the experience of meeting Peruquois, a feminine soul singer, and hearing her sing. Peruquois brought the core of Earth through her body and her voice, and she showed me how to bring sound from my womb and activate my own life force. Until then I hadn't met people as embodied as these two. I didn't know what I didn't know, but I knew I wanted embodiment.

A few years later, having matured into my own embodiment practices, I had the honor and privilege of facilitating my first ISTA Spiritual Sexual Shamanic Experience with founder Baba Dez and Bruce Lyon. Bruce brought his wealth of experience and mystery-school teachings into the field. Sharing the temple arts from an ever-deepening embodied place, I felt the power of this worldwide tribe of leaders coming together to manifest ISTA's vision and create something bigger than us. As we grew and learned, we transmitted our realizations to one another, each of us contributing the best of what we had to the synergy of the whole.

ISTA was developing from an organization into an organism, pioneering new relational models and new ways of living. I could feel the teachings that wanted to come through us, teachings that transcended any individual or philosophy. They came from the core of the mystery, from the void itself. I also witnessed the transformation of those who joined us on this journey as they became fully embodied human beings—more loving, alive, integrated, and openhearted.

We had no idea what the cost of our explorations would be in a world so fearful and contracted about anything having to do with sexuality or freeing life-force energy. At the same time, we felt an undeniable soul pull that gave us no other choice. Out of the foundation laid down by those who came before us, we watched seeds of spiritual sexual shamanism sprout and begin to grow into the rich field that it is today.

I have seen the field of temple arts evolve through many changes, going through a continual growth and maturation process. I have seen the power of sexual energy being wielded in courageous and cutting-edge ways in the ISTA trainings. Together we bring collective, repressed energies into the open and work through the inevitable shadows that accompany them.

The most significant change I have experienced is the emergence of feminine energy in a field where masculine energy had been more anchored, through ritual, teachings, and reflected in the empowered feminine coming into the faculty and lead faculty circles, held and supported by the masculine. This process is still happening in the week-long transformative experiences ISTA offers in communities and temples around the world. Members of the ISTA tribe continue to deepen and integrate their connections with one another on their journey together.

In the past few years, I have served on ISTA's governance circle, a group of three pioneering people who make decisions by listening and inviting love to reveal itself. This model, not based on existing structures of democracy, consensus, dictatorship, monarchy, or corporate hierarchy, is still revealing itself through us. It is alive and dancing with the life force that is the ISTA organism itself.

For me, one of the most potent things about this path is that it is one of remembering. My deepest learnings have come from the path of descent: descending into the body, into the dark recesses of myself, feeling the heights of ecstasy grounded in the depths of the dark, opening the remembering of my soul and accessing the void, so creation could move through me.

My first descent occurred in a ritual space with a beloved friend, mentor, teacher, and soul sister. As I felt myself starting to descend, the stories of fear began running in my head. All of my Catholic conditioning got activated, telling me that descent was the path to hell. I later found this to be true, that Hel was an earth goddess. As I moved through the fear, out of being run by the story in my conditioned mind and into trusting my experience, I descended down, down, down.

Shamanically connecting with Earth and descending into the depths of Earth, I discovered a sacred, compassionate, loving, earthy womb space, beyond anything I had ever imagined or experienced.

The first time I connected with this energy I was truly pissed off. Pissed off that I had listened and believed the stories I had been told. I discovered that the stories I had been told about the dark being evil and a place of punishment were not the dark at all, but distortions of the dark. The darkness I experienced was a place beyond these distortions, a place of deep sacredness. I found holiness in the true energy of the dark, a feeling of deep compassion, groundedness, embodiment, abundant life force, power, and love and an awakening of my sexual, primal life force. I found a place rich in primal archetypal energies, magick, and mystery, deeply infused with spirit and love. Through endarkenment, I found the other half of my soul. I discovered the vastness of the void, the depths of love, and the most unrealized energy of all, the dark light.

As my connection with Earth deepened, I expanded, integrated, and embodied my masculine aspect as well. I noticed how integrating and embodying his capacity to hold my feminine with deep awareness, presence, love, strength, and clarity supported me to explore my passion and soul work: the remembrance and evolution of the feminine mysteries. In particular, I started to access teachings and remember the truth about womb blood and its connection with the lunar cycles and life currents.

For many women, the only awareness of having a womb is during childbirth or when experiencing menstrual cramps and other gynecological issues. But the feminine mysteries, rituals, archetypes, and earth medicine traditions practiced in matriarchal times are reemerging to consciously reactivate the collective womb.

In my own life, this activation manifested as I remembered, in an embodied way, the feminine initiations of menstruation, birth, menopause, and death. I remembered the difference between a disconnected womb that had shut off from its true power and an activated womb that was connected to the feminine, Earth and her ancient, primal wisdom. Teachings came forth revealing the map of the Holy Grail and the portals that we access through an activated womb that take us through the feminine gates to the cosmic womb, the void, the great nothingness that holds the potential for everything and from which all creation is birthed.

As I deepened with this journey, an incident in my life took me back to the existential wound triggered by my father's death all those years ago. I had moved through many waves and layers of grief over the years, but I hadn't allowed myself to feel the betrayal and abandonment that was beyond my father: the betrayal and abandonment by God.

This core soul wound was the ultimate descent. I felt the scar tissue rip open, bit by bit, as my heart felt all the hurt and pain of my separation from the Divine.

This journey opened me to my mystical connection to divine infinite love sourced from within, the twin flame. This genuine union emerged not from a place of platitudes and spiritual bypass, but from an embodied descent into matter. I was no longer looking for love outside myself.

Through this experience, I discovered that betrayal is one of the most powerful initiations for the feminine. The feminine is about living as love and experiencing love. She is about relation, connection, bonding, and attachment. Her soul journey is to know herself as love, and her heroine's journey is to become enmeshed in love external to herself until love finally betrays her.

As I had seen firsthand, the betrayal wound is experienced in the feminine as being staked in the heart, at which point she can either contract or open. The latter option allows the stake to be driven right through her heart, activating it until it cracks open with love and she unites with her inner twin flame.

A key to uniting with the beloved is connecting with the mystical quality of longing. Just like other feminine qualities such as attachment, home, and depth in relating have been misunderstood by the more masculine ascendant philosophies that value nonattachment, emptiness, and freedom, the feminine quality of longing has perhaps been misunderstood the most.

Pure longing comes from the depths of the womb and the heart; it is a yearning of the soul. The womb holds the full physical force of the feminine power.

In restoring my connection within and being in communion with the Divine beyond, I discovered the path of the mystic. The heart longs for the Divine as the beloved, to be penetrated by presence, penetrated by life, to be one with the Divine—that which breaks the heart open into rapture, ecstasy, and bliss.

Not only can sexual energy be expressed as love, creation, seeding, birthing, manifestation, healing, pleasure, transmission, and connection with another; I discovered a deeper place in the mystic journey, the Divine as a lover and sexuality as prayer.

My greatest learning has been how to source myself from the void and connect with the energy that arises from that place that guides my life—the ecstatic current. This is a place beyond polarities, beyond opposites like good and bad, light and dark, right and wrong, masculine and feminine, fear and desire, spirit and matter.

Collapsing polarities means reentering the Garden of Eden and living from a place of wild innocence, aware of duality but living in an integrated way, not polarized by duality. I see this as the ultimate soul journey, with wild innocence as the key.

I have learned how to release emotional blocks in my body that have resulted from cultural conditioning and polarized views, using embodied emotional release practices and shamanic rituals that free the ecstatic current in my body and allow it to flow from the void into all areas of my life.

My life intention now is to live in flow with the ecstatic current, from wild innocence, in sovereignty, synergy, and sacredness.

I experience sovereignty as a place of connection between myself and the beloved within, where I can discern from a place of love and freedom what my unique expression of authentic relating looks, sounds, and feels like beyond labels. I experience synergy as loving interrelatedness and connection flowing through a network of other sovereign beings also moving from this place, inclusive of all relating styles. Instead of relationship dramas playing out as a result of polarization and emotional blocks trying to release and resolve themselves, gifts, love, creativity, archetypes, wisdom, and resources are transmitted and shared through this interrelated network of sovereign beings moving as one organism through the principle of divine synergy.

From this field of love, where people are living from their sovereignty and in synergy with one another, sacredness is birthed—the sacredness of being fully in the moment, the sacredness of feeling moment by moment what wants to be created and birthed, the sacredness of life being fully lived and expressed.

After endarkenment, chop wood, carry water.

After continuing to live in the town of my lineage with my life partner and three children, I felt the call to live in nature, in the wild. I went on an exploration of many different places and communities that I had liked being in over the years, knowing that there was a piece of land calling me that would determine where I lived next. I went full circle and discovered that the piece of land I was seeking was close to where I had lived for most of my life.

I currently live on the Red Earth, which is about 125 acres of wild land. It is covered with Ochre (also known as Gaia's moon blood) and has a womblike canyon through the center. Its wildlife includes kangaroos, echidnas, snakes, spiders, birds, goannas, insects, bacterial and fungal networks, and the odd hidden koala. The area is also rich in sapphires, crystals, diamonds, and, in the past, tin. The history of this land is that it was taken, staked and claimed, and raped through years of tin mining. For decades, since the mining ceased, the land has regenerated itself with ecstatic life force and wild innocence. Not a naive innocence, but one that comes from the devas and elementals and natural ritual spaces. Old mine shafts are now altars to the center of Earth, and every day I receive gifts and teachings from nature.

I see sexual shamanism as an integrated spirituality that includes earth-based medicine, embodiment, and nature cycles; rather than transcending the body, it brings spirit into matter as a lived and embodied present-moment experience. It includes the dark as well as the light, life-force sexual energy, and embodiment.

The vision of this land is to support the descent into deeper connection with Earth and the journey of embodying spirit in matter, to awaken the wildness of the soul though connection with the wildness of nature. This is a place to open into freeing kundalini life-force energy, accessing the power of the dragon, connected through the flame of an open heart. The Red Earth is a place to delve into the feminine mysteries and learn how to connect with the wild and primal, and it is a place for me to celebrate love and life with my tribe.

I spend my time immersed in the land, offering sessions, intensives, and Red Earth Temple apprenticeship journeys. I also spend time traveling to different lands, temples, and places in the world, facilitating as lead faculty with the International School of Temple Arts and deepening with beloveds from a place beyond labels.

Let me introduce myself
I am the being of Gaia
Reflected in this body of water
In this ant, this blade of grass, this tree
I am the being of Gaia and I sing to you
I sing to you the ecstatic song of the soul of Earth
My dark light vibrates
I have been waiting for you, wild earth lover
I welcome your unique soul expression
I breathe you in and I breathe me out
And as I breathe you in
I embrace you ecstatically
In sacred union with the web of life
And we breathe as one

Janine Ma-Ree, the founder of Red Earth Temple, teaches sacred sexuality and feminine womb mysteries. She is lead faculty with ISTA and draws on more than twenty-five years experience as a holistic health practitioner, presenter, author, facilitator, and transformational guide.

EMBODIMENT EXERCISE 16

Moon Blood Ritual

PURPOSE: Moon blood connects us to the mysterious cycles of life and death. When women bleed, their intuitive powers are heightened, and they are connected to all of humanity. When menstrual blood is used in ritual we can access the magic of the divine feminine and reconnect with the wisdom of Earth. Moon blood contains minerals and nutrients that are enriching for the soil.

This ritual is especially healing for anyone who's been taught that menstrual blood is dirty, ugly, or shameful. By breaking this taboo, we can reclaim the sacred. Your intuition is more important than the specific steps of how this ritual is performed.

PREPARATION: If you are in a body that does not bleed, you can do this practice with a lover or a sister. Begin by watching how the lunar cycles may or may not match your own menstrual cycle. Embrace all the stages of the moon, including PMS, cramps, emotional fluctuations, spotting, bleeding, and everything in between. Self-reflect on any negative associations you may have with menstrual blood.

With reverence, during your cycle, begin to collect your menstrual blood. Alternatively, if you are not bleeding, find a woman who is willing to share her menstrual blood for this ritual. You can use a mooncup, which is a soft medical-grade silicone cup that is an eco-friendly alternative to tampons or pads. Or you can bleed into a sponge or tampon, add a teaspoon of purified water, and squeeze it out into a chalice.

Select a space that has meaning for you for your ritual. This can be done in the woods, in your garden, or in your lover's front yard. Or you can even use a potted plant.

PROCESS: This ritual can be done day or night, but it is most potent when performed during the new moon or full moon phases. Blood can be kept in an airtight container in the refrigerator if you want to wait for the perfect time and place.

Set an intention for yourself and your community: release anything you want to surrender, and manifest whatever you desire, as long as it's for the highest good of all.

Hold the chalice up to the sky with your prayers and slowly pour the moon blood into the earth. It is believed that when we feed our blood to a plant that bears fruit or vegetables, the imprint of our DNA can alter the nutrients produced by that plant so that it better supports us and helps our systems to thrive. It can be seen as a synergistic biofeedback loop.

VARIATIONS: Bleed directly onto the earth and think of your ancestors sitting in red tents on straw piles or around dirt holes they dug with their hands. You can also use the moon blood to anoint the third eye and heart chakra, or use it like warpaint on your lover's face. You can build an altar that is specifically dedicated to calling down energies from the moon. Use your moon blood like paint and make a mandala with natural items. No matter how you choose to do your ritual, remember to be gentle and pamper yourself. Moon time is a special time to slow down and tune in.

RESOURCES: If you're interested in collecting your moon blood, these products are sold online and make great gifts: DivaCup, iCare, Mahina Cup, Pixie Cup, InStead Softcup, and Blossom.

IT'S ALL STORY

By Baba Dez Nichols

Carl Theriault

YEAR OF BIRTH: 1956

HOMETOWN: West Los Angeles

RESIDENCE: New Zealand, Australia, and Sedona, Arizona

ARCHETYPE: Sacred clown

SUPERPOWER: Love

SUN SIGN: Aries

LINEAGE/TEACHERS: Julien Canuso, Charles and Caroline Muir, River and Diamond Jameson, the earth, desert, jungle, and ocean

EPITAPH/MOTTO: Love is fully aware, fully present, and totally out of control!

SHAMANIC TOOLS: Vitamix blender, a Hawai'ian nose flute called Pu'u, Voyager Tarot deck, and Presence

HOBBIES: Making love, cooking, playing volleyball, diving, hiking, and enjoying fine wine

I've encountered many mystical experiences on my path. Swimming in the ocean, putting my hands in the earth, disassembling societal programming and receiving support from living and disembodied masters are just a few of the more formative encounters that come to mind. And I'll start this with the first time I realized the true power of making love.

I was living in Hawai'i, growing coffee, vegetables, and pot. I moved to the islands from California at age twenty-two. I lived on a farm with a friend whom I knew from high school. We used to sing together in the concert choir.

His three-acre farm was part of a thriving alternative hippie community in the rain forest of Kona. While living there, I developed a deep bond with the jungle, the ocean, the people, and the earth. The whole environment supported me out of my head and more into my body. I fell in love with life.

During that time, I worked at a local cooperative, delivering fresh produce from our land. There was a woman with long, dark hair named Connie who ran the café. We had a lot in common, like cooking. We had intense chemistry and a natural physical connection.

I remember one time, at her place, making love for an extended period of time. It was very hallucinogenic, like a drug experience. I was blown away.

Afterward, we lay silent, breathing in the afterglow. Once I could start speaking again, I told her how my being was activated while making love. I shared about the connectivity of all things on Earth and to the cosmos. How I felt my life-force energy in an embodied way, and that it felt like some kind of a remembrance and transmission. I spoke of power, magic, and the potential of sexual energy. How, with the right training and intention, making love could be a potent force to cultivate and harness.

As I was sharing, she went silent. She had a worried look on her face, then looked at me like I was crazy and said, "This is really weird. You're freaking me out."

A part of me thought, *Oh my God, what am I doing? Am I crazy? I can't believe that we didn't experience all of this together! Should I stop talking about this? Is she going to be okay?*

Still, another part of me felt, *This is absolutely amazing. I've got to track this further. Maybe I am tapping into another realm of consciousness and extraordinary reality.* Whatever it was, it was powerful. Why isn't sacred sex ritual a part of what we are taught about in ordinary culture?

Connie's fearful reflection reinforced my belief that not everybody is ready to delve into sacred sexuality. We are living in a culture where people are steeped in guilt, fear, and shame around sex. So I manufactured a story that I could not be met.

All my life, I've been telling myself stories about who I am, what life is, who people are, what the planet is, who's in power, and who's in control. And I'm not the only one. All of us constantly tell ourselves stories that create internal fear, abandonment, and suffering, reinforced by the stories we hear in the news and other media.

As I held onto the limiting belief that I could not be met, I kept finding evidence for it everywhere. Frequently frustrated by my business and personal relationships, I encountered a ton of judgment, shame, and fear from my family, friends, and lovers.

But at some point, I woke up to the realization that we can stop telling stories that create separation. I came to see that everything is a story! Therefore, why not start telling stories that support love, ease, and power?

I now have the capacity to radically rewrite my story. So I share my journey in the hope that it helps you awaken to the possibility of rewriting your own reality.

After my experience with Connie, I began my quest for the truth about sex and spirit. In the early '80s, there was no internet, so I started scouting local libraries for anything I could get my hands on. I already had a foundation in Christianity and Native American spirituality from my childhood and teens. Fortunately, Hawai'i hosted some pretty progressive people, so I found manuscripts on divine order, ancient Egyptian practices, Eastern and Western mysticism, meditation, Wicca, sex magic, Hawai'ian shamanism, and sacred sexuality. I read all kinds of esoteric books. The Huna teachings and practices influenced me deeply, as did tapes and books by Osho, the Indian spiritual guru previously known as Bhagwan Shree Rajneesh.

Several years down the road, I began studying with Charles and Caroline Muir, who are among the originators of the modern tantra movement in the United States. Soon, I began organizing their work-shops. They taught a lot of hatha yoga practices and breathwork. Of course, sacred spot work is their most profound contribution. Sacred spot work is a potent healing practice that (among other things) addresses sexual trauma, which is often stored in the body on a cellular level, especially in the pelvic area.

Charles would give instructions and demonstrate a sacred spot session, and then everybody would go to their private rooms and practice separately. Participants were mostly couples, but single people would sometimes join and form triads. If two couples were friends, there might be four people to a hotel room, but we didn't practice all together in the same temple space.

Afterward, the group would reconvene and report on their experiences. Both givers and receivers experienced big awakenings, memories, and healings. The power of this work was less about the technique than it was about bringing intention, consciousness, and love into hands-on sexual practices.

During these sessions, I remember being flooded with memories of ancient temples and seeing both the light and the shadow surrounding this work. I had visions of how these rituals were used for good, healing, and positive manifestation. I also had flashbacks from dark times when these rituals were misused and abused. I saw why sacred sex rituals went underground, and I felt the need to shine the light and bring the temple arts back.

But I knew these powerful practices stirred up a lot of feelings and trauma, and some people would freak out. No one really had the teachings and tools to move their emotional energy safely, and few knew how to ground the experience into deep ease. Looking back, I realize now that these were the first signs of my soul's calling to go deeper, to learn to support people in emotional integration.

After two or three years of working with Charles and Caroline, I came across a cassette tape by River and Diamond Jameson, a husband-and-wife team who founded a research, training, and coaching organization called the Total Integration Institute. As I listened to the tape with Gloria, my tantra partner at the time, our jaws dropped. We looked at each other and said, "We're gonna go hang out with these guys!"

A week or two later, River and Diamond actually came to the islands to teach, so we flew to Oahu to attend their five-day Domain Shift event. It was a wild, amazing, deep journey that combined Werner Erhard Seminars Training, gestalt therapy, and shamanic breathwork.

Coming out of the '70s, River and Diamond wore makeup and bright colors in the rock-and-roll style of Ziggy Stardust. They were part of a group of inspirational musicians and educators called the Alive Tribe, a collective of doctors, life researchers, and shamans living together. At that time, they had taken the last name of Ecstasy, but later, they changed their name back to Jameson.

Music has been a major influence in my journey. A lot of '60s and '70s musicians were powerful spiritual change agents, talking about love as the answer. Artists like Jackson Browne; Todd Rundgren; the Moody Blues; Jimi Hendrix; Pink Floyd; Crosby, Stills, Nash, and Young; and, of course, Marvin Gaye (for his song "Sexual Healing") all planted powerful seeds of change.

I grew quite close to River and Diamond. They were wonderful mentors whose shamanic tools were foundational to the awakening of my emotions. Their work offered an essential piece around the emotional body and energetics, but it didn't directly address deep sexual wounding or sexual healing the way that Charles and Caroline's work did. I became fascinated with merging these two worlds.

I asked River and Diamond about their sexual practices. Although River had studied tantra in India, and they were comfortable with it, they didn't teach it. As a couple, their model was a deep and committed relationship with high integrity. They were impeccable about not judging anybody else's relational choices or life path.

I went back to Charles and shared with him what I was learning about the emotional body and some things I felt could really make a difference for him and Caroline personally and for their teachings.

He replied, "It looks like the student has outgrown the teacher."

So I went deeper into my own process of integrating the tools, techniques, and teachings I had learned from various sources, and I began merging everything together into a more comprehensive curriculum. And thus began my life's work of evolving the temple arts on Earth.

After only a couple years on my own teaching path, I manifested my partner, Heidi, and we dove into a ten-year journey of monogamy. During that time, Heidi and I practiced a lot of sex magic and manifested a multimillion-dollar food supplement company called Pure Planet, which contributed to greater nutritional health on the planet. I'd travel around the world selling products and doing staff trainings or trade shows.

Every once in a while, someone would come up to me and say, "I see what you're doing with these products and everything, but who are you, really? What are you truly about?" It was as though they could see through the businessman and get a glimpse of something more.

That soul recognition accelerated my passion. Eventually, I realized that all the good food and supplements would never help people heal self-hatred and sexual shame, the foundations of health that matter most to me.

So I sold Pure Planet in 2001 to focus on what I really loved, which was sharing the temple arts with the world. I started by gathering as many others involved in sexual healing as I could find for the purpose of talking to one another about the temple arts. I'd say, "Hey, let's collaborate and share our skills and tools and discuss some of the pieces that could make a difference for sexual healing on a global level."

I quickly learned that people doing this work needed a deeper foundation with the emotional body and a broader understanding of who we are as human beings. I got the vision to create a place for people doing this work to come and stay. A place to learn, do the work, and offer sessions. And I would get the benefit of living with my tribe.

I invested my own labor and money to transform my ranch-style house into a nine-bedroom temple, among the magical red rocks of Sedona. It had a swimming pool, patios, fountains, and an outdoor kitchen.

I also bought a building about a block away, a garden center that used to belong to Pure Planet. I renovated it into a school with session rooms and meeting rooms. So now we had two locations; my home temple and what was to become the Sedona School of Temple Arts.

As we grew, we would rent hotel conference halls and theaters to host trainings for sacred sexual-healing work and our annual Daka/Dakini Conference. Over time, the conference became the Sex and Consciousness Festival, and the trainings became the Spiritual Sexual Shamanic Practitioner Training (SSSPT), which later evolved into the Spiritual Sexual Shamanic Experience (SSSEx).

In the beginning, we attracted a high percentage of practitioners from the escort world. These were gifted men and women, some of them true temple priests and priestesses, who didn't know how to cultivate their gifts for their highest use. No avenues existed in modern society for putting these talents and skills to use, other than for purposes of entertainment, sex, and money. In our trainings, we offered a transmission of the temple arts. We gave permission to feel what it means to live in love, freedom, and power. For many, living and working at the Sedona temple was a dream come true.

The vision was working as long as I was there onsite, but when I was traveling, it seemed others were unable to anchor the temple vision without me. I was doing virtually everything on my own, employing practitioners, inviting people to come for healing, and teaching. Seekers and spiritual teachers came from far and wide, all wanting to get something from the temple. But the practitioners I employed weren't able to *be* the temple (remember, I still had the story that I could not be met).

In 2006, I started making a film. Four years later, in 2010, *Sex Magic: Manifesting Maya* was released. Originally it was going to be a documentary about the transformative power of sexual healing, featuring various practitioners and teachers. But over the course of fifteen edits, the directors decided to follow my intimate romance story with a woman named Maya. After she left me, I was heartbroken and driven to get her back. The movie became a monumental example of how nobody could meet me, but this time, my limiting story was being played out on the big screen!

The documentary was widely celebrated and fiercely criticized. Despite winning awards at both the Philadelphia and Chicago international film festivals, people critiqued it for portraying what they judged to be black magic, sex addiction, the objectification of women, and the abuse of power, as well as for betraying traditional family values and commercializing spiritual work.

Most people, including my family and a lot of friends, didn't understand the sacredness of this work and would project their shame onto it. They would totally miss the empowerment and healing because they were focused on the sex and money.

These projections were as much a curse as a blessing. They forced me to look at my own shadow. When I would try to explain the bigger vision, I came off as overly defensive because shadow parts of me still lived in some shame. It took me years to learn to embrace and own my shadow.

Now I can freely say that I love to make love, I love sexual-healing work, and I love being paid well for my sessions.

But I still felt I wasn't fully being met in Sedona, and so I prayed for guidance about what to do and where to go. In 2007, after our book *Sacred Sexual Healing* was launched, I got inspired to travel and take these teachings out into the world. So I decided to hand the school over to a manager to work with the dakas and dakinis who would come and go.

As I started to spend more time traveling and less time in Sedona, more problems started showing up. The dakas and dakinis did good work, but still nobody seemed to hold the vision the way I did. I'd get calls about things falling apart at the temple: people breaking their commitments, negligent tenants, and cash not flowing. Then I'd return home for one or two months out of the year and breathe life back into the temple again.

I needed to be there, but my heart didn't want me there. I wanted to be out planting seeds for temples around the world, in communities like Israel, Australia, the United Kingdom, and Hawai'i. But the temple base in Sedona was floundering. It became an energy drain and a money pit, costing more to keep it open than it was earning. I felt sad and frustrated.

I had held the Sedona temple from 2005 to 2012, but eventually I knew I needed to let it go. At first, I opened it up for group ownership. I thought, *I am going to make it happen,* or rather, *We are going to make it happen, together.* I was able to get two more people interested in investing, but we couldn't find a fourth pillar to sustain the vision.

At that time in Arizona, we were facing a number of political hurdles ranging from city zoning laws to conservative neighbors to the Phoenix temple bust. (In September 2011, a SWAT team raided the Phoenix Goddess Temple, arrested thirty-nine suspects, and booked them on prostitution-related charges, but this is a story for another time.) I took these signs to mean I was to embody the teachings and go seed temples elsewhere.

Eventually, I sold the building to a beautiful man who ran a successful drug rehab center. He and his partner even took an ISTA training or two. So the physical space took care of itself: people are still healing there today and benefiting from all the love we put into it.

This transition was humbling. I knew the loss had to do with my persistent belief that I couldn't be met. I knew I had to shift this self-important story, which in a nutshell said, "As long as people don't meet me, I can continue to feel special and to be a victim. I can imagine myself separate, more evolved, and superior to them." This way of thinking is the essence of the Christ complex or the martyr trip. But the truth is, I deserve to be met, and I can be met.

Another significant thing that happened around that time was that

I reunited with Maya. After a month and a half of being lovers, we realized that being in relationship wasn't appropriate for us anymore. Although it was a steep path, I was able to keep my heart open even when we decided to transition into friendship.

For five months, I became celibate. I interrupted all my old patterns: I didn't let myself go into addiction, distraction, or other relationships. I kept holding space for my own pain and hurt and listening to my emotional body. I held myself in the places where I wanted Maya to show up for me.

In this process, my masculine essence held space for my inner feminine, my own Mary Magdalene (also known as Desiree), and this created a huge deepening of my inner marriage. When my inner feminine came online, I could finally create the external reflection of others meeting me.

Eventually, I started reclaiming everything I had projected onto the external feminine (Maya), instead of going into another relationship looking for a replacement.

As I changed my reality, all my reflections changed as well. The quality and caliber of people who came into my life took a quantum leap. More and more people started to show up and hold the temple vision with me. The change was so drastic that I was able to see, in retrospect, that people had wanted to meet me in the past, but I wouldn't let them.

Now I have amazing friends and lovers who have demonstrated that they actually have my back. Together we're standing up to a culture of guilt, shame, and fear. And not abandoning love.

As I continue to teach ISTA trainings all around the world, I see that people are embodying the teachings faster. Collective consciousness is shifting, and people are wanting to live in love, power, and freedom. Of course, I'm still learning how to show up for myself emotionally, physically, energetically, intellectually, and on other dimensions as well. I'm not willing to pretend to be special or superior anymore. In order to share power, I must be willing to receive people's love.

What I am learning now, through all the communities around

the world, and all my personal mirrors, is how to truly share power. Thousands of people in more than thirty countries are holding the ISTA vision together. I can see clearly that we must do this together, rather than acting as individuals on our own. The vision is a collective one that does not center around any personality. Temples and ashrams that are built around a guru don't work anymore. Sharing power requires a larger vision, and the success of a temple is not focused on some Baba, Osho, or Guru Ma. Rather, it requires everybody to embody his or her own divinity.

This is my new story.

I am here to co-create with other extraordinary beings. I invite anyone who is ready to live in love, power, and freedom to join us!

Baba Dez Nichols is an internationally renowned speaker, teacher, author, singer-songwriter, and transformational guide who stars in the award-winning documentary *Sex Magic*. As founder of ISTA, he supports educators, therapists, and guides into presence and mastery in all areas of well-being, relationship, and sexuality.

Inner Marriage

PURPOSE: This exercise is meant to open an ongoing dialogue between the feminine and masculine aspects of your being. The first time you do this visualization, you may find it's more challenging to see one side or the other. You may find that your male is like an angry teenager or your female is shy and coy. As you repeat this practice and continue to do this work, your inner masculine and inner feminine evolve and become more mature. You may embody more radiance and more responsibility in all areas of life.

PREPARATION: Take a relaxing bath or shower and dress your body in your favorite garments. Even though you will be doing this exercise alone, you want to prepare as if you were going on a date with your beloved. Have your journal nearby.

PROCESS: Lie down, relax, and start to breathe into the right side of your body and notice all the sensations that arise. This is your masculine channel. Visualize in your mind's eye or write quickly in your journal. Be honest. And don't judge anything that comes up.

1. What does your inner masculine look like?
2. What color are his eyes and hair?
3. What is his body type?
4. What kinds of things does he say?
5. What is he wearing?
6. What is he holding?
7. What is he passionate about?
8. What kind of lover is he?
9. How does he react to any given situation?
10. How much space can he hold?

Now drop back into meditation. Breathe into the left side of your body. Begin to feel your feminine side come alive. Ask yourself:

1. What does your inner feminine look like?
2. What color are her eyes and hair?
3. What is her body type?
4. What kinds of things does she say?
5. What is she wearing?
6. What is she holding?
7. What is she passionate about?
8. What kind of lover is she?
9. How does she react to any given situation?
10. How safe does she feel to radiate her essence?

Now that you've personified your inner masculine and feminine, are you ready to have them meet each other? Begin to visualize a beautiful place in nature, like a park or beach that is fond and familiar to you. Imagine a romantic picnic spread with all your favorite foods. Notice the details, such as what color the plates are, or the liquid in the glasses, or the flowers in the centerpiece. Invite your inner masculine and feminine to show up to share the meal together.

How do they feel about each other?

What do they say to each other?

If your inner God were to give a gift to your inner Goddess, what would it be?

If your inner Goddess were to give a gift to your inner God, what would it be?

What do the gifts symbolize?

When you've concluded the session, you can have them thank each other and say good-bye, for now.

NOTES: Many people imagine their inner feminine and masculine are going to be perfect like Hollywood movie stars. But your inner feminine and/or masculine are not the same as your ideal God or Goddess. When you do this exercise, the challenge is to hold space for whatever is real. You can revisit this exercise as many times as you like, for as long as you like.

VARIATIONS: This can be done as a shamanic journey without the journaling.

RESOURCES: Our late friend Robert Frey initiated KamalaDevi into this visualization before he crossed over, and it is reprinted with permission from *Sacred Sexual Healing* by Baba Dez Nichols and Kamala Devi.

18

BEYOND LABELS AND CREDENTIALS

By Komala Lyra

Jasmeen Hana

TRANSPERSONAL NAME: Solar Wind
YEAR OF BIRTH: 1953
SUN SIGN: Pisces
HOMETOWN: Rio de Janeiro, Brazil
CURRENT RESIDENCE: Ibiza, Spain
ARCHETYPE: Unicorn
SUPERPOWER: Being transparent

LINEAGE/TEACHERS: Kashmirian tantra lineage, Osho, Daniel Odier, and Eric Baret
EPITAPH/MOTTO: Live with passion!
SHAMANIC TOOLS: Aromas, oils, colored lights, sounds, and touch
HOBBIES: There is no such thing for me. Life is life! Full on with all there is

The magnificence of cosmic bliss was revealed to me through sexuality at a young age. Since the first time I made love, opening to sexual pleasure sparked an ecstatic current through my bones, pushing me into a universe beyond words. This experience invited further explorations that were not at all common in those days. Flashing back . . .

My parents met on a sailing trip, and I was conceived during their honeymoon, cruising the Atlantic Ocean. My father stood for intensity, freedom, and pleasure, while my mother was guided by intuition, love, and sensitivity. Fire and water! I was born in Rio de Janeiro and grew up between beaches and mountains.

My maternal grandfather left his family to work as a doctor in the Amazon's indigenous reservations and never returned. My grandmother honored his choice with dignity. Mysteriously, he came to visit me the day I was born, transmitting his connection with the spirit of the forest. Though we never met again, his courageous soul remained my innermost inspiration.

Both of my grandmothers were magical witches who spiced my life with kindness, beauty, inspiring stories, tastes, scents, and touch. As a result, I was naturally inclined to explore the arts, dancing, painting, and poetry. I dreamed of traveling abroad and living with an indigenous tribe.

As a child, the smell of sand, salt, and coconut infused sensuality into my skin. The forest and the ocean were my refuge. Surfing with a wooden board, learning to recognize poisonous snakes, and making sure there were no tarantulas in the bathroom when peeing in the middle of the night were part of my tropical education. Riding my horse at a gallop encouraged my adventurous spirit. Sitting under trees for long hours opened my intuition way ahead of my imagination. I was afraid to be called crazy, as I could not explain why I was sitting still doing nothing for so long.

I often cried for something my soul seemed to have lost, though I did not even know what it was nor how to recover it. I knew that this inner state of silent communion was going to be my only aim in life.

In my late teens, I moved to Milan to study art and design. This solo adventure was supposed to last until my graduation day, when I had agreed to return and marry my longtime boyfriend. A few days before I was to leave, I met a man who changed my life's course. What I believed would be my first and last one-night stand turned into a somersault. Within twenty-four hours, I canceled everything and decided to stay with him in Europe. We got married a few weeks later.

This potential Brazilian wife and mother-to-be suddenly became a wild lover of a renowned artist. Passion was at the core of our relationship, along with the most avid desire to live fully, without past references, fear, guilt, or shame, dancing in ecstasy and truth! Yes, I was young, daring, and living fully. Life became an inquiry into what love is.

We immersed ourselves in the world of art. Enraptured by each other's fiery personalities, we dove headfirst into experimentations with our sexuality, emotions, and life intention. We were fierce, without doubt, and naive. We were also ahead of our time in the ways we opened our bodies, hearts, and souls to an unfolding that others much later started to explore, through personal growth movements, gurus, and scientific discoveries.

We drove our Alfa Romeo sports car throughout Italy, Spain, and France. On a sunny day, while moving through the beautiful landscape of Provence, I remember singing loudly in the car, wondering, *How is it possible that so many people settle for confining labels when it is possible to live in magic?* I sang as an invincible warrior of love but with the feeling that something was wrong with me for being so different. Most often, I chose to hide, as few would understand my choices.

Though we were totally committed to our relationship, we sincerely invited other friends to share our love and sexuality. While we were living in Paris, I met a gorgeous man from an indigenous background whose magnetism attracted me in a way that was impossible to deny. He knew the power of his physical and energetic penetration, as well as the depth of silence within his own body. We started spending time together while I was learning to expand my capacity to love and be present.

One morning, we were lying outdoors, naked under the soft sun. As we both relaxed and caressed each other, his penis penetrated me very gently. He remained almost immobile, maintaining his erection inside my body for a long time. I dropped into profound silence and suddenly burst into tears. I could not justify or control it, like falling into a dark, bottomless well.

There is a moment when sounds fade into silence, forms vanish into space, and only openness remains, purity of body-heart-soul pulsing as one infinity. A powerful blast of consciousness dissolves identity into vastness. This taste of nothingness stirred my life's choices. It was like seeing a new color that no one else was able to distinguish. I wanted to live fully in this vibrant stillness, bridging passion with silence.

We kept inviting our closest friends to explore our sexuality, which inevitably provoked a wide range of emotional reactions. Even though we held our fiery love at the center, we lacked the conscious tools to sort through all the confused reactions or peel back layers of identity, personality, constructs, and labels.

Even though my life seemed perfect, there was a dark hole inside that got deeper with each orgasm—and I experienced them frequently. It was as if a portal opened, swallowing me, with subtle vibrations activated all over my body, and I was moving through an endless tunnel. I felt inexplicably alone with these new experiences, unable to share them with my friends. Sex for them was simply a pleasurable entertainment and a way to make babies.

I tried to escape alone to Greece but soon realized that what I was searching for was inside myself. I returned home to our beautiful apartment and love nest. What now?

At the end of our fifth year together, the drama of betrayal was enacted, which moved me to another stage. I invited my closest girlfriend to stay in our house and share our love. Unexpectedly, she and my husband fell in love, and they asked me to leave the house. The lack of understanding and the intensity and provocation of the circumstances, mixed with fear and jealousy, burst our dream relationship and pushed me into despair.

In tears, I decided to move to the beautiful Mediterranean island of Ibiza, off the coast of Spain, trusting the ocean would inspire me to sort out my future and refresh my heart.

The island was a unique sanctuary, an international center for freaks, artists, and musicians who lived communally in old stone houses. This environment gave me a sense of security as well as the freedom I longed

262   ◄◦►   Beyond Labels and Credentials

for; life was magic 24/7. During my first winter months, I retreated
to my new home, with no electricity or heat. I enjoyed my solitude,
bathing in water from a well, lighting candles, and making fires. Food
was abundant, and the silence was nourishing. I painted and danced,
cried and laughed, madly content, profoundly sad, releasing a rainbow
of emotions, as I burst with creativity. I designed clothes to sell in the
market and had no concerns, with more than enough money to live on.

As the spring came, encounters with soul friends happened on the
beach, at cafés and parties, or while hitchhiking. We immediately recognized one another, beyond our different languages and nationalities,
smiling widely. We were a wild tribe living together, sharing music,
drugs, lovers, and the gorgeousness of nature. Babies were born in the
ocean to the sound of drums. We were heralding a new foundation for
ourselves and for society at large.

During these years, I enjoyed sharing lovers with my closest girl-
friends, in a natural and easy way. Having different lovers at the same
time without competition or the complication of romantic projections
was relaxing. Life affirmed that emotional easiness was possible and
delightful!

A few years later, during the winter, our tribe disbanded. By then,
I had studied sustainable architecture, followed by a master's degree in
anthropology. I was still following my grandfather's footsteps, aiming to
go live in a remote place, untouched by rules and regulations.

I decided to revisit Brazil and was invited to spend a few months as
part of a documentary film about an African Yoruba tribe located on a
secluded island off the coast of Bahia. During the day, I sang with the
women while washing clothes in the river. By night, we participated in
traditional rituals, entering deep states of trance induced by music and
invocations to spirits.

As the only young white woman in the midst of polygamous
African men, I felt strong currents of sexual energy, untamed and
potent. They were totally respectful, and yet often gazes pierced my
body with intense desire. I was constantly shaking in ecstasy and fear,

bliss and intensity, past and future. The documentary and the presence of the film crew broke through the tribe's isolation, introducing their culture to the international community.

I realized that there was no way back! I could not return to Europe. With no plans for the future, I went to live in a hut near the ocean on the coast of Bahia, looking at the sky full-time, while my body kept trembling uncontrollably, as if hit by lightning. *What was worth living for?* I asked. I waited for the clouds to answer.

The universe's response to my quest was death. I got very sick as a result of making love on the banks of a river, which was clearly full of bacteria. Death and sex are essentially linked. My body was fading, while my consciousness was blissful. Someone found me lying immobile, in pain and high fever, and the local doctor announced that I had twelve hours to live. I was moved by helicopter to an emergency hospital. Once more, the taste of the void. In this in-between state, I saw my body in India—my next destination—and received the message, loud and clear!

After a couple of months' recovery, I returned to Ibiza, hitchhiked to Rome, and got a plane ticket to Bombay, now called Mumbai. I called my parents from the airport to let them know I was never coming back. I flew alone to the land of colors after giving away my possessions to my musician lover. I kept one handbag with a change of clothes and one hundred US dollars. If death takes everything away, why keep holding on?

India was an immediate remembrance. Coming out of the airport, I saw a crowd dancing and singing loudly, drums setting the pace for the procession. I joined them, elated to be in a place where people danced wildly in the midst of heavy traffic and cows. Soon, I realized that they were carrying a child's dead body on the way to cremation.

Dancing with dead bodies was not part of my refined education, and yet it taught me more about life than years in school. This new perspective invited ecstasy, life, and death to be expressed as a celebration.

In India, which I called Mamaland, life called me to another level of expansion. My body danced between beggars and prostitutes, wanderers and snake enchanters. Trains, buses, and boats led me to Goa. What I had left behind was erased, and my heart was pounding with the thrill. I lost my personality and my bearings. *Who am I?* I wondered.

In Goa, I settled under a large tree in the forest. I slept naked on a straw mat, owning no more than a few sarongs, picking up bananas and mangoes, eating chapatis when someone would offer. I made love with strangers, meeting men and women who had left society, wild and ferocious in their eccentric choices. Without future or words, I sat in awe under the stars, following the engorgement and thinning of the moon, tasting salt on my lips. I danced and danced . . .

As the monsoon season came, I started traveling randomly. I left Goa and took trains without knowing where they were going, getting out whenever someone would invite me for a cup of chai or wherever I liked the landscape. As a sadhulike woman, nobody asked me to pay for anything.

On one occasion, I got lost in a forest in a remote area in South India. A kind man appeared out of nowhere and took me to a tribe near the ocean. They did not speak English and had never seen a white woman. Everything happened through smiles and sign language. I was placed at the center of a circle of women. They were singing and dancing, and some came closer to touch me. My body started to shake, an intense tremor beyond control. I fell into a trance, which opened gateways to vivid memories of past lives. Whether these were soul imprints or hallucinations, it does not matter. I was initiated there into being real, mind lifted, unsealing the portal of infinity.

Only much later, I found out that that I was in a tantric Kali community. This experience integrated parts of my body and heart in a fresh way. I lost the sense of gravity, of my own weight, and soared above my own body for several days. Many images streamed through my consciousness, releasing memories, revealing emotions, and inspiring understanding beyond logic.

As I continued my aimless pilgrimage, serendipity led me to Pune in western India, a noisy and highly polluted city. Before I left Europe, a friend had asked me to give a hug to someone who lived in Pune. He had given me a paper with "Ashram" written on it, where his friend was living. I had never heard the word *ashram* before. I showed the paper to a rickshaw driver and went looking for someone I did not know, simply to give him a hug.

The driver took me to an unusual place, with thousands of people of all ages wearing red robes and looking wild. I went around asking for this guy I was supposed to hug, with no luck.

I stayed at the ashram for a few days, dancing in a large hall dedicated to meditation—another new word for me. A child told me it meant to be happy inside. My dancer's body was delighted to move wildly every night to the sound of live music and to meet people from all over the world who had magically ended up there. The main conversation in the air was about therapy groups, but I was not interested in blah-blah. My heart was still thirsty for a silent lover. I floated in ease, my eyes bright, saying few words, giving and receiving endless hugs, which comforted my body. *Ah!* I thought. *Here they know my language.*

And then death visited me again. I spent a month in a hospital with meningitis and strangely felt like sex and death had merged within the same empty space. In total surrender and pain, I was ready to die. Life, however, had other plans.

After a month's recovery, I returned to the ashram. My body was weak, but my intention to stay in India was fierce. While walking back through the ashram gate, I saw a car coming out very slowly. The long-bearded man sitting behind the driver looked directly into my eyes. As his eyes flashed toward mine, my heart suddenly exploded. Astonished, I fell down with my hands touching the ground. There he was, the silent lover I had been looking for my whole life. I had no doubts or questions. I didn't need to know anything else about him. I was home.

I walked toward the ashram's reception and told the woman sitting at the desk that I wanted to live there. She was not very friendly and described some formalities. I did not listen. I confirmed my intention and offered to do anything that may be requested. She ordered me to come back in a few days. I was told that the bearded man was Bhagwan Shree Rajneesh, later known as Osho.

Soon, I was invited for a ritual of initiation in Bhagwan's presence. About a hundred people were there, in a solemn gathering with intense music and dance. I was called forward. His eyes again pierced mine. He lightly touched my third eye, and ten thousand lightning bolts sparked inside my head. I could not move for a few hours and suddenly burst into laughter, which lasted a few days, almost nonstop.

I received a new name as a way to start fresh and surrender to the mystery. I asked to work in the ashram and was sent to the main restaurant to overview a group in charge of making fruit salads. A few days later, I was asked to offer massage sessions. Shortly after, I received a message from Bhagwan stating that tantra was my path.

Tantra?! Another new word. In those days, my mind did not bother to ask questions. A deeper sense of guidance took over—I just knew I was aligned inside out. I was officially invited to lead a group called Tantric Sensitivity and found myself in a room with about fifty people for a week.

Suddenly, I could see, hear, and feel energy moving inside my body and between people. I followed the flow of electric currents, inviting releases and diving into a sensitivity that inspired souls and vibrated bodies into pleasure and profound awareness. I remembered many lives where I had been trained as a tantrika. I had been ostracized, burned in the fire, and brought back onto the same path, learning to retrieve love's purity.

From there on, magic upon magic, transmission upon transmission, the skies were opening, and profound revelations relentlessly poured into my consciousness. My voice would come out unexpectedly, saying things that I had no recollection of having ever heard before. My body would move and touch others as if guided by invisible forces, clear, precise, and totally out of control. I loved those states of surprise, bliss, and vibrational sensitivity that I had only known before in utter stillness and orgasms. Now these sensations suddenly turned into interaction, responses, movements, dance, invitations, and more!

The next years at the ashram were fully engaged, resting in a samadhi tank—a healing, warm saltwater tank especially designed to reproduce a womblike feeling. I spent my time receiving massages, acupuncture, and hypnosis sessions, recognizing the conditioning that held back my love and expression, releasing fear, anger, sadness, and emotional backlogs, bathing in the wells and river, living in a bamboo hut, and eating little. I was living in paradise, with a little built-in hell to burst old beliefs and activate the inner fire.

I eventually left India in 1981 to be part of a five-year communal project in Wasco County, Oregon—the intentional spiritual community called Rajneeshpuram. Since the March 2018 release of *Wild, Wild Country,* the six-part Netflix documentary series about Rajneeshpuram, the community has been a topic of discussion and speculation. I have not seen the documentary and cannot comment on it. I prefer to have lived it. I was there from the very beginning to the very end in 1985.

In 1986, I joined Osho in India, where he had established another tantric commune, and remained there until his death in 1990. During this time in my life, I felt at home in India. There was nowhere to go. New friends felt like ancient allies. I didn't even remember that I had a family back in Brazil—as if a thousand years had passed.

The commune members were fluid, wild, intense, soft, deep, fun. We lived mostly naked in body and heart, sharing daily meetings with the master, Osho, discovering nuances of our sensuality and sexuality in a totally new way, moving through the emotions that this exploration entailed, now with more awareness and meditation. Working seven days a week, for years in a row, it was amazing to realize the powerful reservoir of energy that human beings are presented with and rarely use full blast. So much delight! Though I worked twelve to eighteen hours a day on a variety of tasks, such as managing the communal bank, laying carpets, giving massages, picking weeds in the garden, I still had more time and energy than ever. I was able to make love as if time ceased to exist.

I explored my sexuality with men and women. Bits and pieces of my personality and ideals were dissolving into joy, wild love, and the gentlest encounters, and this unpeeling was making me feel elated, lighter and lighter. Being with women enhanced my connection with my own body, sensitizing my inner organs in a different way, allowing my pleasure to disconnect from stereotypes. I realized that energy moves when there is resonance. At the core, we are pure, neutral essence, devoid of duality. Polarities alternate to generate contrast; however, energy as expressed in the continuum of life is one unending oscillation. I remembered my fascination with the Möbius as a an industrial design student when I took a course on quantum physics. Finally, I was living that loop, inside out, as a continuing flow.

For a few years, I had solid relationships, while also spending time with different lovers. Within the context of a tantric commune, that was not unusual. However, after a few years, I noticed that my ease with maintaining all these different relationships was an expression or reflection of me avoiding feeling my own reactions and needs when I stayed with one constant partner. Each one of my lovers reflected an aspect I needed to feel inside myself, and yet these parts of my inner world were spread out and not linked inside myself. *Aha!*

This period of exploration expanded the ways I expressed my inner qualities and strengthened my ability to stay present and move with flexibility, letting go of judgments and increasing discernment and compassion while embracing differences. I decided then that it was time to integrate, to face my bits and pieces with one mirror. A sharp surgery was to come.

I had a dream that I was traveling around the world. This was surprising, as I had no intention of leaving the commune.

The next night, on January 19, 1990, Osho suddenly left his body.

I remember standing silent all night as I watched the fire consume his body. I felt awe, sadness, elation, gratefulness, and other swirling emotions wrapped in this ecstatic silence. I was dancing and singing, celebrating life and death as one. This experience stayed with me as a reminder of life's fragility and inspired me to live fully.

During the following weeks, I sensed a profound connection among my friends, as if some invisible cloud had merged our hearts and we had made a compact to be responsible, to ourselves and others. We had lost our outer reminder and now were invited to stand alone. In this protective environment, I had learned to trust my own sensitivity, intelligence, and intuition and to connect with the power of my soul's purpose. It was time to leave and live this inner clarity in the world at large.

I had met a man with whom I immediately felt a profound connection. We decided to leave India and went in different directions. Destiny and intention made us meet again in Europe a few months later. During the following twelve years, we shared the most intimate conscious relationship, embracing all aspects of daily life, living deeper and deeper in alignment with our sexuality, heart, and soul.

Our relating revealed and unpeeled subtle layers of my personality. We both had already explored being with many lovers, so we had enough maturity to focus our presence and face our reactions and shadow aspects. Finally, there was nowhere to go but inside.

I had no doubts that we were to be together for life, not out of formal commitments or constraints but as a result of clarity, maturity, and all-embracing love. Our unfolding love manifested many homes and healing centers around the planet. We facilitated hundreds of educational programs, sharing what we had learned from previous years in commune life, as well as our skills as professionals in the healing arts.

The day that I entered a Venus phase, according to Vedic astrology, my beloved suddenly decided to leave our partnership and move to Europe, concluding this chapter in our lives. The shock was deepened by the death of both our fathers, and I was suddenly swept into a dark dive. Feeling that my soul had failed its love mission, I had lost my life's purpose, so it was not worth staying around. I felt like I had betrayed my soul unconsciously and could not understand how or why. I could only cry and ask for clarity.

Certain that we would be soon reunited, I stayed in California, while months passed by. I was experiencing intense grief. My unique gifts were refined through rivers of tears and cleansing identification with *love.*

I decided to *feel* it fully, not using any of the skills that I had developed around consciousness, which might relieve my sorrow, and instead let my heart rip apart.

I felt the beauty of not understanding nor trying to find out. Seeing the reality of being human helped me recognize my identification with my soul's mission to live as love. *If not for love, what am I here for?* I could not find answers. I had lost what I held as real love, and nothing else was there. Again, there was no way back.

In exhaustion, I was forced to live without any answers. Waves of silence started to wash my tears away. Love started to arise in a totally different way, not directed or inspired by others but bursting from the darkest corners, bubbling from my inner well of being.

One day, I started to laugh again, to feel the little joys, to adventure into coming closer to friends and lovers, grateful for all I had received. By then, I had integrated the arts of Ayurveda, yoga, and tantra as my daily personal and professional practice, as an alive, embodied presence to spirit. Thus, it was natural to invite others to activate their aliveness through these practices and meditations. Suddenly, all of the pieces fell into place. I could see in the dark!

I learned to move through challenges without projecting or blaming. I was able to relate without holding back my aliveness as well as to return to my own source of presence at any time. Both banks of the river of love had been united, the paradox of all and nothing.

A few years ago, I was invited to be part of ISTA, the International School of Temple Arts. As a co-creative partner in this tribe, I am honored to keep inviting new possibilities for individuals to trust their life force and recognize their creative power.

As I get older, the myth of losing sexual drive proves to be another distortion of social and moral structures. On the contrary, I feel more vibrant, free, and clear when expressing love through my body. The gratitude to all who have been part of this journey is inexpressible. My choice to love is unwavering whether it is received or not. The longer I live, the power of eros as a primordial impulse only becomes stronger and more refined.

Sexual energy is the core expression of my creative potential and a direct pathway to ecstatic states. I offer my life and body to the heights of pleasure; it is through this opening that I remember being part of immensity. I keep learning to surrender to my own aliveness beyond labels, romanticism, expectations, or internal and external criticisms.

I seed this future as pulsation through my choices, daring love, and creativity, letting my body fully throb with the rhythm of all that inspires and exhales, all that spirals and expands. I step forward to share this possibility in my own life and invite others to explore their own portals and crystal caves. I dance in poise and quiver. Oh, life—carry me free! It is impossible to let the passion die. Fire is my element; I love to burn.

The richness I am able to receive inspires others to discover their own gifts and taste the fruits of their uniqueness. My heart pierces the truth inside each person's core, and thus I am privileged to share tender moments with many beloveds. I wholeheartedly enjoy this journey with the growing ISTA love tribe, aligning with the power of spirit, alone and together, as earthbound creatures. If the price I have to pay is to be called a sexual shaman, I smile and think, it's worth it.

We are all shamans, connected with spirit by default. How could it be any different? The spirit world is right here, inside our own consciousness. Forgetfulness is the only disease. The remedy is remembrance. We came from infinity and will dissolve back into the void. Meanwhile, we are part of a cosmic reality that keeps sweeping away all of our identity tags.

Komala Lyra is a mystic gypsy, dakini, dancer, author, and lead faculty for ISTA. She is the creator of Women Who See in the Dark retreats. She facilitates intimacy, relationships, and sexuality and lives the continuum of Ayurveda-yoga-tantra. She is based in Ibiza and works internationally.

Osho's Kundalini Meditation

PURPOSE: Osho advocated active meditations for the Western world and recommended hundreds of different movement practices. This kundalini meditation has been practiced around the world for more than four decades. Daily practice increases our capacity for sensuality, physical health, and a heightened sense of aliveness. This sequence of four stages, culminating in stillness, supports releasing deep core tension in muscles and organs, as well as emotions.

PREPERATION: Create the time and space for 60 minutes of free expression where you will not be interrupted. This practice is broken into four distinct stages. It can be guided by a musical track specifically designed to support each phase.

PROCESS: Start well grounded, in standing position with your feet hip width apart. It's best to be barefoot.

STAGE 1: Shake

During the first 15-minute segment, you will shake as if the ground was moving, feeling your legs vibrating and spreading this shaking all over the body. Rather than consciously doing or willing it, allow the shaking to happen through feeling the vibration of the music. The sound penetrates the body, and the shaking can be felt from the inside. Allow the shaking to dissolve tensions and invite the life force and fluidity into your body. You may feel tingling in and around your skin.

STAGE 2: Dance

Allow the body to move authentically and freely in all directions. Eyes can be open or closed. Express the bliss of your being. Keep your body moving for the full 15 minutes. Osho says, "Come into the heart. Let the heart pulsate, let the heart sing, let the heart dance."

STAGE 3: Observe the Silence

Sit still and notice what arises. There may be clear sensations or emotions, or not. No matter what happens, keep watching; relax your inner commentary and allow the inner flow to unwind.

STAGE 4: Savasana

Simply lie down and totally relax. Finally, continue to feel your aliveness throughout the day.

RESOURCES: *Osho Kundalini Meditation* CD with perfect music timed for all four phases can be found online at the Osho website.

19
BOLT

By Bruce Lyon

Sharon Lyon

TRANSPERSONAL NAME: El Aisha
YEAR OF BIRTH: 1957
SUN SIGN: Scorpio
HOMETOWN: Auckland, New Zealand
RESIDENCE: Bay of Islands and Highden, New Zealand
ARCHETYPE: Zeus and temple mason
SUPERPOWER: Igniting souls
LINEAGE/TEACHERS: Trans-Himalayan

EPITAPH: Kneel.
SHAMANIC TOOLS: Tibetan white dragon marble phallic wand
HOBBIES: Studying cosmology, going on sacred land journeys and underwater adventures

Something in me would still like to present this life as a hero's journey, a natural progression resulting from the determined and victorious application of a loving heart and a courageous will. A more accurate metaphor, however, might be tears rolling down the cheeks of night, a lost wrestling match with the unknown, or an often-reluctant and sometimes sulky surrender to the inevitable and undeniable.

What is left of an egoic self can still show up and claim credit for the magic that occurred while it was absent, but I also take delight in the irrepressible nature of the try-hard adventurer. If he had not been so determined to penetrate the divine mysteries, I would not have been able to bring him to his knees and sing my ancient, yet timeless, song through him. He is the hands and feet of my love, and so I will let him write his-story.

It is the role of an adventurer to step beyond the limits of known civilization, to wander off the map, past the warning signs of "here be dragons." The uncharted territories that called me into their mysteries were those of sex and spirit. Actually, it was the reverse order—first spirit, then sex. The journey into spirit was a combination of the desire to escape and the desire to discover; to escape because, like many sensitive souls, what passed for family and social life was a horror to me. I sought first the natural world, and then the inner worlds when the forest and the oceans were no longer enough.

The birth of my daughter inspired my journey back down the mountain. Holding this beautiful being in my arms, my heart exploded, and I knew I needed to retrieve all the scattered bits of my soul and bring them right here, now, into this body, so that the next generation could experience this Earth as the heaven it already is. This, I often failed to do in ways that broke open my heart, but this life is a great adventure into love that I am prepared to keep failing at—forever.

There are many ways to crack the ego. My favorite is the double whammy, both cosmic lightning and kundalini, like a universal defibrillator delivering a double current to restart the heart. For me, lightning came first. My father called me Bolt, pointing to a certain reckless quality he saw in my spirit, and I felt seen, although I never felt comfortable with any identity. Introducing myself and trying to relate to other people introducing themselves was fraught with dread. Call it an overactive amygdala, a sensitive nature, or neurosis. Perhaps this is why my first love was nature, as it didn't need me to "be someone."

Looking back, I see why sex and spirit were powerful magnets because at the root of both experiences is a deep transcendence of the self. In a deep erotic encounter, there is no you and I, only the great dance sweeping both together into the mysteries of love. In deep encounters with spirit, there is the same loss, a flickering on the event horizon of the void and then the sweet release from the burden of identity. The drop slips into the ocean, and all is swell.

I wanted to be a dolphin or a tree or nothing at all because then, somehow, I'd feel connected. This thing that humans had with one another was strange to me, like the ocean living in buckets bumping into each other all the time. The container of the ego and the "handles" of identity seemed to be getting in the way of the water of the soul flowing together. Some deep part of me never bought the program, even though I learned how to survive in bucketland.

Language was the first strange initiation for me. As a child, I recall the wonder of realizing people were not able to sense each other. They had this thing called "words," which I needed to master in order to communicate what I was already saying as loudly as I could with my whole being, such as "I love you." But even that has too many identities, it is really just *love*. Love is the ocean, and as a wave, I had to learn to encase myself in a bucket and get a handle so I could tell the other buckets in the most transparent bucket language I could create that there really were no buckets.

I became a word wizard creating spells to break the great spell of separation. I want to break through the words, scatter the letters, reach straight out through the page or computer screen, and whisper with my whole being into your heart. To touch you directly, to be with you, to be you.

My educational leanings progressed from ecology to psychology, cosmology, and metaphysics. I used the escape velocity of my emotional wounding to fuel my discovery of other worlds, sometimes any other world. The spiritual mysteries, gracious as they are to genuine inquiry, did open to me. I did this through meditation and contemplation, psychedelics and plant medicines, yoga and service, poetry and pilgrimage—all sacred portals into altered states where the descent of grace arrives and the tender arms of love and beauty rock the soul in their eternal embrace.

Sexuality was also a strong call in my system, but I repressed and sublimated this for a mixture of reasons. First, I was following an ascending spiritual pathway that specifically advocated this. Second, it seemed that most sexual activity (and romantic relationships) among my peers were riddled with conflicts. Lastly, but more unconsciously, I was trying to avoid triggering my own sexual and emotional wounding.

I arrived at the university shortly after my sixteenth birthday, and within a year I was totally disillusioned. Learning here seemed to consist of applying more and more layers from other people's buckets to my bucket. I sat through lectures on calculus and rat psychology when I was really wanting to learn how to handle the suffering of alienation. I wanted the mystery teachings. *Who are we? What is the soul? How do we live in harmony with ourselves and others and the planet? What is this mysterious thing called love that keeps welling up inside me? How do I truly connect with that girl with the long blond braid in my chemistry lab who haunts my imagination?*

So, I climbed on a ship to Europe. I tried living in a kibbutz in Israel. I lurked around the pyramids, the Parthenon, and the cathedrals, soaking up wisdom from the stones, the statues, and the frescoes. I meditated and read Hermann Hesse. I lived on the beach at Crete, got drunk, and danced like Zorba. I made love to exotic women and spent time alone in the mountains and the deserts. I wrote a lot. Looking back through the veils of time, I have such love for that young man. He did not know where he was wandering and what he was seeking, but he expected to find it anyway. One day, just before my nineteenth birthday, I woke up from a rough sleep in a Paris cemetery to find a black dog pissing on me. I took it as a sign to go home. The Old World did not have what I was looking for, only the memory of it.

I took my search back to the natural world. There was something about dolphins I loved, so I decided I would go and live with them. I stayed on an island in the north of New Zealand, where I was a fisherman in the morning and in the afternoon an interspecies cetacean explorer. I would find a pod of dolphins, tie my tiller over so that the boat went slowly in a circle, and leap in the water with them. I even made a dolphin tail so I could swim like them. I recorded their sounds and played them back to them. I played flute and Mozart through an underwater speaker and made copious notes identifying their behaviors. I drummed and flashed colors at them and communicated telepathically. In general, I was an overeducated tosser. They indulged me, perhaps sensing my good intentions, and would hang out with me, penetrating my antics with their serene good humor, and then move on. One morning, I woke up in one of those states of pure joy, where every cell feels like it is bursting with life force, and went for a swim off my beach. The next minute, the water around me was alive with a dolphin pod. They leaped all around, rubbed their bodies against me. We played intimately for more than an hour.

After all my attempts to communicate with them, they had finally taught me, with their presence and their bodies, that their language was simply joy. It was a language you had to embody. I consider the dolphins my first tantra teachers.

I loved everything about the ocean: skiing on top of it, surfing the waves, diving into its depths. It mirrored the life of the ocean inside me. Of course, everyone has dreams and visions—an inner life. Learning how to listen, interpret, and speak on behalf of the inner life takes time.

Naturally psychic, I was often flooded with impressions welling up all around me. I wasn't particularly interested in being a channel for dead relatives, as they did not appear to have anything more meaningful to say dead than they did when alive. A lot of subjective experience is just noise, and I learned to ignore it. Some of it is deeply meaningful, like a dream or waking vision that's dripping with numinous power and synchronicity. These, I learned, are best kept to oneself, unpacked slowly and carefully like a treasure from beyond. Some are not personal at all but belong to the tribe. Some are the voice of the whole revealing itself to the whole.

Shamans have this kind of vision. I learned by trial and error, sharing what I should have kept to myself and keeping to myself what wanted to be shared. I found the heart to be the organ of discernment. The heart knows when the bird of the soul needs to sing.

I also had training. In my life, many of my most significant teachers have not been personally embodied but archetypal. The advantage of this was that I didn't have to deal with their human foibles, while the disadvantage was that I didn't get modeling on how to deal with my own.

In my early years, I was self-taught and actively rejected what I perceived as guidance from any source outside myself, loosely defined. My first formal shamanic training was kinesthetic, meaning that I received my training through my body, through feelings and inner visions.

It began one night in my late twenties when I found myself sleepwalking with intent. I was reaching into my wardrobe for a sleeping bag with one hand and had a bottle of water in the other. My ordinary consciousness was shocked when I woke up. What was I doing? An inner voice responded clear and calm: *You are going to this beach to spend the night.* The voice presented me with an image of the beach I should go to. Who was this voice that had such a clear intention? Was it part of me or outside of me? Where is this knowing coming from? I was trained by this time in psychology and the scientific method, but the dolphins had loosened me up a little, so I went with the flow.

A Maori shaman introduced himself to my psyche, giving me his name and lineage, and he seemed to think that we had agreed to work together on some deeper level. More accurately, he reluctantly agreed to accept me for training. He was a traditionalist in the indigenous shamanic schools. There were instructions without explanation, minimalist directions, then silence: *Go here. Look for this [inner images]. Turn left now [tug on the body]. Feel [sensation and image together]!*

So began about three years of experience, which now seems somewhat amusing but at the time was intense, mainly because I had to integrate it into my everyday persona. Once a fortnight, linked to the new and full moons, I would go on a journey, sometimes involving days and hundreds of kilometers. I was on a need-to-know basis, a bit like an orienteering experience without the map and a whole lot of inner psychic territory to negotiate as well. Sometimes it was quite obvious that the journey was a training exercise specifically suited to me and my system. At other times, it was obvious I was being used as part of a mission that I was not at the security clearance level to understand. There was land clearing, ancient battles, buried treasure, greenstone trails, river and ocean cleansing, release of trapped souls, and so on. Each journey was like an episode of *The X-Files* meets *The Teachings of Don Juan*.

Here I will share an example of one such journey from the late '80s. I was shown an island and a particular pyramid-shaped rock structure in my inner vision. Under this rock was a dark hole, and inside the hole some kind of treasure. I got an image of a flax basket rotting away, and inside it a stone that was alive and glowing.

I set out not knowing where or how far I needed to travel in my trusty old Citroën. I simply came to a crossroads and asked, "North or south?" and then trusted my body's response. I drove through the night and most of the next day until I came to a peninsula that narrowed to a point. In the distance, I saw an island, which no doubt was my destination. Too far to swim. What to do? *Go left. Stop. Ask that man.*

"Er . . . excuse me, do you know how I might get out to that island? I'm doing some . . . botanical research."

"Well, I do have a couple of kayaks, but it's tricky to land there, particularly in these big swells. I can come out with you if you like and show you the way through the rocks."

I landed, drenched after a hairy ride. He waved cheerily. "See you tomorrow."

There was a large rock face to climb to get to the top, and so I began. Halfway up, my body froze on a ledge and refused to go any farther. The sun was setting, and suddenly I was flooded with everyday sanity. I thought, *I am in a dangerous place. I am petrified. What the fuck?* I was chasing some inner chimera. I spent half an hour allowing my body to shake through the fear. I climbed down, lit a fire on the beach, crawled into my sodden sleeping bag, and reflected on my crazy life.

In the morning, I decided to abandon this particular mission and managed to get into the kayak. I was paddling away from the island when I turned back and saw it: the pyramid-shaped rock from my vision. *Bugger.* I returned to the island, and three hours later, I had made the ascent. Bruised and exhausted, I approached the rock, and as I bent down, I cracked my head on the stone and fell, slamming my knees into more rock. Now I was crying with pain and in full resistance. I looked up through my tears and there was the hole. I gently reached in until my arm slid all the way in up to my armpit. I felt something . . . something moving! As I pulled my arm back, a young tuatara ran up my arm and sat on my shoulder.

Visions flooded my mind: a huge pyramid-shaped mountain covered with snow, a large piece of greenstone carrying all the ancient stories of a race like a library, ancient boxes being dug up from the desert, Earth itself in space, whales singing. Huge grief and great joy were thundering through me at the same time. Several hours went by. I began the daylong journey back to my home, my family, and my psychotherapy practice.

The tuatara is the most ancient living reptile on the planet, truly a living stone. It is said in Maori mythology to be the "guardian of the upper jaw," a keeper of the wisdom of the cosmos and cosmic origins. It has a fully functioning pineal gland on the top of its head when born and is linked to an awakened third eye.

Six years later, I wrote about the tuatara in a book on the soul of New Zealand.

Ten years later, I was called to the snow-covered pyramid-shaped mountain Kallash, in Tibet, the site of my next significant shamanic initiation.

Seventeen years later, I went to the Gobi Desert in Mongolia, carrying a large piece of greenstone to give to a shaman who, seventeen years before—at the time of my vision—had dug up his great-grandfather's boxes from the desert and established a temple.

Twenty years later, the whales came to call. And so on . . .

Each of these shamanic visions was like a concentrated teaching that slowly unfolded its meaning, in the body, through time and space.

This first period of shamanic training lasted three years. Even though it was "old school" in some ways, it was not focused on me specifically but on how I, as a unit within a greater whole, could be used to serve that whole.

Afterward, I had a period of being taught by sacred geometry. Every three years, on a certain date, October 19, beginning with the stock market crash in 1987, I received a complex geometrical symbol. It was kind of like an inner crop circle in 3-D. It would take me three years to decipher, just in time for the next one, and when twelve years and five symbols had gone by, they all slotted together beautifully in my consciousness to reveal the energetic signature of my life.

In 2000, I made a journey to the Himalayas, more specifically the sacred Mount Kailash in Tibet. What opened up for me was a connection with a Tibetan teacher who was also part of a preincarnational soul contract. The effect of his consciousness on mine was humbling and at times overwhelming. Unlike the more traditional direction of my earlier shamanic training, I was completely free to engage as I wanted, to ask questions, and to eventually collaborate in the experiment. I was cautious, at first, and scientific. I set aside an hour a week for that particular relationship and monitored the quality of what emerged and its effect on my life and environment.

Within a month, I was certain that the love and wisdom I derived was greater than I had ever experienced from any embodied teacher I had met. We began a seven-year collaboration, which involved the creation of a modern-day initiation school and the writing of six books.

My sense of the process was a soul communion where my consciousness was raised through our interaction so that realizations poured in. It was then my work to convert essential energy into ideas and concepts that could be written down. The grounding of the earlier training and the practical requirement of a project on the physical plane helped anchor the deep awakening of cosmic perspective that accompanied these seven years.

For one year, in 2006, I woke and slept with the rising and setting of the galactic center instead of the sun as I wrote a book on occult cosmology. Some nights, the fire moving through my body was so intense that I felt like a sparkler.

Contact with this teacher accelerated my soul journey enormously and culminated in a deep opening to the void, so that what lies beyond both soul and body became a stable reference point. At that point, we concluded our connection with his injunction: "Now just go into the world and be love."

At the very point I finished one journey, a new one began. On a visit to Delphi, I was surrounded by ravens and had a waking vision of Zeus's eagle hit by a reverse lightning-bolt serpent coming up from Earth. The bird dropped straight down, and at the last minute Earth opened to receive it and it entered the womblike core. The journey with my masculine guides complete, it was now time for initiation into the feminine mysteries. I began to work with a Jungian analyst who specialized in the dark feminine. We almost never talked, just moved, wept, laughed, sang, journeyed, and bowed to each other.

Following the flow of my feminine intuition through a series of powerful synchronicities, I met a woman in Montreal who offered to give me a sacred spot session. The way she touched my body, the flow of energy from her hands, and the tenderness she showed me all helped me deeply relax and open. When she reached the rosebud of my asshole and gently held her presence there, I began to sob, and I wept steadily for the next hour as she gently opened and entered me with love. Without a doubt it was the current of love flowing through her that touched me so deeply. It was not the clinical prostate check I had once experienced from a doctor, nor was it part of sexual play. It was loving touch and embodied presence in the very place on my body where shame, tension, and fear were stored. All of the spiritual experiences my soul had tasted over many years seemed to land in and through the body. I came home in a profound way. Who knew that a finger inside the one place that my soul had never thought to look could bring me back to Earth and the experience of belonging here.

That initiation began a decade of in-depth soul work with the body, sexuality, and the mysteries of Earth. I felt like I had penetrated the mysteries of the cosmos, of the subtle worlds, and of spirit symbolized by the symbol of the black hole at the center of the galaxy. With the opening of the singularity in the base of my body, the door into the center of Earth opened, and I fell like a stone through the core of matter to find the same experience and then nonexperience of the void as I had on the ascending path. Once more I endured a form of social suicide as all of the soul companions I shared the ascending journey with stepped back in alarm, believing me to have lost my way and fallen into the snares of maya, the allure of sex and the dark left-hand path. Black holes and assholes, *sunyata* and sacred shit. Such is the beauty of the world.

In my inner worlds, I began to be accompanied by feminine teachers. They were not conveying perception and direction as my earlier shamanic training had, but instead what I might term *energetic penetration*. A presence I interpreted as Mary Magdalene sometimes approached, seated at the center of a set of seven spheres. As she passed into my aura, I experienced a distinct sensation as each of the spheres interacted with my energy fields vibrationally. Now my energy fields and bodies were being upgraded and stimulated in the same way that my consciousness had been in earlier years. It took a period of seven years for this relationship to move from an energetic kiss to making love in a kinesthetic experience that made me understand what a dakini really is. When I taught groups, I would often experience her presence accompanied by a group of women wearing deep blue robes and holding roses. As the temple processes deepened and individuals surrendered to new levels of heart, emotion, or sexual healing, the priestesses would throw the roses down into their bodies.

I began to understand that only so much can be conveyed through consciousness and that touch in both the physical and metaphysical sense is required for the direct transmission of awakening.

When I first established a mystery school, my rule was "No sexual interaction between teachers and students," for obvious reasons: the power differential, the potential for trauma, transference, shadow desire, exploitation projections, and so on. I was well trained in the psychotherapeutic models of human development. After spending three years in a global group of empowered young people living together in a huge transformational field, I knew there had to be another way. There had to be a deeper way, one that embraced the full intimacy among human beings, restored our sexuality to its rightful place in the temple, and reunited it with a spirituality that honors and celebrates all aspects of our being. I went back into the world investigating all the different offerings in the realm of sexuality and spirituality.

When I met the ISTA tribe, I felt that I had found a starting point I could be part of and help co-create with. No one has all the answers in this repressed and powerful part of human experience and no one is immune to his or her own shadow drives. At least here we are a group of people who were willing to risk getting it wrong for the sake of love, willing to challenge each other and grow practices together so that future generations can have a healthier relationship with their bodies and their life force. My own touchstone when I became part of the governance of ISTA was that I wanted to feel that these were programs that our children and grandchildren could attend and be treated with the care and respect that every human being deserves.

A personal test came for me when a young woman wanted to engage with me sexually. She was on a training that I was leading, and I took my usual stance of support for her process psychologically and energetically. Mostly my experience was that transformational work around sexuality was best done energetically and that physical engagement often triggers unconscious processes, which may be counterproductive as well as having potential for entanglements. She pressed the issue and was very clear what she wanted, not to be treated as a therapeutic case but met authentically as a human being on her journey who was being brave enough to follow and explore her desire to be met in that way by me. When I checked inside, I found that this was also my authentic truth, not just in my desire and in my heart but also my soul intuition that included my sense of care for her in the role I was in.

This was a crisis.

Do I follow my own deep truth or do I follow collective wisdom? The risk is great, both to me and her, if I am misguided. Surely it is better to follow the path of caution. I meditated on it, consulted my peers, and kept coming back to this truth. On one side was my clear and definitive yes, which felt loving. On the other side was my caution, which also felt loving. On the side of my caution, however, I also felt fear for myself. If I take this step, I cross beyond a barrier. I open myself to potential danger—psychological, social, legal, spiritual. If I choose to follow my inner knowing, I step beyond the normal restraints of the society I am part of; I break a taboo. This fear for myself helped me make the decision.

I stepped away from safety and into a new place of freedom. I went to stand with her at the root of all experience. Our meeting initiated her into a new and deeper relationship with her sexuality. Our meeting in this way initiated me into a new and deeper relationship with my integrity. We acknowledged our roles and chose to transcend them. We were two naked human beings who had something for each other that could only be given and received in that sacred act of intimacy that lives at the core of all temples. We met in that field Rumi talks about, out beyond right and wrong. It was a beautiful meeting, and it changed us both forever. It did not change my caution around physical engagement with others on their journey of sexual empowerment and integration; what changed was the place I go to make all of the most important decisions for my life. It restored the trust between my soul and my sexuality that modern society has done its best to interfere with in such painful ways.

It was not enough to simply offer my soul and heart to love. All of my subtle bodies wanted to be in on the gig, surrendering all those energies locked up in the lower chakras: sex, possessiveness, money, survival, belonging, self-worth—all of the ancient traumas and fears from growing up in a world where love was exiled from so-called material reality. It was the goddess, veil by precious veil, revealing that matter itself is spirit and as sacred as any inner experience or state of awareness.

Ultimately, the role of a sex shaman, as I see it, is to touch you in the deepest, most intimate part of your being, to get you to confess and surrender to the most profound longings of the body and soul alike. It is to be known, penetrated, and called forth into expression in the world so that we cannot help but stand up and become visible as the love we are. This is an erection of the human spirit. This is soul arousal. We are not just at the "great turning" on Earth but the "great turn-on." We are the erectile tissue of the planet, able to first feel the rush as the loving life blood of the human spirit returns. We are not just the universe becoming self-aware or self-realized, but the universe enjoying itself, reaching out and touching itself intimately under the veils of space and time, exploring what feels good, beginning to tremble, breathe heavily, and cry out together. Then it will not be the note of suffering that this planet sends out into the universe, it will be the irrepressible sound of life liberated and love being consummated. It will be a shameless, orgasmic cry of freedom.

Bruce Lyon explores places where the personal, planetary, and cosmic meet, guiding others on initiatory journeys around the world. An international teacher and author of numerous esoteric books, he is a member of the wisdom council that advises ISTA's governance and a lead faculty member. As cofounder of Shamballa School, he is seeding a modern temple and mystery school called Highden in New Zealand.

Naked in Nature

PURPOSE: Nature assists us to remember that we are part of the web of life. Plants, animals, and minerals exist in the present moment. The natural world is happening now, and it is in harmony with the natural rhythms of the planet. By getting naked in nature, we strip off our limiting human identity, remember how we were born, and enter into a state of wild erotic innocence. This practice can heal imbalanced energies in our bodies and help steer our nervous systems back into clarity and creativity. It can also give us a greater appreciation for the world in which we live.

PREPARATION: Scout for a secluded area in nature where you can be fully expressed. Bring anything you might want during this time, such as water, raw fruit, sunscreen, a journal (for recording any messages), any sacred objects, and a blanket to lie on.

PROCESS: Take your time disrobing. Consider that your clothes are like a costume to represent your identity. As you strip off each layer, allow yourself to drop out of ego and move into essence. Envision yourself letting go of judgments and mental constructs.

Feel your bare feet against the earth. Notice the quality of the ground cover. Is it dirt, grass, or pebbles? Is it wet from dew or rainfall? Feel the pulsing of life below you. Deepen your breath, exhaling with sound. Melt deeper into your connection to the ground. Invoke the guides of this land. Let nature know that you came here to remember. Set the intention to experience yourself as an inextricable part of nature.

Start by listening to your surroundings and decide on a position that optimizes your connection. Try squatting with your hands on the earth or crawling on all fours. Allow yourself to follow any impulses that move through your body. Are there trees? Rocks? Water? How does your body want to connect deeper? Eventually, allow yourself to have belly contact with the earth. This could be on the ground or against a tree or boulder. Breathe into your belly, and then sink deeper into your pelvis. What wisdom is nature sharing with you? Notice any messages that may enter your awareness through visions, words, or sounds. Notice any and all animals that journey with you, even the creepy-crawly ones. Allow yourself to have a spontaneous conversation with nature. You can be still or silly. Sit, walk, dance. What is the full expression of your true nature, in this moment?

VARIATIONS: Though ideal, getting completely naked may not always be possible. In this case, strip down to the degree that is possible, to underwear or a bathing suit, and make contact with your body through the textiles.

Take this exercise deeper with an ecosexual encounter. You can activate your eros with orgasmic breathing and PC pumping during your invocation, then allow yourself to commune with the elements as if the earth were your lover. The possibilities, positions, and practices born out of love and eros in nature are infinite.

RESOURCES: See the ecosexual manifesto by Dr. Annie Sprinkle and Dr. Elizabeth Stevens, who also guide groups on ecosex walks and tours.

MY FUCKING GOD

By Mia Mor

Anne Lomberg

TRANSPERSONAL NAME: Dancer in the Dark

YEAR OF BIRTH: 1987

SUN SIGN: Virgo

HOMETOWN: Oulu, Finland

RESIDENCE: Earth

ARCHETYPE: Forest nymph, temple dancer, and Melpomene, goddess of song and tragedy

SUPERPOWER: Turning everything into poetry

LINEAGE/TEACHERS: My grandmother, Prem Baba, Osho, Bruce Lyon, the earth and fertility goddess Pachamama and all Earth's inhabitants, and ayahuasca

EPITAPH/MOTTO: Find the center through the polarities.

SHAMANIC TOOLS: My hands: they listen and learn, see and feel, bless and move masses of energy.

HOBBIES: Going second-hand shopping, getting lost, making and eating exotic fusion cuisine, wild harvesting—and I can always dance more.

Photo credits: Anne Lomberg, photos on pages 293 (bottom), 294, 296; self portraits by Mia Mor on pages 293 (top), 295, and 297.

This is me, in my flesh,
owning my felt-experience of GOD
through all my cells:

You *CANNOT* hold an Empire on God.

So tired of the arguments on how to worship,
lessons on how to pray, how to cleanse and repent
and all that good and evil nonsense!
That got us all kicked out of the paradise
of THIS EARTH as IT IS . . .

The might of his R*evol*ution
will be felt *ON YOUR KNEES.*

When the true majesty of my being
open to a higher consciousness

is present, all I can do is weep,
grasp the ground, and shake
and destroy all that is NOT
in alignment with LOVE

This God created us,
the world, everything,
and so he will take it away.

Behind the visions
is the *VOID.*

A place of no-time, extending across dimensions,
dark matter, complete stillness,
penetrating through all matter,
like the eye of the creator

At times I long to escape the sensate reality
to this place of nirvana . . .
wishing everything could just STOP . . .

The deep yearning for both
destruction & rebirth

RE-EMERGENCE
from the Earth

**

Until all the lessons are learnt,
this place exists.

But the Gods are coming
The GODS are coming
The Gods are COMING!

. . . and even they will bow down
to the Truth,
of what MATTERS.

The moment is arriving
Bombs ablaze
for the nuclear destruction
of this *CANCER*
that is eating us,
our carcasses
barely qualified
as alive

**

IT HURTS so much to be alive,
Sometimes.

The course of our bodies . . .
the flooding of our hearts . . .
it is SO HARD to find that insight.

But there is an essence
that will change everything

When you give up ownership
of earth, the body and sky,
the soul & everything
in between.

All is breathing with spirit.
It is all sacred.

MY *FUCKING* GOD

IN MY *FUCKING* BODY!!!

Alive with the magic from within

Resonating with everything

GOD pushing through my cell walls
annihilating facades, corners, doors
Pushing through,
pushing through
keep pushing through . . .

Birth the new Earth.

Mia Mor is a gypsy soul dedicated to the path of an open heart. Her arctic roots with plenty of solitude and connection to wilderness have gifted her a channel to mystic poetry and dialogues with Earth. She travels the world awakening bodies to divine sensations and embodied soul communication.

Sacred Sexual Storytelling

PURPOSE: What life-changing experience have you had that deserves to be immortalized, not only in your journal but as a personal narrative for your family or friends? Reflecting on your own experience with sexual shamanism is like creating a treasure map to how you became who you are, now. There is gold at the end of this exercise! By remembering where you came from, you can release an old version of yourself and start a whole new chapter. This can help you find your voice and allow others to connect even deeper with yours.

PREPARATION: Give yourself multiple days to draft and revise and polish. Don't pressure yourself to finish it all in one sitting. Start with a brainstorm or a rough outline. Make a list of the turning points in your sex life and/or spiritual journey. Do not start with your earliest memory and try to tell your whole life story. Fast-forward to the end of your life, perhaps seeing yourself on your deathbed, and ask yourself what were your most significant moments of awakening in the area of sex or spirituality. You may want to seek support and accountability in a creative ally or coach to support you through the inevitable resistance of this vulnerable practice.

PROCESS: To get your juices flowing, answer the following questions in technicolor detail, into your journal or a voice recorder. These are the same prompts that were given the authors of this book. Afterward, focus only on the most interesting answers and pick a place to start your story.

- When did you first become aware of your sexuality and/or spirituality?
- What early messages did you get about sex and/or spirit during your childhood?
- How has your life been different from what you'd imagined?
- What were the greatest challenges or wounds that your soul has wrestled with?
- What was your darkest hour? Is there time in your life when you felt betrayed or alone?

- What is your personal shadow or karmic pattern?
- Do you have any secrets or regrets?
- Who are your greatest teachers, and what is the hardest or most important lesson you've learned in your life?
- Are there places you've traveled that have changed you?
- What final wisdom or moral to the story would you like to share with others?

Focus on at least one central scene instead of a list of many. A story must have a beginning, middle, and end, held together by a central theme. And a good story has a conflict with high stakes. What is the risk you are taking and what do you stand to lose? Remember, you are taking the reader on a journey.

Use your emotions and your sensations to add sensual details. Listen to the smells, tastes, and sounds that arise as you lay them down on the page. Write from your belly, your heart, and your body. Use your mind only when it is time to rewrite and edit. The major thrust of the piece is to express your own sexual awakening.

VARIATIONS: If you prefer, you can express yourself through poetry, performance art, or even paint!

RESOURCES: Joseph Campbell's *The Hero's Journey* is a wonderful guide to help with the development of your plot.

ACKNOWLEDGMENTS

It's one thing to support your partner's soul calling, it's another thing to hold their hand as they walk the path, sometimes pulling them up when the climb gets steep. My husband, Michael McClure, has not only been there through every step but even dreamed up the title of this book!

Next, I want to thank Daniel Schmachtenberger, Roxanne DePalma, and Cheri Reeder, who've been the holy trinity of muses. Our weekly dates were a mixture of writing, sensual play, and inquiry into the mysteries of the universe.

Thank you, Jon Graham, the acquisitions editor at Inner Traditions, for taking a risk on this controversial collection and fanning the flames of my creative fire. And big kudos to our visionary project editor, Jennie Marx, for all her compassion and patience while working with the particular eccentricities of this wild band of artists.

I'm overflowing with gratitude to all twenty of the contributing authors for their courageous and vulnerable storytelling. I honor what is said within these pages as well as the experiences that expand beyond this frame. Big thanks to those who submitted but whose work is still being refined for future volumes.

Special thanks to Ohad Pele Ezrahi for mentoring me in the field; if it weren't for your fantasy oracle and fiftieth birthday, I might not have found my way back home. ISTA is my soul tribe.

Other mentors who have supported this book in nonlinear ways include Ray Stubbs, Mystic Mother Tracy Elise, Charles Muir, Caroline

Muir, River and Diamond Jameson, and, of course, Bruce Lyon.

I also acknowledge all the students and apprentices who've heard the calling to support this work, especially those who pitched in to help with this book: Ria Bloom, Matooka MoonBear, Liz Morris, and Mia Mor.

Further, I feel supported by a vast web of long-term lovers and metamours. This is my family of choice: Daniel Schamchtenberge, Roxanne DePalma, Sharmilla Graefer, James Schamchtenberger, Harry Judge, Viraja Prema, Summer Athena Fah, Stacy Ellis, Kamela Peace, Toree Love, Jennifer Norton, Jesse Norton, Tahl Gruer, Alix Lowe, Triambika Ma Vive, Anthony D'Aula, Kenny Benavides, Ria Bloom, and everyone else in the San Diego Super Pod.

Next, I'm grateful to my blood family for putting up with my absence for all the hours I've poured into this passion project: my son, Devin; my mother, Rosa Knapp, for originally initiating me as a curandera; my father, Spencer, and my other mother, Laurie, who both constantly inspire me to contribute bigger. My in-laws: Grandpa Frank and Nana Linda. My brother-in-law Christian for being my beta reader and cheerleader. My blood brother Carlos who started a journey of recovery from addiction this year. And my big brother Miguel, who married Kim while I was publishing this. And to my nieces Kaylani and Mikayla, who are graduating from high school.

This book would not be the same without the tremendous technical assistance from my editors and author assistants: Lori Masters, Jen Moreno, Estrella Paracelsus, and Josh Zuchowski.

Gratitude also goes to my beta readers: Josh Zuchowski, Azura Cottier, Paul Hanrieder, Lisa Parker, Jim Wood, Kirsten Young, Annie Mangan, Serena Anderlini, Sophia Leva-Marie, Tim Weaver, Devla Imperatrix, Paul Hanrieder, and ManDrake.

In loving memory of Mukee Okan, Mead Rose, Mary VanMeer, Deborah Taj Anapol, and my grandmother Mama Terry who, at age one hundred, crossed over into the great Mystery.

About the Cover
Artist

In Loving Memory of Mukee Okan, who was initiated into a tantric yogic lineage in 1984 and left her body in November 2017.

Mukee Okan was a wisewoman, grandmother, artist, and teacher of sexuality for more than thirty years, known to her closest friends and mentors as Muktananda, meaning the "bliss of spiritual freedom." A certified surrogate partner in the Western medical model of sexual healing and a Quodoushka spiritual sexuality teacher, she was known as Your Orgasm's Best Friend and can be seen as the sexuality educator in *The Vagina Diaries,* a documentary made for the Australian Broadcasting Commission investigating why so many women, especially young women, undergo cosmetic labiaplasty in Australia.

Mukee Okan's purpose was bringing peace on Earth through transforming the discourse on sex. Her greatest legacy is the creation of *The Pussy Talks,* a fifty-five-minute documentary of twenty-eight women sharing their most intimate sexual anatomy. This documentary instigated a new standard of excellence in multimedia production. For women in particular, viewing *The Pussy Talks* encourages them to witness and connect with the most intimate and sacred part of themselves, to realize that their sexual well-being is a natural expression of the divine design, and to discover what is possible when they are at peace with the power of sex: see "The Pussy Talks" website.

For more art by Mukee Okan go to https://thepussytalks.com.

TEMPLE ARTS TERMS

Words are used in prayer as well as curses. Specific phrases in certain circumstances have been known to intervene with the cause and effect of physical phenomena. As ISTA travels the Earth studying and teaching the temple arts, our vocabulary of occult terminology is naturally evolving.

The following is a list of words, phrases, sounds, and symbols that often arise in our ongoing exploration of sexuality and spirituality. Many of our collaborating authors have trained in a variety of shamanic schools that teach only through oral tradition. We do not claim to read, write, or speak all of the languages referenced here. Also, keep in mind that definitions vary widely in different circles, and this is an interdisciplinary work-in-progress. We offer only brief and partial definitions here, with an emphasis on how our subcultural meaning differs from that of a mainstream dictionary.

You may feel an immediate resonance with some concepts, while others may take many years to develop an embodied understanding. Each of these terms deserves deeper study. If you are called to research further, we've included some relevant keywords in italics. We encourage you to work with a spiritual teacher to go beyond mere intellectual understanding. Remember, words have the power to create or destroy life.

ahimsa. Do no harm. This is one of the cardinal virtues of Buddhism, Jainism, and Hinduism. Mahatma Gandhi popularized the concept of harmlessness during his nonviolent resistance against British rule.

Akashic records. An etheric library that contains universal knowledge, including a history of all past, present, and possible future lives. These records can be accessed through shamanic journeying.

alchemy. The art and science of transmutation, split into inner (esoteric) and outer (exoteric) studies. The inner aim is achieving gnosis. The outer aim is to alter the atomic structure of matter; examples include changing base metals into gold or formulating the elixir of immortality. The shamanic alchemist sees both esoteric and exoteric alchemy as complementary practices.

aliens. Visitors from outer space who sometimes travel and interact with shamans through inner space.

allies. Ancestors, angels, animal spirits, aliens, and ascendant masters who can each be called upon for guidance and protection during ceremony. These spirit entities may or may not be separate from the shaman's alter egos. (*entities, guides*)

altered state. Any state of consciousness that is significantly different from a waking beta-wave state. Hypnosis, dreaming, and deep meditation are some self-induced examples. Some states can be externally created through exogenous drugs or near-death experiences. (*mind alteration, nonordinary awareness, shamanic state of consciousness [SSC], trance*)

amrita. Sanskrit for "divine nectar" or "elixir of immortality." The term is commonly used for female ejaculate. It is considered to be a powerfully healing substance. In contemplative practices, the term is used to describe the subtle energetic substance emitted from the pineal gland during meditation that produces a sweet taste in the back of the throat. (*nectar, serpentine drops, soma*)

ananda. Sanskrit for "bliss, joy, spiritual ecstasy."

androgyny. A healthy balance of masculine and feminine energy. Describes versatility in energy, fashion, lifestyle, or sexuality. (*Ardhanarishvara* *[composite male-female form of the deities Shiva and Parvati], fluid, gender neutral)*

animal guides. Messengers and symbols from the world of spirit that provide wisdom and guidance. Shamans can commune with animal spirits spontaneously or at will by invoking them, meeting them in journey, or through biomimicry. (*animal spirits, power animals, totems*)

animism. A system in which the spiritual realm is considered inseparable from the physical and all natural objects, creatures, places, and phenomena are considered animate. By praying to the spirit within plants, crystals, lakes, clouds, and so on, practitioners may invoke cooperation with these forces of nature.

apprentice path. A committed pursuit of experiential learning (or unlearning) that trains the body, mind, and soul toward inner mastery. An apprenticeship involves observation, feedback, initiation, and guidance from a master or multiple mentors. ISTA's apprenticeship requires three mentors and emphasizes embodying the void. (*journeyman, master system*)

archetype. The universal energetic prototype that is embedded in the collective unconsciousness. Carl Jung's and Joseph Campbell's work looks at quintessential characters found across different cultures' mythology, such as the wounded child, sibling, lover, warrior, scapegoat, artist, wizard.

aspecting. An energetic dialogue in which one or more aspects of the shaman's alter ego is invited to manifest and speak freely. A therapeutic healing method that resembles voice dialogue, parts therapy, psychodrama, gestalt, transactional analysis, subpersonality work, and/or theater role play.

assemblage point. The unique perspective or viewpoint through which we perceive the world, our sense of centrality or where we experience the highest concentration of self. To experience other worlds, we must become aware of our programed perspective and consciously move to different points that may include or transcend the mind, body, and spirit.

astral plane. The realm our souls pass through upon birth and death. A world inhabited by entities, landscapes, and astral artifacts that cannot be seen by ordinary human vision and may or may not have direct connection to the material plane. (*celestial realm*)

aum. The feminine counterpart to *om*. The primal sound or vibration that constantly emanates from the entire universe. It is the sound of creation and destruction, representing the beginning and the end.

aura. A luminous electromagnetic field that surrounds the physical body. It can only be seen through the open third eye or an activated fifth chakra.

avatar. A spiritual messenger or emissary who incarnates for the benefit of humanity. (*incarnate*)

ayahuasca. Meaning "vine of the soul," this entheogenic brew combines the stem of one vine and leaves of another plant and contains DMT and MAOI. Used by indigenous people of the Amazon basin for diagnosing and curing illness, communicating with the spirits of plants, animals, and human beings (dead or alive), traveling to distant places, and prophesying.

bardo. Purgatory, a transitory state between death and rebirth. The Tibetan scriptures refer to the bardo state as a transition between planes of existence.

BDSM. This broad term is an overlapping acronym for Bondage and Discipline (BD), Dominance and Submission (DS), as well as Sadism and Masochism (SM.) It is also includes a wide variety of kink, sensation play, and fetishes.

black magic. The use of power and the manipulation of matter for selfish ends, or magic that is overly focused on materialistic forces. Any magic conducted without the informed consent of all involved.

black tantra. A tantra practiced by the Aghori, a Hindu sect of ascetic sadhus who have transcended social taboos. They have been known to engage in postmortem rituals, such as using bones from human corpses in their ceremonies, and often practice in secrecy. They are respected and feared for their magical powers.

blood mysteries. A body of teachings that considers menstrual blood and birthing to be holy. A deep reminder that life comes from the Goddess and that moontime blood is full of the void and can be used for healing, ceremony, and to help nourish Earth. (*moon blood, womb blood*)

bodhisattva. One whose essence is enlightenment. *Bodhi* is the Sanskrit word for "enlightenment," and *sattva* means "essence." The bodhisattva vows to stay on the earthly plane to help liberate all sentient beings from suffering.

body memory. The body's capacity to hold memories of past events that may not be readily available to the conscious mind. Often, as a natural defense mechanism, memories associated with emotional, physical, or sexual violence can be repressed from conscious recall but held and released through somatic therapies.

boundaries. Guidelines that define the permissible distance in which we allow people to make contact in order for us to be at our best. Personal boundaries include physical, mental, psychological, spiritual, and sexual limits. Boundaries are flexible.

bubble. A practice for dropping into presence and authentically communicating boundaries, fears, and desires. It begins by creating an energetic field around yourself or others at the beginning of a ritual, sexual scene, or conscious communication practice. This practice was popularized by Margo Anand.

cacao. Used as a medicinal elixir and drunk by royalty during sacrificial rituals in ancient Aztec and Mayan times. Mythology says cacao was derived from the heavens and gifted to the people. Today, cacao is used to open the heart, facilitate connection, and accelerate intentions.

calling. When someone feels an insatiable pull toward a spiritual path, a natural impulse, like that of a migratory animal. Often, a calling is preceded by a crisis or a discovery of psychic abilities. It is not to be confused with a thirst for ego gratification or external validation.

celibacy. The sacred path of renouncing sex (and sometimes romantic relationships), which may or may not include a practice of self-pleasuring. Classical yoga schools teach *brahmacharya* as a virtue for a holy lifestyle. (*abstinence*)

central axis. The channel of energy that runs up the spine, extending from the perineum to the crown. (*central channel, column, djed, pranic tube, sushumna pillar*)

chakra. A Sanskrit word meaning "wheel" or "circle." Refers to the energy centers or points of spiritual power that reside in the body along the spine and compose the astral or subtle body.

channeling. A natural form of communication between humans and nonphysical entities, animals, plants, or minerals. Similar to a language translator or interpreter, a channel senses nonverbal communication from another being and then translates it into human words. When the practice involves allowing one's body to be controlled by the entity, it is called *mediumship* or *skinwalking*. When it involves summoning dead humans, it's called *necromancy*.

Chulauqui Quodoushka. A body of shamanic teachings popularized by Harley SwiftDeer Reagan who studied the nagual tradition. The work holds sex as natural, sacred, and profound. Its unique curriculum includes a system for classifying types of genital anatomy. Also known as the Q.

compersion. Taking pleasure from seeing or hearing about another's pleasure; the opposite of jealousy.

consensus reality. The agreed-upon concepts of reality that members of a culture or group believe are real. Our understanding of reality is determined or influenced by consensus, what the majority of our group determines is normal, which may be a culturally constructed illusion. (*consensual continuum*)

consent. To unambiguously agree, voluntarily, to the proposal or desires of another, without pressure, coercion, or manipulation. Sexual consent differs from legal and medical contexts because it requires an individual to be able to say no or stop the activity at any point.

cord cutting. The practice of releasing energetic attachments with other people, places, or experiences. This shamanic ritual is a healthy way to reclaim and maintain autonomy and power.

cords. Energetic fibers that extend between people through their subtle energy bodies, like a child's umbilicus toward its mother or branches or vines between plants. Not all cords are negative. (*attachments, bonds, emotional ties, karmic connections*)

core. The central, innermost essential part of anything. Also the name given to the annual ISTA gathering of worldwide faculty and organizers, which occurs at different sacred sites around the world.

core shamanism. A set of principles and practices that are shared by shamanic cultures from all around the world. Anthropologist Michael Harner's research and lifework has been to empower Westerners with access to universal shamanism that is not bound to any specific cultural group or perspective.

crone. Despite the definition in *Merriam-Webster's Collegiate Dictionary* that she is "a cruel or ugly old woman," in shamanism, a crone is a powerful healer. Her body is no longer fertile, but her womb holds the mysteries of life and death.

cult. A spiritual or religious group with a charismatic leader who is unaccountable for coercing, persuading, or exploiting its members, sexually, economically, or otherwise. This is often a pejorative label used against controversial communities or groups. (*sect*)

curandero/curandera. A folk healer from Peru or other pre-Columbian magico-religious areas. They are healers who cure illness using herbs, psychic powers, and hallucinogens.

daka/dakini. Sanskrit for "sky dancer." These supernatural beings act as intermediaries, connecting shamanic practitioners to the transcendental. They either test the practitioner's ability or act as a muse for the shaman. Elusive by nature, they transcend intellectual concepts. In modern times, a daka (man) or dakini (woman) is someone who has been trained in the tantric healing arts. An adept shamanic practitioner can embody both daka and dakini (male and female) and also be a spiritual consort to the practitioner.

dark matter. An invisible substance that is theorized not to interact with light photons. This dense matter holds galaxies together with its heft and gravity. Scientists estimate dark matter comprises up to 85 percent of all mass in the universe.

darshan. Receiving a blessing or transmission from a deity or holy person.

descent. The action of moving downward, dropping, or falling into denser energies, embodiment, earth, or primal vibrations, commonly labeled dark. The opposite of ascent.

dharma. Spiritual obligation or divine duty. That which one must do to fulfill one's soul's purpose. In Buddhism, dharma is seen as a universal law or ethical doctrine.

divination. The act of foreseeing or foretelling future events. A psychic prediction made through a variety of rituals such as dreams, tarot cards, fire ashes, scrying, sacrificial animals, casting lots with ears of maize, and so on. (*prophecy*)

DMT. N-dimethyltryptamine is a chemical compound naturally produced in the brain at death and believed to be responsible for near-death phenomena. When ingested, it crosses the blood-brain barrier, causing hallucinations and affecting human consciousness.

Dreamtime. The conceptualization of the beginning of knowledge, time out of time, or the collective stories of all of existence from Aboriginal ancestors of Australian regions.

ecstatic current. A current of life force that arises from the void when we are moving from the center beyond concepts of masculine and feminine, good and bad, light and dark, right and wrong. Polarized viewpoints create contraction, whereas the ecstatic current brings aliveness and creativity. (*eros, kundalini, sacred fire*)

embodiment. The experience of mind, body, and spirit as one. The physical sensations that result from the soul incarnating or merging with the corporeal.

emotional release. A transformative practice that uses breath, movement, and sound to open doorways in the body that release stuck energy manifesting as anger, guilt, fear, shame, or any other emotion that was not safe to express. It can be combined with the seven shamanic tools, bodywork, shaking, and/or aspecting.

empath. Someone with the gift of feeling what another person is feeling by means of paranormal sensitivity.

empowerment through pleasure (ETP). A sexual-shamanic method of utilizing the trance states of high sexual pleasures for visioning and rewiring of the brain, developed by Dawn and Ohad Pele Ezrahi.

endarkenment. A play on the word *enlightenment*. A rebellion against fundamentalist views that prescribe strict adherence to any path that transcends the body. Endarkenment suggests that God can be experienced in the dense, dark realm of matter, through the senses, and even in scientific phenomena.

entheogens. A Greek word meaning "generating God within." A plant or chemical ingested for ceremonial purposes to enhance spiritual consciousness. This term is used to contrast with recreational connotations such as *psychedelics* or *hallucinogens*. (*medicine journey, plant medicine, sacrament*)

erotic trance. A hypnotic state of arousal induced by sensual stimulation, sexuality, and/or eros. An altered state of consciousness that predisposes the spirit for flight.

etheric double. An energetic duplicate of the physical body that exists outside space-time in subtle or psychic form. It is a perfect replica of the physical body, except made of energy. It appears as a luminous being, a white, phantomlike emanation. Egyptian alchemy focused chiefly on the transformation of the *ka* body. (*dreaming body*)

evolution. The gradual and continual process of development from simplicity toward complexity that unfolds within all life. A natural urge or impulse to change, mutate, and merge into ever-higher states of consciousness.

extraction. A shamanic healing ritual whereby pain or illness is energetically removed from a person with the help of a power animal or spirit teacher.

eye gazing. An open-eye meditation practice of sitting before a mirror or a partner with the intent of seeing beyond form into essence. Benefits include becoming more present, opening your heart, and expanding your awareness of the Divine in all beings. (*soul gazing*)

familiars. A soul mate in an animal's body. Many witches and sorcerers are deeply bonded to pets that help them in their metaphysical pursuits. They are living creatures and animal guides.

four directions. Many native traditions create sacred space by calling in the north, east, south, and west. Depending on the lineage, each direction has a special guardian, element, meaning, and color associated with it.

Gnosis. Direct knowing, wisdom. (*Sophia*)

guru. Sanskrit word meaning "dispeller of darkness." A spiritual teacher or master in metaphysical doctrines.

heaven on earth. A concept in embodied spirituality that emphasizes the here and now, that heaven can be found on earth, and that one's state of being is an accurate reflection of one's spiritual reality. This contrasts with some religious dogma, which believes heaven and hell are places we go after death.

hedonism. The doctrine that pleasure or happiness is the highest good. Devotion to pleasure as a way of life.

holding space. The willingness to be present with another person, to be physically, emotionally, mentally, and spiritually available for someone else's process. It also implies listening without judgment. This is a quality of the divine masculine.

hook. An energetic attachment that is barbed and sometimes painful. It is usually the result of an unhealed relationship with someone or something that is needy, manipulative, or toxic. (*drains, energy leaks, vampires*)

huna. Means "secret" in Hawai'ian. Kahunas are the secret keepers or priests who have healing powers and are known to work with *mana* to increase spirituality and energy. This ancient metaphysical system was made available by the modern American researcher Max Freedom Long. (*ho'omana*)

ida. The subtle pathway up the left side of the spine that runs lunar energy and is connected to the left nostril.

immortality. The deathless principle in all beings. The feeling that you can live forever, now. Living fully and making necessary changes to stay healthy and alive.

impeccability. Beyond the common understanding of being without sin, Carlos Castaneda defines impeccability as the proper use of energy, born of a delicate balance between our internal being and the forces of the external world. It is an achievement that requires effort, time, dedication, and being permanently attentive to the objective.

initiation. An intense personal experience, often a death and rebirth that marks a transition from one level of consciousness to another. A memorable benchmark that acknowledges the successive attainment of mastery. Can be a ceremony given by a spiritual teacher. (*ceremonial gateway, rite of passage*)

intention. The energy of the soul expressing itself into form. To firmly fix one's personal will on a thoughtform until it crystallizes into an aspect of the shaman him- or herself. When clearly formulated and powerfully activated, it materializes into reality.

invocation. The calling, often aloudly, to allies for assistance when *casting a circle* or *summoning* for ritual, practice, and/or meditation.

journey. A shamanic practice of deliberately entering an altered state with the clear intention to vision, heal, reclaim power, or communicate with nonphysical entities. (*ecstatic flight.*)

kabbalah. The mystical wisdom tradition that was carried within Judaism for centuries. It's true origin, in the mystery schools of Assyria, is far more ancient than Judaism itself. The ultimate purpose is the perfection of self.

karma. The accumulated effect of deeds and actions in this life, as well as past and future lives.

kedesha. A sacred woman or priestess who served the goddess Asherah or Ashtart/Astarte in ancient Israel. The *kedesha* uses her sexuality as one of her many tools, to perform rituals of service to the goddess. Kedeshas were persecuted in the seventh century BCE by the king and his zealots.

kink. Unconventional sexual desires, practices, or fantasies, including a range of preferences and fetishes, such as leather, rope, spanking, role-playing, and so on. (*BDSM, power exchange*)

kriya. A spontaneous movement that purifies the body's energy channels. It can look like twitches or seizures.

latihan. A spiritual practice of moving into the unknown. From Subud, an Indonesian-based international spiritual movement, *latihan* means "following inner guidance." Beyond preconceived notions of sex and love-making, stay open to existence and allow energy to flow through; anything can happen. (*authentic movement*)

law of attraction. A universal law that our vibration—beliefs, visions, feelings, and thoughts—magnetize our experience.

left-hand path. An approach to magic and ritual that opposes conventional morality and espouses the breaking of taboos. This path includes sex magic and embraces satanic symbology. (*heterodox, left-handed attainment*)

life force. The most primal and potent energy that creates and sustains life. This is the fuel for alchemy. It creates the foundation of matter, into which spirit incarnates. (*chi, ki, mana, prana, shakti*)

lineage. Descent from an ancestor or predecessors who share their accumulated knowledge. When specific spiritual practices are handed down from teacher to student, in an unbroken line, for many generations.

lingam. Sanskrit for the male sexual organ, meaning "wand of light." The phallic symbol of masculinity, associated with Shiva.

lucid dreaming. To become awake in the dream and reclaim the ability to consciously navigate dream spaces with awareness and create by choice.

magick. Focusing on the spiritual essence of all matter and working with natural forces to bring about a desired outcome. The archaic spelling of magic is used to denote ritual magick as opposed to stage magic. In his book *Magick in Theory and Practice,* Aleister Crowley defined it as "the Science and Art of causing a change to occur in conformity with will."

mantra. A pattern of syllables used rhythmically to quiet the mind and balance the inner body. A form of prayer to be recited over and over again to magnetize or intensify a divine frequency.

mechanistic. When phenomena are analyzed only in terms of their physical or mechanical components without consideration of their metaphysical significance.

medicine wheel. A map of how life moves with seasons, moons, and virtues in each divine direction. Since a number of Native American traditions use it, there are variations on the symbology. It can be a spiral pathway to ever-increasing levels of awareness.

memes. Cultural attitudes, ideas, symbols, practices, or behaviors that are transmitted from person to person through writing, speech, gestures, rituals, or other viral phenomena with a mimicked theme. They are analogous to genes in that they self-replicate, mutate, and evolve.

metaphysics. A branch of philosophy that examines the fundamental nature of reality and the relationship between underlying reality and physical forms, mind and matter.

moksha. Ultimate spiritual liberation from the bonds of suffering and the cycle of birth and death.

morphic fields. A resonant field that enables memories to pass across both space and time from the past. The theory that all self-organizing systems, such as molecules, crystals, cells, plants, animals, and animal societies, have a collective memory from which each individual draws and to which the individual contributes. See Rupert Sheldrake's work on morphogenesis for details. (*morphic resonance, field of consciousness*)

muggles. Nonmagical beings from the Harry Potter series. Some are not even aware that magic exists, and those who do are afraid of it. Often used to refer to mainstream mentality.

mundane. Worldly, ordinary, common, simple. Pertaining to the Earth plane.

mystery school. A gathering of mystics who study spiritual teachings, occult practices, and rituals that speak directly to the soul.

na. A sorcerer believed by various Middle American Indians to be capable of transforming him- or herself into animal form.

nagual. A Mesoamerican sorcerer who is capable of spiritually or physically shape-shifting into an animal. In Carlos Castaneda's series the term also refers to the unknowable that lies outside human perception. Miguel Ruiz writes in his book *The Four Agreements: A Practical Guide to Personal Freedom* that in the Toltec tradition, naguals guide an individual to personal freedom.

namaste. A traditional Hindi greeting that means "I bow to the divine light in you, which I recognize as the same light that animates me." Can be said nonverbally by bringing the palms of the hands together before the heart.

nondualism. A state of consciousness in which dichotomies disappear, where things appear distinct but are not separate.

obstacles to flight. The psychological impediments to spiritual evolution. These can be real or imagined. (*resistance*)

occult. Deep paranormal studies that extend beyond physical sciences. Hidden knowledge that is only known by a few, not only because this wisdom has been persecuted but also because not everyone is ready for the power that comes with this knowledge. (*arcane, esoteric, huna*)

open relationship. A committed partnership, sometimes a marriage, where all partners are open to sexual or intimate relationships with other people. This umbrella term can include polyamory and swinging.

out-of-body experience (OBE). When one's consciousness continues outside one's physical body and can travel through will or intention. (*astral projection, mental projection*)

pachamama. The experience of planet Earth as a living goddess who is waking up through our bodies. She is responsible for divine intervention through fertility, weather, earthquakes, and volcanic activity.

parapsychology. The interdisciplinary study of that which is beyond the field of normal psychology. The scientific branch of occultism.

path. An approach, method, or system to spiritual growth or mystical knowledge.

PC muscles. Pubococcygeal muscle group in both male and female anatomy that runs from the pubic bone to the tailbone in a figure eight shape around the genitals. Strengthening these muscles is vital to the orgasmic response. (*kegels*)

pineal gland. A pine cone–shaped endocrine gland tucked between the two hemispheres of the brain that produces melatonin and is responsible for circadian cycles. It's responsible for our empathetic capacity and holds a key to higher states of consciousness. (*conarium*)

pingala. The energetic channel that runs up the right side of the spine and ends at the right nostril. (*solar circuit*)

pink tantra. A heart-centered path that embraces both spiritual and sexual practices. Can encompass transcendental lovemaking, Taoist sexual healing arts, and the sweet, sensual exercises in modern tantra pujas. (*full path, middle path, violet tantra*)

placebo effect. Belief in results can cause results. The most powerful, cheapest, and therefore least-researched method of healing. (*positive expectancy*)

plastic shaman. A pejorative term for a deceptive or incompetent individual who attempts to pass him- or herself off as a spiritual leader but who has no genuine connection to the tradition or culture he or she claims to represent. (*charlatan, chicken shaman, pseudo-shaman*)

plug-in sex. To "close a circuit" with penetrative sex. A term used to distinguish physical penetration from energetic sex. (*penis in vagina*)

pod. A playful term used to describe any group of three or more lovers. It is a reference to how dolphin's play and mate in groups. Other politically correct terms for nonmonogamous relationship structures are *circle, family, intimate network,* or *polycule.* This term is also used in ISTA to describe intimate sharing circles.

polyamory. The capacity to love more than one person with the informed consent of all involved. The intimacy and nature of the relationship varies greatly between individuals and groups. Connections may be sexual, emotional, spiritual, or any combination, according to the desires and agreements of those involved. Deborah Taj Anapol popularized the term in her landmark book *Polyamory: The New Love without Limits.*

polytheism. A religious belief in many deities of varying power and of many lesser spirits as well who are considered real and worthy of respect and worship.

power object. A sacred artifact imbued with unseen forces and energies used for ritual or healing. A shaman can also extend his or her personal power into crystals, rattles, and wands or staffs. (*altar item, amulet, talisman, shamanic tool*)

practitioner. A person actively engaged in the art and discipline of his or her spiritual practice. A practitioner may adopt a variety of roles, including the shaman, priest, priestess, daka, dakini, or community leader. The practitioner is continuously working on his or her own evolution and upholds an ethical and professional standard that includes working with intent for the highest good of all.

practitioner training. An in-depth training designed for ISTA graduates to further their skills in facilitating somatic sexual-healing sessions for others. It emphasizes how to use the power of sexual energy as a framework for wholeness. It includes skills in touch, emotional embodiment, and shamanic practices as well as teaching integrity and compassion.

priest/priestess. An official representative of a given religion, sect, or cult who is responsible for leading people in rituals.

psychopomp. A guide who escorts souls through other dimensions, such as newly deceased souls into the afterlife, but who can also serve as a guide through various life transitions. Common in mythology, religious texts, sacred narratives, and near-death experiences around the world.

recapitulation. A shamanic death and rebirth process wherein a person relives his or her past and disengages from anything that drains power, enabling them to go forward on their path with renewed energy. (*purification, rebirth, throwing off the world*)

red tantra. An aspect of tantra that sees the sacred in the profane. It relates to the mastery of passion, desire, and sexual skills. It can be liberating for the sexually repressed while helping moderate the sexually obsessed. Practices may involve taste and touch and intensify primal impulses leading to intense purifications and awakenings. Instead of bringing the kundalini energy up to the crown, the red path draws spiritual energy down into the root. (*California tantra, cult of ecstasy, left-hand path, vama marga*)

right relationship. Being in harmony with ourselves and all life around us, such as plants, animals, or humans. In a sacred partnership, mutual agreements are made between autonomous beings without coercion or control. The relationship is dynamic, and all parties seek to bring out the best in each other. (*reverent participatory relationship*)

sacred space. A place of tranquillity created through intention, respect, and focus and by cultivating an environment filled with energies that support, uplift, comfort, and transform our inner and outer awareness and benefit our highest good.

sacred spot. This is less of an exact spot and more of an energetic access area where all of the energy of the sex chakra is stored. Roughly located on and around the G-spot in women and on and around the prostate in men, when stimulated, it often fills and swells and may produce strong sensations along with a release of emotions.

sacred spot ritual. Charles and Caroline Muir were pioneers in originating this ceremony, which is designed to heal past wounds and awaken cosmic pleasure in the sacred spot. One partner offers conscious touch and loving presence while the other receives. It can be incredibly pleasurable, yet sometimes it may burn, be painful, or induce numbness. Each ritual is unique to the individuals involved. It can be performed energetically, without penetration. (*sacred spot session, massage work*)

sacred union. A tantric rite that involves physical or imagined sexual union. This does not require opposite genders; both partners can hold both masculine and feminine polarities. An etheric lingam can penetrate an etheric yoni. (*hieros gamos, mahamudra, maithuna*)

safer sex elevator speech. To communicate with current or prospective partners, Reid Mihalko developed a brief script that includes sharing STI test results, relationship status, sexual orientation, safer sex protocols, preferences, boundaries, and more. The acronym R-BDSM is used as a variation of this practice, and it stands for R-Relationship Agreements, Boundaries, Desires, Sexual History, and Meaning. This final word reminds us that sex has different meanings for different people, so it is valuable to ask potential partners what it would mean to them if you were to have sex.

samadhi. God realization. The final goal of yoga. (*enlightenment, satori, nirvana*)

Saturn return. A period of astrological time when Saturn returns to the place in the sky where it was during a person's birth; this occurs every

29.5 years. It signifies reaching full adulthood, with new challenges and responsibilities. (*quarter-life crisis*)

seeing. The act of viewing the world according to its true nature, without illusions and expectations.

seeker. A person or aspect of the self that is in search of the authentic truth. An explorer motivated to find and attain higher purpose, enlightenment, or love.

self-activating. The art and practice of turning oneself on, igniting one's own life force or sexual desire. (*self-pleasure, solo practice*)

self-knowledge. Being familiar not only with the strengths and weaknesses of one's own personality but also having a relationship with one's own soul.

set and setting. The context for shamanic journeying: the mind-set (set) and physical and social environment (setting). Preparing or creating this context for magic. (*creating safe space, setting the container*)

sex magic. The deliberate use of orgasmic energy to fuel manifestation. A ritual or practice of infusing ecstasy for the purpose of creation. It may also refer to the inner alchemy that transforms consciousness itself. Can be practiced solo, with a partner, or in groups.

shadow. The unconscious, disowned parts of ourselves. These parts tend to be primitive, negative, and socially unacceptable impulses, but the shadow can also include our genius and brilliant potential, so it is not a synonym for evil or dark. Shadow also likes to manifest as a projection of judgment onto other people.

shaman. Any being who is called to walk beyond ordinary awareness to use magic and psychic ability for personal and tribal benefit. They might also be priests and priestesses of specific lineages who work with the unseen world of spirits. (*medicine person, self-healed madman*)

shamanic breathwork. A form of breathwork developed by Linda Star Wolf that synthesizes ancient shamanic practices with current breathwork modalities and relies heavily on group process techniques.

shape-shifting. The shamanic practice of changing the luminous body to match the frequency of a natural entity such as a mineral, plant, or power animal. This may give the shaman the ability to travel a great distance or through difficult environments. (*soul shifting, therianthropy*)

sharing circle. A group of people sharing feelings, experiences, and insights with a set theme and guidelines, such as maintaining confidentiality and not allowing cross-talking. (*talking stick*)

Shekinah. The divine feminine fullness of existence in kabbalah and Jewish mysticism. Everything that is energy, matter, and appearance *is* her. She thrives on connections among all that exists, and thus she is love. She is dynamic, cyclical, and unpredictable. She yearns to be penetrated by the divine masculine, which is the unwavering consciousness, nothingness, and total awareness.

soul. The unique essence or subtle self that exists beyond personality, found in our wild core.

soul contract. Agreements made by the soul before incarnating on Earth. A curriculum with specific lessons that helps the soul realize its potential. It may include subcontracts to work with specific people, places, or things.

soul loss. When the physical trauma is too much to bear, a part of the essential self can seek safety in the nonordinary reality. Although this can be a helpful survival mechanism, a problem arises if the soul gets lost or stolen by another entity or doesn't know when the trauma has passed and it is safe to return. (*dissociation, susto*)

soul retrieval. A healing ritual in which a shaman enters into an altered state of consciousness to remove any energy that is not in harmony with the seeker's soul and restore lost energy or power so that the recipient can be whole again. Written about extensively by Sandra Ingerman. (*soul catching*)

soul tribe. An intimate network of spiritually evolved friends and lovers who support one another's soul's evolution. People who bring out the best in one another and can be called on during times of celebration as well as times of challenge. (*fellowship, sangha, second skin, soul group*)

sovereignty. Free from external conditioning or influence, a shaman becomes self-governing by independently sourcing power within. Authority over self comes from a connection with one's core.

spiral dynamics. A psychological model that explains human development as an unfolding, emergent, spiraling process. Evolution is not just physical but also psychological and sociological. The model illuminates developmental worldviews or systems of thinking held by individuals, organizations, and societies. For more information, see the work of Clare W. Graves (*The Futurist*), Don Edward Beck and Christopher C. Cowan (*Spiral Dynamics: Mastering Values, Leadership and Change*), and Ken Wilber (*Integral Psychology: Consciousness, Spirit, Psychology, Therapy*).

spiritual bypass. A defense mechanism to avoid facing unresolved emotional issues, psychological wounds, and unfinished developmental tasks by distracting oneself with spiritual ideas or practices.

stalking the shadow. The act of pursuing our unseen, self-destructive behaviors and habits, proceeding in a steady, deliberate, and intentional manner to bring these disowned aspects into the light. Carlos Castaneda advocated the use of cunning, sweetness, patience, and ruthlessness. (*shadow work*)

subjective. Interior phenomena that occurs within an individual, such as thoughts, feelings, opinions, and visions.

superpower. Any of a variety of extraordinary abilities such as shape-shifting, time travel, clairvoyance (including clairaudience, clairsentience, and direct knowing), spontaneous healing, prophecy, bilocation, teleportation, and levitation. (*siddhis, yogic powers*)

suspension of disbelief. Temporary interruption of one's critical faculties for a specific purpose such as a performance or ritual. Afterward the participants are encouraged to analyze, question, doubt, and wonder.

sutras. A religious text or collection of condensed wisdom. (*aphorisms*)

synergy. Beyond Aristotle's concept that the whole is greater than the simple sum of its parts, the ISTA community relates to others (humans and nature beings) from a place of resonance, following the guidance of the ecstatic current.

Tantra. An esoteric system within Hinduism, Buddhism, and other Eastern traditions that involves the integration of opposites. The literal translation from Sanskrit means "weave on a loom," referring to the fabric of reality.

The term is commonly used to describe energetic sexual practices, yet it transcends the sensual experiences of the body.

Tantra Theater. Performance art that it done as an act of embodied worship by the performers as well as the audience. The intention is to offer improvisation, song, dance, music, or other temple arts on stage. Cofounders KamalaDevi and Michael McClure's mission statement is to use Tantra Theater to transmute sexual guilt, shame, and fear into art, healing, and liberation.

telepathic agreements. Transmissions of information, thoughts, and feelings shared in a relationship, group, or culture that have the power to influence behaviors without verbal or sensory means.

temple arts. Ancient and modern practices encompassing spiritual and sexual rituals designed to heal, awaken, and enhance life, relationships, and living.

transpersonal. A form of relating to oneself or another beyond the personal. By extending beyond one's mundane identity, a shaman can consciously embody certain universal archetypes—such as the divine feminine, mother, father, church, dragon, inner child—to commune with deeper aspects of humankind, the psyche, or the cosmos.

underworld. The extraordinary realm within Earth where shamans go to commune with animals, plants, rivers, and all natural entities. Also the realm through which dead shamans may help with many levels of healing, learning, and exchanges of energy and knowledge. (*otherworld, spirit world*)

universe. The sum total of all the states of all of existence. All there is. The unknown. The absolute.

upperworld. The dimension where angels, winged entities, star nations, planetary beings, celestial guides, ascended masters, and archetypes live. Our higher self and superconsciousness are connected to this realm. (*cosmos, heavens*)

vajra. A Tibetan term for "thunderbolt" or "scepter of power" used to refer to the male sexual organ. (*lingam*)

void. The emptiness and nothingness from which all form manifests and contains the potential of everything. (*empty center, shunyata*)

wheel of consent. Betty Martin created a four-quadrant framework to separate doing from giving and to find deeper layers of receiving. The main focus is to become clear regarding who is doing and who it is for and become solid in creating agreements before the action. It evolved from the three-minute game by Harry Faddis. (*wheel of desire*)

white tantra. An ascetic yogic spiritual discipline that builds etheric energy to help transcend the earthly plane. Through postures, hand gestures, internal muscular exercises, chanting, meditation, and breathing, the practitioner accelerates awareness of the realm of the soul. Physical touch and sexual practices are not essential to advance on this path.

witch. A practitioner of magick who may engage in divination, herbs, and healing. One who works with the land and moon cycles and can see in the dark. This term is often used pejoratively to identify and persecute someone who is thought to worship the devil.

womb work. Rituals and energetic experiences that clean, purify, and enliven the sacred energy portal of the womb. Through intention, touch, movement, and sound, womb work can heal chronic illnesses, brokenheartedness, unhealthy attachments, negative sexual experiences, and abuse.

yab-yum. A tantric position in which a woman sits astride facing her partner, heart to heart. The literal translation from Sansrkit means "mother-father pose." In this position, all of the chakras are aligned.

yantra. A symbol of cosmic forces, used to support concentration, meditation, and visualization. (*mandala, sacred geometry*)

yin-yang. The Taoist representation of how opposite energies come together in divine union to form the universe. The symbolic interplay of two paradoxical energies that both battle and harmonize.

Yogaboxing. An emotional release practice inspired by a variety of modalities, including martial arts, tantra, and yoga. It combines sound, movement, and energy discharge and is taught by Joshua Smith and Laurie Handlers.

yoni. In Vedic texts, the vagina is regarded as the passageway to the womb and the source of all life. The term *yoni* translates to "sacred space" or "temple" and includes the vulva, labia, vagina, clitoris, and sacred spot. It is physical in women and ethereal in men.

yoni worship. Honoring the divine feminine through the doorway of her genitals. Any practice of adoration that can range from gazing on the vulva to consensual touch to oral pleasure depending on the goddess's boundaries. (*yoni puja*)

RECOMMENDED READING

Collectively, the contributing authors have compiled this list of transformational books and DVDs for sincere spiritual sexual shamanic seekers. For a list of the contributors' own works, see the "Want More?" chapter that follows.

Anand, Margo. *The Art of Sexual Ecstasy: The Path of Sacred Sexuality for Western Lovers*. New York: Jeremy Tarcher, 1989.

———. *The Art of Sexual Magic: Cultivating Sexual Energy to Transform Your Life*. New York: TarcherPerigee, 1996.

Avinasha, Bodhi, and Sunyatat Saraswati. *The Jewel in the Lotus: The Tantric Path to Higher Consciousness*. 3rd ed. Arroyo Grande, Calif.: Ipsalu, 2002.

Brown, Bernadeane, and James Strole. *Just Getting Started: Fifty Years of Living Forever*. Scottsdale, Ariz.: People Unlimited, 2017.

Bryant, Dorothy. *The Kin of Ata Are Waiting for You*. New York: Random House, 1971.

Cameron, Julia. *The Artist's Way: A Spiritual Path to Higher Creativity*. 25th anniversary ed. New York: TargerPerigee, 2016.

Campbell, Joseph, and Bill Moyers. *The Power of Myth*. New York: Anchor, 1991.

Castaneda, Carlos. *The Art of Dreaming*. New York: HarperCollins, 1993.

———. *The Teachings of Don Juan*. Berkeley: University of California Press, 1968.

Cheng, Patrick S. *Radical Love: An Introduction to Queer Theology.* Fayetteville, N.C.: Seabury Books, 2011.

Chia, Maneewan, and Mantak Chia. *Healing Love through the Tao: Cultivating Female Sexual Energy.* Rochester, Vt.: Destiny Books, 2005.

Chia, Mantak, and Michael Winn. *Taoist Secrets of Love: Cultivating Male Sexual Energy.* Santa Fe, N.Mex: Aurora Press, 1984.

Dangerous Beauty. Directed by Marshall Herskovitz. United States. Warner Brothers. 1998. Film.

Dodson, Betty. *Liberating Masturbation: A Meditation on Self Love.* Self-published. Betty Dodson, 1974.

———. *Sex for One: The Joy of Selfloving.* New York: Random House, 1996.

Douglas, Nik, and Penny Slinger. *Sexual Secrets: The Alchemy of Ecstasy.* 20th anniversary ed. Rochester, Vt.: Destiny Books, 1999.

Dyer, Wayne. *The Power of Intention: Learning to Co-Create Your World Your Way.* Carlsbad, Calif.: Hay House, 2005.

Easton, Dossie, and Catherine A. Liszt. *The Ethical Slut: A Guide to Infinite Sexual Possibilities.* Emeryville, Calif.: Greenery Press, 1997.

Eliade, Mircea. *Shamanism: Archaic Techniques of Ecstasy.* Later reprint ed. Princeton, N.J.: Princeton University Press, 2004.

Ensler, Eve. *The Vagina Monologues.* 20th anniversary ed. New York: Ballantine Books, 2018.

Feuerstein, Georg. *Tantra: Path of Ecstasy.* Boulder, Colo.: Shambhala Publications, 1998.

Finney, Lynne D. *Reach for the Rainbow: Advanced Healing for Survivors of Sexual Abuse.* New York: TarcherPerigee, 1992.

Frater, U. D. *Secrets of the German Sex Magicians: A Practical Handbook for Men and Women.* Woodbury, Minn.: Llewellyn Publications, 1995.

———. *Secrets of Western Sex Magic: Magical Energy and Gnostic Trance.* Woodbury, Minn: Llewellyn Publications, 2002.

Harner, Michael J. *The Way of the Shaman.* New York: Harper & Row, 1980.

Ingerman, Sandra. *Soul Retrieval: Mending the Fragmented Self through Shamanic Practice.* San Francisco, Calif.: HarperSanFrancisco, 1991.

Kenyon, Tom, and Judi Sion. *The Magdalen Manuscript: The Alchemies of Horus and the Sex Magic of Isis.* Tom Kenyon Orb, 2006.

Kraig, Donald Michael. *Modern Sex Magick: Secrets of Erotic Spirituality.* Woodbury, Minn.: Llewellyn Publications, 2002.

Kramer, Joseph. *Evolutionary Masturbation: An Intimate Guide to the Male Orgasm*. Oakland, Calif: New School of Erotic Touch, N.d. DVD.

Levine, Peter A. *Sexual Healing: Transforming the Sacred Wound*. Louisville, Colo.: Sounds True, 2003. Audio CD.

Long, Max Freedom. *Secret Science at Work: The Huna Method as a Way of Life*. Camarillo, Calif.: Devorss & Co., 1953.

McKenna, Terrence. *The Archaic Revival*. New York: HarperCollins, 1992.

Muir, Caroline, and Charles Muir. *Tantra: The Art of Conscious Loving*. San Francisco, Calif.: Mercury House, 1989.

Osho. *From Sex to Super-Consciousness*. India: Rebel Publishing House, 1996.

Primal Man Nude Massage. Directed by Joseph Kramer. Oakland, Calif.: Joseph Kramer, 2007. DVD.

Roberts, Jane. *Emir's Education in the Proper Use of Magical Powers*. Newburyport, Mass.: Hampton Roads, 2000.

Sanella, Lee. *Kundalini Experience: Psychosis or Transcendence*. Buckingham, Va.: Integral Yoga Publications, 1987.

Spanbauer, Tom. *The Man Who Fell in Love with the Moon*. New York: HarperPerennial, 1992.

Stubbs, Kenneth Ray. *Women of the Light: The New Sacred Prostitute*. Secret Garden Pub., 1994.

Wanless, James. *Voyager Tarot Cards*. Beverly, Mass.: Fair Winds Press, 1986. Card deck.

Woodroffe, Sir John, and Arthur Avalon, trans. *Mahanirvana Tantra: Tantra of the Great Liberation*. Martino Fine Books, 2012. Facsimile of the 1913 edition.

WANT MORE?

For a full list of ISTA events, teachers, and trainings go to
www.ISTA.life.

Contributing Authors' Resources

(alphabetized by first name)

Baba Dez Nichols

Search on "Baba Dez" for website

Sacred Sexual Healing: The SHAMAN Method of Sex Magic, by Baba Dez
Nichols and KamalaDevi (San Diego, Calif.: Zendow Press, 2008)

Sex Magic: Manifesting Maya, documentary directed by Eric Liebman and
Jonathan Schell, with Baba Dez Nichols, Maya Yonika, and KamalaDevi
McClure (2010)

Thank the Moon, music CD (2007)

Bruce Lyon

Search on "Shamballa School Bruce Lyon" for website

Agni: Way of Fire (Wellington, New Zealand: White Stone Publishing, 2004)

Mercury: The Mercury Transmissions (Wellington, New Zealand: White Stone
Publishing, 2004)

Group Initiation: The Mercury Transmissions (Wellington, New Zealand: White
Stone Publishing, 2005)

Journey to Shamballa Land (Wellington, New Zealand: White Stone Publishing,
2008)

Working with the Will (Wellington, New Zealand: White Stone Publishing, 2007)

Occult Cosmology (Wellington, New Zealand: White Stone Publishing, 2010)
Raiding the Inarticulate: Essays (Wellington, New Zealand: White Stone Publishing, 2003)

Crystal Dawn Morris

Search on "Tantra for Awakening" for website
Making Love to Life (prepublication)

Dawn Cherie Ezrahi

Search on "KabaLove" for website

Deborah Taj Anapol, PhD

Search on "Love Without Limits" for website
Love Without Limits: The Quest for Sustainable Intimate Relationships (Intinet Resource Center, 1992)
Polyamory: The New Love Without Limits (Intinet Resource Center, 1997)
Polyamory in the 21st Century: Love and Intimacy with Multiple Partners (Lanham, Md.: Rowman and Littlefield Publishers, 2012)
The Seven Natural Laws of Love (Elite Books, 2010)
Articles online at Loving More Magazine and Psychology Today ("Love Without Limits" blog)

Ellie Wilde

Search on "Ellie Wilde ISTA" for website

Janine Ma-Ree

Search on "Red Earth Temple" for website
The Clearing Generation (out of print)

KamalaDevi McClure

Search on "KamalaDevi McClure" for website and see page 320 listing

Komala Lyra

Search on "Komala Lyra" for website
The Califa & Iemanjá (novel; available on website)
Intimacy: Ayurveda, Relationships & Sexuality (Mantra Books, 2012)
On the Way to NowHere (Lincoln, Neb.: iUniverse, 2005)
Chakra VIVA, DVDs by Komala Lyra and Sidd Murray-Clark

Laurie Handlers

Search on "Butterfly Workshops" for website

Sex & Happiness: The Tantric Laws of Intimacy (Butterfly Workshops, 2007)

Lin Holmquist

Search on "Art of Love Lin Holmquist" for website

We Choose Love, MP3 by Fredrik Swahn and Lin Holmquist (2018)

Matooka MoonBear

Search on "Matooka Moonbear" for website

Mia Mor

Search on "Embodied Poetry Wordpress" for Mia Mor's blog: A Dakini Poetess Soul

Ohad Pele Ezrahi

Search on "KabaLove" for website

Kedesha: A Timeless Tale of a Love Priestess (CreateSpace, 2018)

Cosmic Snake, music CD

Something out of Chaos, music CD

Patrik Olterman

Search on "Theo-Erotic" for website

Raffaello Manacorda

Search on "Fragments of Evolution" for website

Relationships: The Art of Bringing Awareness to Intimacy & Sexuality (FoE Publishing, 2016)

Ria Bloom

Search on "Welcome to My Riality" for website

Stephanie Phillips

Search on "Tantric Synergy" for website

Sex with Your Light On (ebook available on website)

Other Books by Author/Editor
KamalaDevi McClure

Don't Drink the Punch: An Adventure in Tantra (San Diego, Calif.: Zendow Press, 2006)

Sacred Sexual Healing: The SHAMAN Method of Sex Magic by Kamala Devi and Baba Dez Nichols (San Diego, Calif.: Zendow Press, 2007)

Earning your BLACKBELT in Relationships, DVD directed by Kamala Devi and Reid Mihalko (2009)

52 Fridays by KamalaDevi McClure and Roxanne DePalma (Cleis Press, 2020)

Polyamory Pearls: Invaluable Wisdom on Open Relationships, Jealousy, Group Sex & Other Spiritual Pursuits (Amazon Digital Services, 2014)

Sacred Slut Sutras: Radical Insights on Sex, Love, Tantra, Kink & Other Spiritual Pursuits (San Diego, Calif.: Zendow Press, 2014)

KamalaDevi McClure is also available for appearances and speaking engagements and select private healing sessions. To inquire about her availability and services please email Bliss@kamaladevi.com.

Books of Related Interest

The Sexual Practices of Quodoushka
Teachings from the Nagual Tradition
by Amara Charles

Slow Sex
The Path to Fulfilling and Sustainable Sexuality
by Diana Richardson

Tantric Orgasm for Women
by Diana Richardson

Tantric Sex for Men
Making Love a Meditation
by Diana Richardson and Michael Richardson

The Complete Illustrated Kama Sutra
Edited by Lance Dane

Tao Tantric Arts for Women
Cultivating Sexual Energy, Love, and Spirit
by Minke de Vos
Foreword by Mantak Chia

Healing Love through the Tao
Cultivating Female Sexual Energy
by Mantak Chia

Sexual Reflexology
Activating the Taoist Points of Love
by Mantak Chia and William U. Wei

INNER TRADITIONS • BEAR & COMPANY
P.O. Box 388
Rochester, VT 05767
1-800-246-8648
www.InnerTraditions.com

Or contact your local bookseller